MW00627427

The Way Out:
A Guide to
Being Free
From the
Prison of Your Mind

The Way Out:
A Guide to
Being Free
From the
Prison of Your Mind

Cory Roussel
with **Denise Roussel**

Cory's Dream

Publishing

First edition published in 2015 by
Cory's Dream
Publishing

"The Jail Break Project"

To loose the binds of men whose minds,
Keep leading to the "Bank of Time",
To credit for the time that's served,
For Starving Spirit, an hors d'oeuvre,
To bring to health the ailing mind,
For common good- in time we'll find,
And though we all will make mistakes,
Sentence long, can't truth replace:

We choose day in and day out- ONE
Naught or best that could be done.

- Cory Roussel

Sincere gratitude to Tammy Watkins, Brian Tohana and Angie Trampel for their assistance in transcribing letters.

Contents

Chapter 1: Introduction

This book is primarily the brain-child of my son, Cory Roussel, who passed away on October 26, 2014. A prolific writer, he wrote most of this book while serving a one-year federal prison term for smuggling an illegal immigrant across the border. I outline Cory's life in my book, *Beyond This Space: My Son Cory's Story and How He Changed My Life[1]*, so I do not feel it appropriate to tell his whole story here. But to give context of when and why this book was written, I will share some highlights of his life.

Cory was raised in a loving, safe and nurturing home with a strong sense of spirituality and morality imparted by a strong Christian upbringing. Yet, from the beginning, he proved to be quite DIFFERENT. He didn't think, behave and operate like most. Life was an exploration for him, as he invented things, learned about things in nature and always seemed to be getting into some kind of mischief. He began as a preteen to be ostracized at a new middle school, which led to anxiety attacks. Later, early into high school, he was introduced into drugs and alcohol and quickly fell into the trap of addiction. This path led him and our family through a difficult journey. As his life progressed into adulthood, the radical shifts in the nature of his life became more pronounced as he moved into arduous circumstances like consuming addiction, homelessness, near fatal bicycle accident and prison time to name a few, AND periods of serenity, service, profound insights, clarity and a powerfully loving and compassionate presence. The last few months of his life, he wrote a book, along with his many other numerous writings, called *The Seed Collection[2]*, and he developed a document called "The Way Out". Both of these important works of his are collections of truths and inspirations by which he lived. "The Way Out" was his way of giving back to prisoners what he gained from his experience, in the hopes it will help others to find the liberty and passion for life that he found while in prison. This book is a collection of edited letters that he sent us over the span of a year and his document, "The Way Out".

The story behind the title: One day while in prison, Cory was conversing in his rudimentary Spanish with Juan.

"Juan, I know the way out," Cory whispered to his friend.

"Really?" Juan's eyes widened.

"Yes...We wait, and we wait, and we wait, and we wait...And one day the doors will open," Cory finished with the sweep of his hands.

"Hah! That's great!" Juan laughed. "Hey, Marcos! Cory says he knows the way out!"

At the time, it may have seemed funny, but Cory actually meant it. He knew from the many hours he spent reading, writing, meditating, sharing and praying that liberty was a process that was not instantaneous. It begins with changing our thinking and progresses from there. His hope is that he can bring you along a similar journey into freedom from the prison of your mind.

The significance of this book cannot be understated because it is my firm belief that the principles outlined in this book can completely transform ANYONE's life. I know it did mine. Although written by a prisoner and partially to other prisoners, the concepts and ideas presented are applicable to ANYONE who finds themselves captive to the prison of their mind. May we hear what Cory is trying to share with us, knowing it has come from a place of deep knowing, experience and suffering- understanding he came to this earth to help us grow and evolve. Enjoy!

- Denise Roussel

Chapter 2: Letters from West Baton Rouge Prison

The first batch of letters were written March to May 2012 while Cory awaited where the Federal government would ship him. The prison term was actually a revocation of his time-served conviction of alien smuggling in San Diego. As part of his probation, Cory was required not to drink or use drugs. The year while he was on probation proved to be a nightmare for a number of reasons, namely you can't force a person to get well. Each person has unique needs and if those needs are not met, no amount of threats, punishments or demands can bring the sick person to health. So, Cory's probation got revoked for a dirty drug test. At the time of his arrest, he had already begun a profound process of liberation that he shares early in these letters. He was arrested in mid-March and sentenced in late April, but they didn't actually move him back to San Diego until May. What I find interesting is his progression of thought and insight the more time he spends in prison, which prison he was in and the effect of his time in solitary confinement.

While compiling these letters I made the decision to keep certain passages in that may be offensive to some regarding Christianity. It is not my intention to offend anyone. These letters were personal letters written to us his family while Cory was undergoing transformation and soul searching. These passages I feel show a progression of his journey. It is my understanding (as well as Cory's) there is no one way to do this thing called life. We each choose our own path. It is my hope the passages in question can be viewed objectively, understanding they are not intended to make any statement for or against anyone's journey.

3

March 2012
Amanda,

Hello. How are you? Personally, life is very good for me right now. I'm in a small parish prison in Louisiana, as you've probably heard. I've been sentenced to one year of federal prison for violating my probation. For a number of reasons I feel like I've won the lottery. God has an excellent and incomprehensible, beautiful plan for this year and the potential it represents. I won't get into all of it, or at least all I perceive of it, but if nothing else, I'm sure you can envision finding some great use, even enjoyment in a year free of distraction or responsibility, during which you have virtually unlimited access to books, people to help teach and help, and writing implements. I asked Landon, but I'm also curious to hear your idea of what you would spend two years in prison doing. Personally, I think my one year in prison will be more beneficial than even two spent in college was for me. But I'm quite curious -- what would you do with two years of prison?

Would you tell me what the ten most profound books, preferably nonfiction, you've ever read are? My purpose in asking is to help populate a list of books to be a part of a prison book program. So far we've been able to introduce six great books into the general population- two suggestions from my mom, some of her top most profound, impactful books, as well as one from my aunt. I'm very excited at the difference those books are making for people, as they likewise did for me, especially Eckhart Tolle's *A New Earth*[1] -- so good.

Do you have any suggestions of what kinds of things a prisoner should read? Eventually, I seek to compose a resource guide, as well as a book on the incredible potential the collective minds of our incarcerated represent, as well as a manifesto on beginning to activate that collective potential -- over six million in the U.S. alone, I believe. I believe very soon that number will quintuple or more, if the way the U.S. has built special prison camps and their capacity, greater than 30 million, are any indicator, maybe even worse. What do I know? I'm just a - behold, a pale-white-horse-toting-conspiracy-theorist-truther. What do you think?

Anyways, I've got to go -- much writing to do.

With love, Cory

4

April 2012
Dad,

It's about 9:30 PM on Friday night here. I am sitting here talking with my roommate. He's a 24-year-old college football player that graduated from Alabama A&M last year. His name is Corey, and we are the same age. Out of our 30-man tank (almost all blacks, 4-5 whites), three of us share the name "Cory". One of the first guys I met was also named "Cory" in a different part of the prison. I suppose it's God's humorous way of reminding me: "You're unique, but not different." I scratched out "cellmate" in favor of "roommate" because I find the living arrangements feel to be extremely reminiscent of my days at Kirby Smith [LSU college dormitory]. The same white cinderblock walls. The same hoard of loud unruly young men acting childish all day just outside. The same atmosphere of academic/philosophical conversation all day. Both of us spend hours taking notes on books we've read and share common interest in books. I've found that the majority of inmates have read some, and many, like Corey and me, read A LOT. The most valuable/shared/read books are non-fiction on improving one's self through spirituality or business. It's a great thing to see otherwise uneducated young men taking advantage of this great opportunity to improve themselves. I've also seen folks on the other end (being released from prison) who had taken their time in prison to educate themselves and became aware of life-changing spiritual practices. It seems to me this faction, who has had the benefit of exposure to powerful ideas, receives, by far, the greatest benefit from incarceration. There are many who are receptive to these sort of ideas but simply never have had a chance to get their hands on the books.

The past three months have been a strange mixture of external misfortunes (ultimately of my own creation), yet internal fortunes. Windfall really. Lost a job, got beat up, got locked up, all in a short period of time. The first two results of living with wing-nuts, the last a result of being a wing-nut. Nevertheless, internally, it's as though I've won the Powerball, which really makes the misfortunes seem not only trivial, but complements, providing sharp contrast to the recent blessings, making their value even more glaring.

I speak of having a great darkness lifted off of my mind, physiologically, psychologically and spiritually. Physically, I , despite

5

not really feeling "sad" or "sorrowful", accepted my counselor's suggestion that I may be "depressed", even if only chemically. I read of the German's success with St. John's Wart and ordered a supply. I also began taking the amino acid supplement 5-HTP, a precursor to serotonin. Wow! The results were amazing! My energy level shot up, but not at all in the stimulant way; my mood increased exponentially; my mind became clear. I experienced no side effects whatsoever and no crash or withdrawal when I was admitted here. The 5-HTP also seemed to really help sleep restore my mind more effectively. Since the two are considered very safe and don't require a person to be depressed, I recommend you try them. If your mind/brain is ANYTHING like mine, a small natural improvement in serotonin levels will prove revolutionary.

The second aspect, of greater and lasting consequence, was the implementation of radical, rapid forgiveness, as described and catalyzed by a book Mom gave me. At various times in my life, I've undergone extensive "4th and 5th step" processes to try to address resentments and reoccurring negative emotions, but for some reason, none so effective as this. It was though my words and desires was to "forgive", but my emotions would not follow. I was subconsciously bent on retaining my resentments, so I could use them as weapons to defend myself against future similar attacks. If a person accidentally hurt me, I held onto that emotion to use it on them in the future. It is an effective strategy, but the problem is: it has the side effect of poisoning the mind, cluttering the temple of thought with dangerous thoughts that I felt I would be a sucker if I forgot them, since with many I had sincerely tried and failed when the feelings resurfaced. What I have discovered (on Mom's suggestion, as well as the book she gave me) is that these persistent resentments require an EXPEDIENT, PERSISTENT resolve to forgive, as well as a persistent commitment to let go of that feeling. And finally, I felt a relief far superior to what I have ever felt with the over-analytical 4th and 5th steps. I would recommend you also read the book Mom bought. It's good stuff, even for every day "annoyances". Anyways, this mental and spiritual housecleaning had the effect of skyrocketing my mental clarity and fixating my mind in a positive place, unshakeable by the oppression of the Federal Government or some instigating gangster who decided to blacken my eye. I could literally take it all with a smile.

The U.S. Marshalls came on Monday morning, and I knew it meant I was losing a considerable chunk of my life's precious liberty; but my confidence, disposition and resolve was UNSHAKEABLE. They got in my face and threatened to "make me choke on my front teeth," and it just didn't matter. (The federal government is very evil whether you accept it or not.) Later that day, after a long wait in an empty courthouse cell, I was escorted into the courtroom, still sporting a wide "You can't scare me" smile. For this hearing, I was given no lawyer, so it provided an uncommon opportunity to speak directly to the judge, a quite empowering being. There's something human about speaking for yourself and being taken well. The prosecutor laughed at my quips. Did I mention with mental clarity comes wit? And even the judge let off a surprised chuckle. It was obvious to me all the people involved in the revocation were surprised/confused by the lighthearted way I was taking their attack. My probation officer was so embarrassed she had to do this to me, she wouldn't even look my way, though we were 15 feet away from each other. I understand. The version of me she spoke to last would likely have sent her a death-stare, not a friendly smile.

I know that eventually my mood must settle into contentment, but for now I feel unstoppable. Even a three-year sentence doesn't scare me. It helps that I perceive a great few opportunities within these walls. More on that later.

The inmates here at West Baton Rouge Prison got a kick out of me smiling for my mug shots. I was given a green ID card, denoting my "federal" status. Here, being a "fed" is a great badge of honor. It sets a man apart from common thieves and drunks. Deserved or not, everyone from guards to inmates respect feds more. Despite what would normally be a mark of shame- a black eye- the other inmates seemed to respect the non-chalance with which I entered each successive "tank" I was moved to, until I finally made it to my cozy new cell. Even such a serious potential mark of vulnerability, which if coupled with a vulnerable disposition would have spelled certain permanent damage to security and respect, coupled with a strong air of confidence and joviality, it went virtually unnoticed.

I rather like it here, even if it is loud and most of my peers are young ignorant kids. Jails group people different ways, and I guess I ended up in the "immature" tank. Fortunately, completely by chance, I ended up here instead of the infamously dirty, un-air-conditioned Tangipahoa Parish Prison, the normal place federal inmates go. Just a chance glitch. I also am fortunate enough to be in the "maximum security" portion, which means I have a cell with a door I can retreat to at will, a silent sanctuary with my quiet respectful cellmate, an infinite improvement over being in a room full of bunks 24-7 for four months. Also, I love the food- much of it is grown here on the grounds. We get lots of vegetables and tasty properly cooked, quality old-fashioned southern-styled meals: Turkey necks with rice and okra. Most meals include fresh made rolls, red beans and rice, squash, cauliflower, fried chicken. Really some of the most wholesome institution food I've ever had.

A large part of the reason prison no longer scares me- I have a plan. No- it's not a plan like in the "Shawshank Redemption". It's a plan on how to make the most use of my stay here. How to not waste time and come out of this situation better off in ways that wouldn't be possible without, and more importantly, to make a difference that wouldn't be possible without. (More on this later.) I've collected a series of aspirations, all very achievable, over the years for this specific purpose. If anything, there is more danger I won't have long enough in prison to do all I want to do. However, I've also (so far successfully) renounced any semblance of excessive diversion- TV, cards, vulgarities, idle chatter. I've filled my time with these things:

- Meditation three times/day
- Prayer
- Mental exercise
- Physical exercise
- Studying/reading
- Writing/Note-taking on reading
- The occasional game of chess- but I must be careful. Chess tends to arouse great anger in people. I've actually seen more conflict from it then any other game. When certain people lose, they feel insulted and sometimes get violent. They see chess as an intellectual game and hate to be played for ignorant. Since I'm by far the best player in our tank, I gotta' watch it. Certain people I won't even play out of a resolution towards peace.

Mental exercise I perform are of these varieties:

- Attempting to do difficult calculations in my head without paper (especially useful in solitary confinement). I can calculate 3^7 mentally (2,187). This skill has proven valuable in the past, so I'll continue to perfect it.

- Visualization (often combined with meditation and idea articulation). The process of describing the place I intend to be/experiences I intend to have in great detail. It is said this technique is most effective for realizing goals.
- Writing business plans/articulating ideas/preparing them for execution. My recent submersion in texts on entrepreneurship and business/marketing execution has me itching to put some long-developed ideas into motion. This is a great opportunity to refine and design them further and hopefully continue to study and learn about executing such ideas.

Earlier I mentioned an idea, really a vision I have, the execution of which will provide me with a very meaningful purpose. I've had the benefit of receiving/reading a great array of truly soul-changing/life-changing/game-changing books during my various stays in prison. The books Mom, Landon and Bethany have sent, which I've left behind, give me the great pleasure in knowing they'll be read, and have a positive effect on people's lives, hundreds if not THOUSANDS in time. Somewhere in San Diego, an inmate is learning how to live a life of devotion to God with Landon's *Devout Life*[2]. Another is learning to redirect anger reading a book by Gandhi. Another is sharpening his mind with a book of mind games and puzzles. Thousands and thousands of hours of positive therapy and often LIFE CHANGING exposure to ideas. (I've met hardened criminals that learned how to meditate and became completely reformed, all from reading a book.) Trouble is, quality books are few and far between. Most books are very old donated fiction novels and other books of little redeeming value. My vision is to court publishers, authors, churches, individuals, friends and family to donate books selected for their powerful spiritually and intellectually empowering quality. A $5 book is literally worth its weight in gold in terms of the impact it will have on this captive audience. The book will pay for itself many times over in positive impact on not just the prisoner, but the lives, communities, families and culture that surrounds former inmates.

April 3, 2012
Mom,

How are things? Things are going very well over here.   The book you gave me[3], which I haven't received the new copy yet, has in fact played a

9

significant role in a broader transition out of the prison of my mind, in perfect timing, directly before I moved into the prison of the law.

I'm quite at peace about the circumstances, even optimist about the potential of my incarceration, despite pessimism about the duration I'm expecting. My mind is free, and not just because I'm forgiven, but because God has seen fit to clear my mind of its dark, enveloping shroud. This shroud had to be lifted before my mind was even capable of forgiveness. I had made many attempts, even continuously made attempts at forgiveness/mental housecleaning, but to no effect. My mind was so clouded that my conscious decision could not affect my subconscious resentment. It was like pulling weeds without their roots. My mind was so fragmented, no amount of analysis and rationality could be effectual. I thank you profusely for your ongoing prayer and support in this regard, and it was a great idea to give me that book.

I've been studying avidly during my week this far. With new-found clarity, my mind is more receptive to ideas. Reading and writing will be my keys to freedom, and this imposed solitude will be the vehicle which will take me towards my destiny. Can you think of one time in your whole life you've gone a week without distractions? Even one day without responsibility? The truth is, my weakness is distraction, and being strongly encouraged to focus only on the task at hand will do me a world of good. Already I've written almost 25 pages of letters, another 25 of notes, introspections, meditations. Our room, me and my roommate, Corey, has an air of spirituality and academia to it. My 24-year-old same-named roommate and I are alike in many regards, so we get along well.

I have read and am now avidly rereading and studying what is perhaps the most profound, eloquent, perfect book on spirituality I've ever read. I consider it of even greater impact than the Bible in its short 124 pages. Its tenets are entirely congruent with the Bible and draw from Christian, Jewish and Buddhists teachings, offering what amounts to a very eloquent, poetic summary of salvation. I strongly encourage you to read it. It won't teach you anything you don't know, and I doubt it contains even a sentence you won't agree with, but it does it in a new way. It's called *From Poverty to Power*[4] by James Allen.

What are the most profound five books you've ever read?

I've noticed in my experience with incarceration a certain openness to new ideas, fertile grounds on which spiritual concepts grow in the minds of the troubled, whose vanities withered as weeds in the darkness of a prison cell, compost the soil. Here people read, they share ideas, they adopt religions, and become educated on subjects otherwise locked away from them in the free world.

I've seen fighters learn passivity, drug dealers learn to work the stock market, the godless find religion…all with a shoddy collection of old hand-me-down, antiquated books. Anything worthwhile is few and far between. Once a good book makes it into jail, it will last 10 to 20 years and be read probably at least once a month. That's 240 to 480 times! For a $5 book like *From Poverty to Power*[4], that's one cent per person whose whole thinking has changed.

How can we go on letting opportunities to change people's lives slip by the millions? Imagine if every prisoner had access to such books. Prison could become a place of rehabilitation! I seek to take initiative to make that a reality. Prison is too valuable a mass of humanity to be ignored as a place for castaways. On the contrary, it's the perfect place to start rebuilding communities in the minds of the ones who are inclined to take initiative, in the minds of the ones who reject the status quo.

My plan is as follows:
- Make a list of books that could improve the average prisoner's mind, body or spirit.
- Contact counselors and probation officers to distribute surveys to identify influential books/get suggestions for books.
- Write authors and publishers asking for discounts in dollar-matched donations; raise funds to purchase books.

Any ideas, suggestions?

I would love to write more, but it's late, and I've been writing all day. I'll write more in about a week.

Love,
Cory

11

April 2012
Mom,

Things are still going great here. Making me think everyone could benefit from a period of incarceration every now and then. I go before the judge on the 19th of April, Thursday, at 10 a.m. I'm curious to know what I'm looking at. Hopefully, the public defender will be able to tell me more. We'll see.

In other news, not only do we both have the same name, age, political, spiritual, ethical beliefs, but we even have the same blood type --O Positive. He's also on the same page with me on our business and entrepreneurial endeavors, so we have big plans for the future. He's probably getting out on Wednesday, so he's going out to "pave the way", so to speak, and generate some start-up capital. When I get out, God willing, he's going to get me situated right away and get right to business. We're a match made in heaven. He's got the access to capital and collections, and I've got the idea and knowledge of how to make it all happen. It's very promising. He's got a heart for helping others like me and is aware of all the stuff I know about. I have to admit I was used to seeing this sort of "I'm a Christian but I believe there are other ways" modern American spiritual but not religious hipster Christianity as weak and self-negating. The Bible is pretty explicit about exclusivity and its sole proprietorship on salvation. But now I see the "accept everything" crowd of Christians are really only wrong in one thing… the existence of Christ and authority of the Bible. I never understood why people talked about Gnosticism and the "symbolic" nature of the Bible. Now I see. Yes, it's highly symbolic, and the symbolism holds the key to its own revelation as a fraud. A text written by Anglo Saxons to assist in the control and manipulation of the masses… as was Jesus. There's a reason why so much of the Bible contradicts itself, and the Old and New Testament seems to contradict each other. It's because they were entirely composed of recycled and repurposed Egyptian (Kemetic) wisdom, designed to aid an oppression of the masses… Muslim included… It's a hoax… Once the truth is unlocked, the entirety of history and colonialism makes perfect sense.

Thanks for the book on chess. It's great. I sent Bethany a list of books I want sent in. Perhaps y'all can work together to identify and purchase these books with my money from the tax return card. Let reviews be the main evaluating factor. These books will be passed around here from my friends, and ultimately the general population. Certain ones I won't be leaving behind, so they can be of a more educated nature, i.e., not limited by being suitable for high school level readers.

12

Here's the list:
Two books on meditation techniques
Numerology
Sacred geometry
Four-Hour Work Week[5], and one other book by Timothy Ferris
Eckhart Tolle (two of his highest-rated books)
Math Techniques and Tricks
Kemetic and Ancient Egyptian Knowledge
Mental Math Techniques/How to Do Math in Head/Shortcuts

April 2012
Mom,

Hello.   How are you? I'm doing well over here, just enjoying peaceful life.
Read anything worthwhile lately?
Yesterday I stepped out on a limb and went to "church."   It started out
good.   We sang "Amazing Grace" and had a brief prayer.   The reverend
said a few good things about grace and mercy, then it all went downhill from
there.   Without going into an in-depth analysis, let it suffice to say he did a
good job reminding me why Christianity is so silly and the Bible is a book of
disgusting blasphemies mixed with priceless truths. The doctrine of the
infallibility of the Word is about as silly as the doctrine of the infallibility of the
pope.   Oddly enough, the more I read about the history of the church and
its foundations and illumination and politics, the more free I feel to pursue
God in His true, approachable form. After the service, I was talking to my
roommate about the blatant fabrications in the Bible that talk about a
personified god using temporal verbs and reactionary language to describe
God: "And they hid from God in the garden."   "Heard his footsteps."
"Jacob wrestled with God!"   "God's wrath was aroused."   "When God
saw..."   All these statements imply imperfection, vulnerability, reactionary
thinking.   It's silly, if not maddening. So we were talking about that, and
out of the blue, our Muslim friend comes in with a book wanting to show us
a certain passage about THIS VERY SAME CONCEPT, talking about
Adam and Eve and how God was supposedly walking with them in the
garden, looking for them.   He had absolutely no way of knowing what we
were talking about.   He had just received this book in the mail and wanted
to show us.   Talk about confirmation. But things like this "divine
serendipity," as I call it, are becoming so common, we're almost becoming
expectant of it.

If you think to, see if you can collect some prayer requests from the drop-in center for some of us to pray for.   I've started an intercessory prayer group; so far, it's just me, but God's shown me it will grow as time goes on, eventually becoming a virtually constant team of guys praying and interceding on behalf of the world and select issues.   So I will need some issues to pray about, especially something I care about. I feel like prayers about an issue one can relate to are more effective.   Thanks.

I know you must be spending a lot of time trying to line all this up. I hope you don't forget it's all for the good.   God has blessed me with an opportunity to be of service, but my ability is limited by the execution, or at least initiation of certain minor tasks: Ordering books, helping me connect with people who will help, gathering prayer requests, etc. Any effort you put in helping me is multiplied in its impact on others.

April 11, 2012
Mom,

It's 11 p.m., and all is quiet for a change in the POD. I sometimes use the technique of staying up late and waking up early to cut as much of the almost deafening but certainly peace-threatening sound of the 24 other inmates playing like children, who just happen to have booming deep voices, out of my day. The purpose of my prison stay is to be productive, and all that commotion only slows down my focus. So late night and early mornings are crucial.

So far my stay has been excellent, mainly because of the powerful alliance/deep friendship I've made with my roommate, Corey.   It's truly amazing how much we have in common personally, spiritually, aspirations, beliefs, etc. Then, there's almost spooky stuff like same age, shade of skin tone, experience with moms turning us in, name, blood type.   And then we differ in exactly the perfect ways to work together towards financial prosperity.   I've got exactly the strengths he lacks. He's got exactly the strengths I lack.   He's needing exactly the experience I've got. I need exactly the experience he's got. As long as neither of us has a super-long sentence, we've got some serious money making, secure, legal wealth and lifestyle plans cut out perfectly for us.   I can't even express how much of a divinely serendipitous meeting this has been. Plus, we're both adamant about creating a spiritual gathering place at a homeless shelter with our proceeds. And we've got a comrade, who is a solid Mexican, who can help us set up secure ranches in Mexico with our first 50K.

14

The truth of "to succeed in life is all about knowing the right people" is ringing so, so true. Even in a worst case scenario, we've shared enough crucial info to improve each other's profitability ten times. If I can just recover from drugs and alcohol, I'll never be poor or anything but secure and thriving again. I've set myself up through what I've focused on learning and experiencing for this. All I've needed has been at least one of these things to turn my knowledge into a raging success and long-term catastrophe-proof security. Sobriety or capital.

Now it appears not only will I have access to both, I've also got a solid, super-connected brother to execute my plan with. The primary focus of the rest of my stay will be to seek God's help and prayer and meditation to overcome any addictions and personal shortcomings once and for all. In this regard, this opportunity of seven months to three years of relative solitude is unprecedented. Never before have I had both an ideal opportunity to recover and God's peace and blessing in my life. To solidify my goals, I'm taking a 13-day fast before sentencing on the 19th of this month, Thursday, at 10 a.m. Speaking of, I would do good to have at least two people present at sentencing -- the revocation hearing on aforementioned date. I've got no idea who might be available, but perhaps you can ask around. It doesn't even have to be family, just a couple of faces to show the judge I'm not a complete rogue. It would help a lot. The proceedings will probably last no more than twenty minutes at 10 a.m., Thursday the 19th. I will understand if no one is willing. This is my mess, not my already skeptical family's. It's just too bad all of you are in Europe for it. I may try to get it pushed back for this special reason.

This (being incarcerated) is nothing to be sad or discouraged about. This is a miracle, and in time will be revealed as such. Now that's not to say I won't lose two years of my life, be beaten to a bloody pulp a few times as payment for it, but it will be worth it in the end. My friend, Corey, plans to use some of his powerful contacts to get me some protection and protection money while I'm down as well; so maybe not. We'll see. I do know a white guy just got jumped a few weeks ago, by some of the same idiots that are already beefing on me (at odds with).

One thing I've learned about being Cory Roussel, even when I'm a hundred percent respectful, I'm a lightning rod from adversity in these kinds of environments. For example, we're allowed to wear whatever we like in our pods. If we want to wear boxers, no problem, no rules. We can walk around in just boxers. I ordered some thermals last week since a common outfit is thermals -- just thermals, top and bottom. Well, I put mine on and go downstairs for lunch.   I don't even think about how I look.   I know others wear the exact same stuff every day. Well, I go back upstairs, and Joe, this big, tall white crack-head gets to making some homo comments about my long johns.   Another black guy says, "What, are you gay or something?"   And he (white guy) immediately starts swinging on him -- pow, pow, pow.   Well, the little black guy is weak, and he hits back, but is clearly the prey to this situation.   The blacks start to move around like they're fixing to defend the little guy and maimed the big guy, Joe.   Joe runs frantically to the button and starts demanding that the guards take him away.   He senses a danger. Point being, I don't want you to worry, but being different, especially smart and white and colorful, can stir up lots of controversy, and even incite violence, for no explicable reason other than pre-existing tensions getting shook up, and that's with me staying in my cell 22 of 24 hours.   So I almost plan to get beaten at least once or twice. Oh, well, my task is to become God-centric enough to be too like-able for anyone to get away with maiming or killing me politically.   If I can accomplish that, I'm brave enough to take a beating, and if need be, dish one out.   God will protect me, if I keep my heart pure and be vigilant about removing malice from my heart.

Now, Corey is probably the fiercest and strongest, most respected fighter in the dorm -- former Maryland State wrestling champ.   So, as long as he's here, I'm golden.   But he may be leaving soon on either bond or dropped charges, but whatever the case, God will protect me.   For every two knuckleheaded predators, there's one fierce fighter who hates parasites, predators.   We fight not against flesh and blood, but powers and principalities in high places. Ever thought about what that really means? Principalities in high places?   That doesn't sound like something entirely supernatural.   Heck, that almost sounds like they're talking about powerful, political factions. I have learned so much in the past three weeks about God and man and everything in between.   I can relate to George Jackson of *Soledad Brother*[6], whose letters written from prison are filled with what his parents considered wildly speculative, conspiratorial ramblings. I can relate to the black powers' hatred for colonial exploitation and brainwash and oppression tactics.   In the world of modern European-American totalitarianism masquerading as democracy, it's not just the poor blacks and prisoners that are being poisoned, raped, manipulated, cheated, deceived, brainwashed and robbed of God's truth, and the power of spiritual identity, it's you and Dad and Landon and Bethany and me. It's so much deeper than you think -- so, so much deeper. I suspect it's also deeper than I think, and I think it's very deep. No wonder I participate in crime, drugs and self-destruction.   Everything down to my religion has been carefully designed to destroy me and rob me of the understanding of God, history, health, our

16

origin as humans, psychology. I encourage you to get out of the cushy, comfort zone that is the life Dad and you built and at least put forth a minimum of effort entertaining the possibility that our own culture, the rest of the world included, is unsustainable, and not only that, but diabolical designs on planned obsolescence of our population are in the works and will be enacted in our lifetimes. The purpose for this awareness is not to be discouraged, but to take some, at minimum, reasonable precautions. In fact, a moderate level of preparedness can be achieved for only a few thousand dollars -- water purifications, stockpile a few months' worth of food, a couple of weapons, a motorcycle, transferring equity into tangibles, leaning towards tangible investments, often more profitable than the highly vulnerable paper-based investments Dad's got his retirement in. These are the things that the very wealthy are doing. Billionaires are hedging their bets against the recession with gold, land and other tangibles, as we speak. Anyways, it's late, and I'm rambling.

With love, Cory

April 2012
Mom,

I received your letter and also read *My 8,344th Day in Prison*[7] by Michael Santos. It's good. His perspective on ways to avoid conflict could be helpful to some people. He strikes me as a very troubled and doubtful person who I wish I could help to see even greater freedom. It's encouraging to know he's been such a great success because it's a demonstration of the "state of the art" of doing time. It confirms the value and need for promotion of a better way to freedom. I'm very tired from not eating for four days, so I'm probably not going to write as much as I normally do. I did include a lengthy articulation of the method to move towards progress (in the prison project). The next step is creating the blog and uploading the explanation of the project in the form of the outline that's included. Can you please mail it to the Louisiana Book Project after copying it for use with other potential collaborators?

Well it turns out the book Sue suggested is probably the single most profound book I have ever read. *A New Earth*[1] by Eckhart Tolle is about... You know what? I want you to read it. I'm not even going to tell you all about its numerous great truths. It's also a pretty easy and poetic read. Lots of good examples and stories.

Thanks, Cory

April 2012
Mom,

Thanks so much for your letters. I've read them and the research provided and am overwhelmed with the things I want to respond to, but I am learning to accept and work with the limitations I've got as far as timing, memory and the limits of written expression.

We had a big day yesterday. The cell block based facility I was in was evacuated and turned into an isolation/disciplinary wing for people involved in recent violence/trouble makers. As a result, we all begrudgingly packed our stuff and got ready to move into strange new dorms. Everyone was very anxious, but I was not- I knew it was somehow part of God's plan. Sure enough- it was. The new dorm I'm in is a much larger, open-style dorm. Although I refuse to stay in an open-bunk style arrangement for long (sensory overload/ lack of solitude/ inherently detrimental to longtime spiritual purity), I am willing to accept the benefits for my few short weeks left. The benefits are networking with more folks, socializing, playing more chess. (My celli had been my only opponent. Now I've got many who can challenge and beat me.) As a divine bonus, prayer groups are held THRICE daily, with almost half the dorm participating and amazing results being seen in people involved lives, even exoneration and unprecedented mercy being shown. My celli, Corey, is across the hall, so we at least have a chance to "telephone" each other (sign language).

I am very thankful you sent those books. They're going to be a great asset to the people in here. Many guys are very receptive to this sort of Christian self-help/ God-help books. So I'm sure they'll have a profound impact much like *The Shack*[8] and *Purpose Drive Life*[9] have already for sure. I hope you weren't expecting me to read them because I've got three books I'm reading now and two more in the queue. Just no way I'll have time to read them all.

In a divine confirmation, shortly after I wrote a response defending my egoism and narcissism, I came across a book on overcoming shame (the approximate cause of narcissism). It's very revealing, and I hope I have time to read and digest it before I go. It's called *Healing the Shame that Binds You*[10]. Also the Tolle book, *A New Earth*[1], is proving incredibly profound and revealing. It's basically a book debunking "the deception of identity" (Freudian "Ego") and awakening our Oneness with the creator. It references Jesus,

18

Buddha, etc. and explains salvation and many of Jesus' crucial concepts in down-to-earth psychological terms and opens a way to enlightenment/ transcendence that's essentially the condensed B.S.-free version of all true religion in a beautiful and poetic way. I see why people consider Tolle such a profound person, writer- He's a big deal. I highly recommend it.

Your research has effectively opened the door for many great manifestations of the goal of freeing people. It's also left me almost overwhelmed with the great possibilities. As a result, as you suggested in a previous letter, I intend to focus on networking- that is exploring FIRST ways I can help with existing projects and information I can gather and pass along to others on these resources. I may get cut off at any minute.

Cory

April 17, 2012
Mom,

It's morning now, one of the two times during the day it's really quiet enough to give something complete attention. Oddly enough, the habit is this around here: At 5 AM, everyone must stand for count. At 5:30 AM, breakfast is served, always a very carb-heavy plate of toast, cereal, sugar, grits, etc. Then everyone just gets back in bed and sleeps until noon. On full stomachs. Very crazy thinking if you ask me. Why even bother eating a huge breakfast if you're just going to sleep on it for six hours? As a result, my celli skips breakfast. He's completed a 28-day fast during which he ate only two slices of bread and still did intensive aerobic workouts every day. Quite impressive. He lost a bunch of extra weight, but more importantly, got back in control of his diet. No meat. Stopped eating at every opportunity like so often, as Americans, we do, and eat to fullness. Restauranteurs admit, the key to profits is "crave-ability" of items, not wholesomeness, quality or even taste. It's crave-ability. That is-similarity to a drug. If restaurants find an appetizer that makes you get addicted, that's dollars. So we as a culture, in 40 years of time, went from restaurants almost exclusively as special occasions venues to regular providers. We, myself included, struggle with eating too much of everything. The food ingredients contribute too-veggies devoid of their normal nutrients, carbs all but empty of nutrition, meats of the lowest grade. We get more toxins and less

19

nutrients than ever before. As a result, it's crucial (as it always has been, but even more so) to fast. Fasting is crucial to true purification of the body. It's impossible to convey how incredibly important and useful it is to the soul and mind as well. Mentally, its benefit is three-fold: First, it forces the mind to break heavily reinforced reward cycles that naturally get out of control over the months, (heaven forbid going years without a fast). No one is immune to the eventual corruption of the pleasure centers of our mind. Like a communist dictatorship, the ruler who sits in power, however just, for years and years unchallenged, slowly is corrupted. He needs to be challenged every now and then. A strike, if you will, to get him back on track. If you believe as every major spiritual teacher says- the self is a tyrant-seeking subtle sabotage of our best intentions. Fasting rewires that circuitry, since subconsciously and consciously one must reinforce a higher motive every time the body says "eat". ("No, I'm striving towards a greater goal, body. I won't eat.") It's a shortcut to the primary means every spiritual leader suggests is the key to attainment of any kind of spiritual worth- self-abasement. Few if any other methods can come close, since fasting is tied directly to denial of our very life energy.

Second, it clears the mind incredibly well. Whereas before, our brains are preoccupied with the running of a metabolic powerhouse, in fasting, the city of our mind is "shut down" to all unnecessary commerce, and its inhabitants are free to take on all sorts of tasks they otherwise never would in a state of constant business. Can you imagine how debilitating it would be to never even have one solid week of vacation time? Anyways, the mind becomes a big beautiful empty vessel, open and ready to receive God's ideas- with beautiful agility and crystal clear clarity and vigor. It's a feeling superior to the best experienced otherwise. Everything gets organized and nothing is out of balance. Instantly the mind becomes wide open for communication with the Creator and the feeling of connection with the universe. We comprehend the shortcomings of self and get a new clear-minded perspective.

Third, time slows down. It's difficult to explain this one, but somehow a 24-hour day turns into a 34-hour day. With our mind's frequencies fixating on a much narrower band, and not wasting untold (and otherwise unperceived) amounts of efforts on metabolism, it makes time begin to seem of much more substance. Suddenly, you've got even more time to do good in a day, and focus becomes more effortless.

Physically, fasting is completely invaluable. The huge stores of toxin-laden fat reserves in the body are cleared out and ridding us of otherwise detrimental poisons that were releasing themselves on a deadly daily regimen. Even the thin have toxic fat reserves, brain, cardiovascular and vascular system. Anywhere fats are present, so are accumulated toxins. I liken it to a house or pantry. Even the best kept pantry will accumulate unused food over the months and years and eventually stuff pushed to the back will rot, contaminating the integrity of the whole pantry. Only by removing it all, piece by piece and putting it back, can we effectively identify and remove the bad stuff. It also gives us a chance to reorganize. I believe God calls us to be excellent stewards of anything he entrusts us with. As we both know, this I have not been- disorganized, wasteful and ultimately unaware of everything I own. "If you can't measure it, you can't manage it." So, I've taken to the habit of arbitrarily removing every single item I own from its "home", cataloguing it and putting it back. To me, if I can't give God's possessions enough respect to keep close track of where every single one is, I'm unworthy of possessing it. Same with money. As a result, I, for the first time in my life, am organized. To the "T". It's the same with our bodies. We must stop just adding and subtracting food to it daily and take time to let our bodies REORGANIZE and purge. It's a proven fact there exists certain powerful restorative mechanisms in our bodies, even mechanisms which restore our very constantly degrading DNA, that cannot and do not activate until day three of "starvation". Hence the natural "glow" you see on a person who has been fasting for three weeks or a month. Their very DNA is being repaired. The bodily benefits of fasting continue long after the fasting period is over- once our millions of cells have "experienced scarcity" they learn to operate frugally and efficiently, much the way children of the Depression paved the way to the prosperity of the 60's and 70's becoming Warren Buffets and George Soros. Our every cell needs to "learn" to overcome its "sinful" (I no longer believe in sin) nature. This simply isn't possible without fasting, much like God simply can't do anything with a prosperous person who knows not brokenness. Too much self holds him back. (Think the rich man who asked how we can get into heaven.) Sad to say, but as Americans, we are ALL that rich man. Anyways, after fasting, one is overcome with energy and vitality- as well as the new natural ability to rise above our natural and imperceptible inclination towards inoptimal consumption.

Our spirits too benefit immeasurably from a fast. This is why every major religion incorporates fasting into their practices and history. The Bible describes afflictions that can only be removed through prayer and fasting. The Catholics say fasts make your prayers immeasurably more effective. Buddha fasted 40 days to know the true nature of God.

Personally, I'm on day 10 and feel excellent. It's been an excellent fast, really helped me clear up my mind and address dietary concerns. I would go longer but without proper nutrition to break the fast, I think it is not the best idea. On my last month, I plan to do a 28-day fast. So, I can break it up properly with fruits and veggies and good nutrition.

Even with how thin you are, I think you would greatly benefit from a one-week fast. It certainly won't hurt you, and you can even play tennis on it if you wish (though you'll find it's a challenge, and you'll become wiped out afterward). It's a part of being a good steward of the body, brain and spirit we're borrowing. I fast at least one week per year, but would like to increase that number in both duration and frequency, since it's proven so powerful a vehicle for strengthening my body, spirit and mind.

I hope you'll get the list of books I sent to Bethany from her. I am getting very close to the end of my rope in terms of good reading material and have been waiting for someone to get on Amazon and send me a few ASAP. If nothing else, please send two of whichever are Eckhart Tolle's most highly recommended books.

By the way, the chess book you sent was PERFECT. Great selection, thanks. I read it and my game and understanding shot up, as well as Corey's. I know it will enter circulation as a prized commodity when I leave or pass it on. The first of many.

Also, any highly rated book on "logic" that covers and explains "symbolic logic" operations. I had a college textbook on this subject, but I don't remember its title. Preferably a book which includes sample problems and exercises and speaks of proofs using symbolic logic. This is a college level subject, but if you can just select a reasonably priced used, best-rated book that would be great. Thanks so much, I better wrap up so this catches mail call.

With love, Cory

April 23, 2012
Landon,

Hey, how are you? How is everything? Everything's going great here- life in prison is exceedingly simple/easy yet also full of amazing serendipity and interesting experiences. I'm very happy here, and often think I might have voluntarily admitted myself if I knew it would be such a great thing. I was too caught up stressing about potential negative aspects of incarceration to just step forward and revoke myself (to kill the probation) and enjoy the positive aspects, which are many.

Yes, it is prison, and full of sin and violence, but it's also full of peace and holiness too- just more extreme. I had created a couple of enemies two weeks ago (almost unavoidable) and felt sure an eventual showdown was imminent with them. I was at peace about it though and just prayed for the guys and forgave their transgressions. A few days ago, I got word that confirmed my suspicions that one of them was plotting against me- just waiting for the right opportunity. I just shrugged it off, knowing God would handle it- even if it meant me getting stomped. Then yesterday a friend of my enemy disrespected a Muslim brother while he was in prayer. A fight broke out, which quickly turned into a 2 vs. 10 riot- and guess who one of the two was. My enemy. I did not wish violence on them, but that's the energy they put out, and guess what? God sent it back 10-fold. Luckily, they survived, but only because they got spared. I've got a newfound faith in God, and am almost daily experiencing wild serendipitous confirmation of His work.

I've also been shown a way to make the most out of this situation- a comprehensive plan to come out bigger, better, faster, smarter, wiser, richer, stronger, healthier and more well-rounded. More importantly, God's shown me a variety of profound ways to help others in a variety of meaningful ways during my stay. I've got NO EXCUSE for boredom nor can I feel anything but deep gratitude for this year- for it will be my most meaningful yet. Perhaps you'll have some kind of input of my ideas.

The ultimate plan is to use otherwise undirected attention to help inmates improve themselves through spirituality and the accumulation of knowledge/education. This is accomplished a few ways:

23

Book/Magazine program- This will start with me purchasing a variety of informative, educational and uplifting books with my own money, based on recommendations and requests of others for the purpose of refining intellects and exposing inmates to beneficial practices, beliefs and ideas, i.e. meditation, self-awareness, spiritual practices, self-improvement, etc. Any book which will be read AND directs people's attention towards improvement or intellectual pursuits is a candidate. Through this process, books with the greatest potential will be identified; publishers will be requested to offer it at a discounted price and ultimately donors will be sought out to fund large scale prison distributions. The beautiful thing about the idea is: in prison the average book is read over 100 times. If a book costs $15, that's $.15 to potentially have a major impact on someone's life for the better. Ten dollars could literally expose someone to a huge wealth of empowering information- 60 "book reads". The only limiting factor is identifying the most impactful books (balance of interestingness to impactfulness). I know this will make a MASSIVE positive impact on the world, even if NOTHING ELSE it never gets past me spending a couple of thousand on 100 books for wisdom-hungry inmates to read for years to come, (10,000 book reads). I already know of certain books that profoundly improve almost every person who reads them's lives- so this is a win-win sure-fire big impact idea.

Then, I also plan to show people who to fix their credit through the mail while locked up. (Someone showed me.)

Then, I also plan to help inmates connect to pen-pals through pre-existing websites, whether just for fun or some other beneficial purpose, i.e. finding an AA sponsor that will help them change and recover through the mail. (Nothing new. I just know how to make it happen.)

Then, I also am going to start soliciting prayer requests and get our informal Bible Study group to start a prayer team for people outside who send in prayer requests. If prayer works (of course) and prison is full of devout Christians (it is) who are just dying to do something meaningful with their lives (they are) and have free time (you know we do), then this could turn into a viral idea. Either way, like all my ideas, even if it turns out to be just me and one other person, it will still be great.

I am also on the lookout for any productive, potentially marketable uses for idle minds willing to work via correspondence. I know personally I could help Mom's ESL [English as a Second Language] students revise/edit essays via email, but I know there's some kind of way I can put moderately smart people to work doing something via correspondence. To make $3-$5/day for 8 hours of work would be a fortune in terms of prison pay grade. (Many jobs pay <$.18/hr.) Surely there's some kind of editing work/proofreading/something I can get some people doing for money while in prison. Let me know if you think of anything.

Anyways, my work is cut out for me. I'm downright busy with ideas and can't wait to see them slowly grow with Mom's help doing legwork. If you have any input or suggestions about these initiatives, please do tell. I can use all the help I can get.

April 23, 2012
Mom,

Hello, just wanted to check in and say hello. How are things? I'm not sure if I turned in my visitor approval slip in time to have you visit Thursday. If I didn't, I'm sorry. Things are going well. I've been experimenting with my diet, trying to find a healthier way to live in prison. When I broke my fast Thursday, I did exactly what I intended not to do and went overboard on food for a few days. Eating is such a precious luxury. We take it for granted with our everyday three-meals-a-day diets. It's so important to properly time eating and force the body to "learn" new ways to metabolize food. The norm of three meals a day for years completely neglects the way we were designed. Finally, I've been getting back on track, focusing on cutting caloric intake down to 1,500 calories/day or less and timing it so as to spend as little of the day digesting as possible- ideally one meal. People don't realize being in "digest mode" actually requires a certain subconscious mental preoccupation that ultimately clouds the mind. This is why the medicine man in *Eat, Pray, Love*[13] eats only one meal a day. Anyways, I'm enjoying teaching my body and mind to submit to greater purposes, defy our American culture of sin and weakness. I've started working out with my roommate, Corey. My entire body is sore from the intense workouts. When I get out, I plan to be bigger, stronger and leaner in every way, so physically is no exception.

Remember the enemies I told you about? I knew God had a plan. This morning there was a riot, and let's just say homeboy isn't a concern anymore. I came downstairs to see what the ruckus was, and there was like 10 guys just punishing them. They're very lucky they're not comatose right now. One enemy still lives in this block, but he's so scared he's going to be next in line that I could probably tell him to leave if I wanted and he would leave our block. Although violence isn't great, it's the inevitable, and events like this morning are the finest expressions of physical justice. Two troublemakers were taught a lesson, made it out alive and our block grew in respect and camaraderie. The one problem-maker left has been turned harmless. I know that security is just as much a matter of mindset in here as it is circumstance. My responsibility is to keep a pure heart and a keen mind. If I do that, God will take care of the rest.

I'm getting a bit restless and ready for my move to B.O.P. (Bureau of Prisons) custody so I can really start diving into books and my projects. I'm somewhat curious where I'm headed as well, since it could be anywhere. Anywhere will do though. I just need books, people and a pen, and I'm good.

April 23, 2012
Dad,

Hey, How are you? I'm doing great here, prison life is actually pretty nice when you're in the right mindset. There are some things you mentioned I wanted to take some time to write on/inquire about...

First, Why are you or were you sad about me being locked up?

The truth is, with three years probation, revocation was all but inevitable. Any number of objective perspectives on my chances for completion looked very unlikely, even if I could triple the longest I've ever been sober. Truth be told, the government just plain doesn't like me, not just for non-compliance, but for who I am and what I stand for. The system is set up for population control, not understanding or assistance becoming healthy, joyous and free. I know you don't agree with this thinking, but it's the truth and without accepting the real dynamics of what's going on, you're never going to see me as anything more than a misled rebel chasing worthless causes. I have to stick to my guns and follow what I believe, as you do too, but I think a little understanding could go a long way.

26

I am in very good spirits about my situation here. In fact, the biggest concern I have right now is YOU and how YOU'RE dealing with the shame of me and how things may appear to you and others. I know you're ashamed of me, and given what you know, I don't blame you. It's what you don't know and what you can't see that leaves me powerless to do anything but apologize and try to help you understand, at least for long enough to get you through until you can actually SEE what I mean and have meant all these years, hard as they may be. I am very sorry to have shamed you. I know that the way I spoke to the judge did not help. I went into the courtroom with a much different demeanor than my interactions with him portrayed. He caught me off guard with his adversarialism- particularly his abuse of confidential psychologist notes taken out of context and his failure to recognize the full implications of the disease model for alcoholism. He also had the audacity to accuse me of "thinking I was smarter than everyone else." I assert I don't think myself smarter until you give me good reason to believe I am. If you demonstrate a far inferior collection of beliefs and understanding of a particular subject, which I have studied and listened to the whole gamut of expert opinions on, then Yes, I will consider myself smarter than you in that subject, until you prove otherwise. That would be like me arguing which catalyst is superior for polymer synthesis with you, and then getting angry when you demonstrate a superior understanding on the subject.

What's more, I do not recognize the authority of the U.S. government over me. They're acting in stark opposition to the spirit and letter of the Constitution, the spirit and letter of our fore-fathers, and the spirit and letter of the Word of God. They have become a tyrant and are daily committing despicable atrocities against God and humankind. I know you disagree, but that's just my belief. I did not chose U.S. citizenship- and if it weren't for you, Mom, and Bethany, I'd renounce immediately and flee. If you knew half of what I know about our government, you'd completely understand. It's not crazy. If it were, then you'd have to say all of our fore-fathers and all of Western European history were crazy and a complete fabrication.

With that said, I have the utmost respect for the individuals I've interacted with who have represented the U.S. Court system for their integrity, heartfelt compassion and patience dealing with me. They mean well. Their roles however and the legislation they enforce is nothing less than disgusting.

27

You mentioned unfamiliarity with the "four prerequisites" for recovery I mentioned.

- Environment
- Desire to quit
- 12-step involvement
- Support system

Yes, these things I've found 100% necessary for recovery. This is not a cop-out. It's the same four things treatment experts and 12-step sponsors have taught me. Twelve step involvement can be replaced by religion, and environment and support system can be built, but all four must align for lasting recovery to happen. I was denied meetings, denied access to support systems, denied the request to go to an environment I knew to be healthy (Austin), forced to stay in environments I knew to be unhealthy (drug infested half-way house in Baton Rouge). It was a recipe for disaster. I know I can and will recover, but I gotta' stick by what I know and do it the only way I know how.

You also mentioned something that hit a sore spot. "Money is never a problem when you don't have a drug problem." I agree with this statement 75%. I think you have a skewed idea of my life and its struggle. I've frequently had money problems even when not on drugs. I've also been in extremely difficult situations because of drug use and spent months desperately trying to get help, but was unable to do so because some minor expenses forced me to spend my time and energy trying to just meet my basic needs- food, water, shelter, mortal safety. Point being, NO, drugs are not to blame for all my money problems. A combination of not being taught proper money management technique, irresponsibility, mental problems and cultural toxicity have all worked together to undermine financial success in my life. Believe it or not, my plight is far from unique. The generations my age and younger are, on average, completely incapable of sustaining themselves financially. It's an issue I'm determined to address this year along with many others.

I would go so far as to say I'm excited about this year in prison. I'm at peace, and God's given me a way to use it to the MAXIMUM for self-improvement and the improvement of others. You'll see in time.

With love,
Cory

28

April 2012
Dad,

Hello, how are you? Thanks for your well thought out response to my letter. I am very impressed.

In an update, every initiative and goal I've set towards the ends God has shown me to pursue has been progressing at a MIRACULOUS rate, flowering and growing every hour of every day with every conversation, every person I meet, letter I write and letter I receive. It's as though I've been rocketed into a dimension of the "highly improbable"/miraculous. Divine confirmations are a DAILY occurrence. I can't tell you how many times we'll be studying or talking about some spiritual principle when not five minutes later someone comes in with a book to show us a page talking about the EXACT VERSE or concept we're discussing in an undeniably miraculous twist of destiny. We'll be discussing a business idea when suddenly a person comes into the dorm who happens to be an expert in that particular field. Things you and Mom mention to me in your letters will be expanded and explained in a bizarrely direct way in books I read or things people tell me about. The way God shuffles us around the prison is another way we've got a constant stream of divine confirmation. I was just telling Mom, we began a fast Monday night. I told my celli, Corey, "Man, I've got that feeling. It's like the feeling before a workout I know will be grueling or a big tough day at work." He says, "Why?" I answer, "I can just tell sometimes when God's fixing to put adversity in our lives. Perfect ease and comfort are always broken by trials and adversity when one's striving after God." Sure enough, not eight hours later an almost unprecedented reshuffling of prisoners occurred, breaking up our cohesive and harmonious block into various others throughout the compound, which hasn't happened in > five years. Needless to say, it was a trying situation; most of the dorms aren't nearly as relaxed as ours. The dorm I'm in just got done beating a man (convicted that day of molesting multiple 11-year-old girls) to the point of disfigurement. Then when the C.O.s (correction officers) came to break it up (so he wouldn't die), they restrained the aggressors and he ran back to his bunk and got a knife and proceeded to slash his attackers repeatedly. Needless to say, it was very gruesome. Fortunately, God protects. God has shown me how to conduct myself, from the hours that I sleep to the way I purify my heart of resentments to minimize risk. He's also put me in a position to connect with some of the most respected warriors in my various

29

dorms- something that's saved me at least once. I feel about like the possibility of getting hurt in anything more than a trivial way, the way you probably feel about getting in a wreck. Yeah the roads are dangerous, but a little defensive driving and you can be at 100% peace overall about taking a calculated risk. I'm not above having myself put in isolation if I feel a threat is imminent.

You mentioned "not projecting expectations/ideas of what's best for me" in life. Yes, this is good, but raising concerns isn't bad and in fact is a very valuable even priceless form of help that I've got very limited access to. My close-mindedness/spiritual oppression has severely limited my ability to respond positively/accept this sort of help from y'all in the past, but hopefully I can overcome this, as I have been with various criticisms and concerns Mom has raised: narcissism, authority issues, God-centrism, non-judgementalism of religious beliefs/ tolerance, various concepts about the manifestations of my spiritual mission. Though I often respond reactionarily and inconsiderably to such criticism, I always retain them, even when I'm spiritually incapable of digesting them easily (or at all). I'd like to think now that my spiritual self is healthy, I can digest anything wholesome, however difficult. All those things Mom mentioned were confirmed by things I read soon after they were brought to my attention, another form of confirmation by God. All have to do with misdirections of the "ego" in the form of identity and coping mechanisms designed for healthy pursuit of God pushed off balance by adversity. Fortunately they need not be "adjusted", simply exposed and they more or less vanish (until and unless I revert back to sin). Such WAS the nature of the recovery I recall in Austin. I really never dealt with my problems. They were merely pushed aside and replaced with God-centrism in every area I submitted. This is why psychology, AA/NA and other active-resistance-based methods have proven ineffective. It's all about the grace of God. All that stuff has its place, but is only potentiated by grace and catalyzed through grace.

I think what I speak of when I talk about conflict in the way to help is a breakdown in our abilities to help each other- an area of my life I've felt lacking severely, mostly because of my having driven any form of interaction with you out of my life- due to a combination of factors, mainly misinterpretation of your actions and shame of letting you down. Truth be told, I know that I've got some ways to help you achieve your life's purpose as you have me. I need your insight into life to succeed, as I need Mom's and my support systems. I resolve to be more open about it.

You wrote about your investment strategies/insights. I appreciate that very much and plan to research those thoroughly when I get to the Fed. I recently read a book about George Soros and Warren Buffet, a comparison and contrast book that outlined a few of their insights on wealth/investment. They too speak volumes about preservation of capital/frugality. Warren Buffet still lives in his old house from before he made his first million (now >$45 billion). He still picks up pennies and change. He pays himself a salary of $100,000/year and lives on even less. I found that very amusing. He complains some of the most costly financial decisions he's ever made involved visits to the corner store when he was young. He estimates his $.50 worth of snacks, after appreciation over 40+ years, would be millions today. It also talks about how very wealthy people love creating wealth, not spending it. I don't know if I'll ever be very wealthy, but I do know that crucial to my financial success is: letting go of my flesh. Something that even in prison with God's will coursing through me every minute and extremely limited temptations, I still struggle. I do things like collect cornbread and eat it addictively and get addicted to thinking about ideas, especially entrepreneurial ones. I just can't escape the oppression of the flesh, only shift my focus away from it and give it to God. Still, it leaves me apprehensive about my ability to be free. If I can't quit eating compulsively (and only experience true relief in a fast), how much more so will I gravitate towards real vices? One solution I've conceived is to live overseas in places with minimal costs of living. These places will also offer the opportunity to help others greatly with limited resources. I am reluctant to want to invest charity in Americans who need hundreds, when mere dollars can cure and save children in other countries. Either way, I've determined I'll have no excuse not to net an excess of $100,000/year once I'm released. Through networking I've gathered a huge wealth of opportunities that could only be compromised by my return to old ways. I also know now why my repeated whole-hearted attempts to recover were unsuccessful. The Bible speaks of one who falters from his salvation being repossessed by seven demons where before only one existed. It goes on to say the person will not be able to lift himself from his dilemma and will require help from other believers to be brought back into the light. This is why I felt so helpless. I also now know that being locked up is better than life out there in addiction. So, if I were to falter, I know that just trying to recover on my own with AA/NA is impossible. I would need a team of prayer warriors to free me. I also know living lawlessly and being arrested is superior to just failing repeatedly. It sounds crazy, but if given the choice between a life of freedom without abstinence and a life in prison, I'd choose prison happily. God's given me a way to do time gracefully and purposefully, so why even shy from it?

I seek to find a healthy, free-man's substitute for the cure that is prison. It's really the suspension and elimination of sensory depth and richness, distractions and temptations that makes prison/jail so powerful of an experience. Every bit of benefit a "retreat" offers- ashrams, temples, fishing trips, etc.- all offer and capitalize on this in watered down ways. Prison is just the purest- well almost purest- form. There are places that offer more, like a place in Dallas where you go to meditate in silence for week-long visits. No talking. No moving around. Just meditation. I'm interested in doing all I can to divert the possibilities of failure to recover, but back-up plans are important too. Life's a never-ending battle.

Anyways, back to investments. I have to say, while I can appreciate your reasoning for not investing in an apocalyptic possibility way, I assert that though it may be okay with you if "we're all in the same boat" when it goes down, which will most likely manifest itself in a political way not a natural way, why not protect yourself in some small way if the cost is low? If I could show you some of the research I've read and studied on the laws passed/institutions in place that point to nothing less than the wealthy and the government taking steps to "gear-up" for something huge, why wouldn't you take out a small insurance plan? Even if it only saves you for a week or helps you have resources when everyone else is desperate (think Katrina or a Baton Rouge levee break). It's worth its weight in gold. Emergency preparedness. Taking the same precautions "those who know are" seems reasonable enough even without seeing the actual congressional bills made to institute extensive oppressive population management measures and intentionally sabotage our normal resource infrastructure to ensure cooperation. I'll tell you right now there are actual laws on the books that: establish a legal way for the indefinite suspension of the constitution in an emergency, enactable by the president at will; confiscation of our private property during an emergency, for any reason; prevention of escape from the U.S.; creation of prisons capable of housing one third of the U.S. population; withdrawal of all currency and requirement to participate in government programs to allocate

32

resources; existence of a list of over 30 million Americans slated for detainment as "risks" to implementation of martial law"; creation of extensive SWAT team-like police force called LEAF within the ranks of the National Guard and state police designed to neutralize any resistance to martial law's implementation and constitution suspension; laws that allow any person who even speaks against the government during such an emergency to be executed or shipped to a concentration camp.

The writing is on the wall. No, you can't stop the rising tide, but you can get in a boat. Many politicians are spending millions storing up pure water and building underground cisterns for food-grade water storage. Why?

These are signs of a coming catastrophe whose effects can be reduced through some careful research and planning. Why not?

Yes, the country is great. Its government contains a certain cancer that is malignant, incurable and fatal, so hopefully after the dust all clears, all will be well again. But in light of the clearly written reports on what's fixing to happen and happening, I can have no other opinion on the Fed than EVIL. A puppet for families and organizations who have no other interest but maximum exploitation and will kill, steal, poison, torture and destroy to ensure it. Anyways, it's late. I hope to hear from you soon. For now, I'm out.
Much love, Cory

April 2012
Mom,

How are you? Over here things are going splendidly. It seems I've created some hostile enemies, and may find myself the target of an attack if I can't get transferred before it precipitates. But I've got no fear and am also confident in my position in the issue. I've been wrongly accused by simple-minded thugs who feel threatened by my personality and smarts. What's new? They aren't going to kill me, and I won't give them reason to make a justifiable attack that doesn't put them in the light of the rest as anything but predators (an unpopular and dangerous role to play). So, I'll just go on doing me, staying in my cell reading and praying like normal, occasionally visiting with my new-found friends. There are more who respect me than hate me, so I can't see an altercation getting very serious.

33

None-the-less, pray for the well-being and prosperity of my enemies, if you will. And worry not. As I have described before, hatred towards me is almost inevitable simply because some value not all the things I embody and will naturally desire to harm that which they don't understand. It's actually a great opportunity to make a display of God's love- for myself and others.

My roommate, Corey, is probably leaving soon, which is a blessing and a curse. A curse because he's my back-up plan body guard. (He's pledged protection, and he has the ability to enforce it.) I'll lose a confidante and thinker to converse with. But a blessing because he's going out to get started paving the way for our future collaborative business efforts. He's also going to make sure my books and phone stay loaded up and any other loose end I've got outside gets tied up. He's also offered to send books in. In exchange, I'll be helping him with investment planning and research, as well as networking with other prisoners in the Fed to build our business. It's incredible the kind of knowledge and networking that can be done in jail. People have tuned me into some beautiful opportunities, as I have likewise given insight to others that'll prove crucial to their future livelihood.

Yes, in addition to the outpouring of spiritual treasure, it looks like very soon (perhaps before I get out of prison) financial progress will become a reality. It's all beautifully tied in with my main goal for this "retreat", too: HELPING OTHERS.

As I shared with you in previous letters, I've been given a powerful and confirmed dream/vision for what this medium-length prison stay could be turned into. The great Reverser of Setbacks is offering me an opportunity far superior to anything I've thus far experienced to make a difference in people's lives and the world as a whole. As you predicted, God has given me an opportunity to turn my struggle for mental and spiritual freedom into a chance to help thousands of other inmates be "broken out" of intangible prisons: bondage to self, ignorance, "boredom", poisonous pop culture, diet, criminal mentality, etc. Through my experience at the halfway house, I saw the value of knowledge to give people new ways of thinking, acting and living. I saw people, crippled by rage and criminal thinking, be exposed to books on self-denial and turn into mini Buddhas and Gandhis. I saw people who only knew the drug game learn to be entrepreneurs, pursue nursing certificates and get good jobs. The opportunity is there.

34

Here as well as other places I've seen, a certain hunger exists for a better way. People DO want to change- find God, change patterns and become healthy productive members of society. Sure, some don't care, but some really do.

They do all they can with the limited resources that are available. Good books are voraciously consumed, traded and treated as sacred jewels. People turn an eager ear to business opportunities that could be an alternative to crime. The Bible and Koran being the only two main spiritual books available are read cover to cover. And then discussed.

What this place and others lack is RESOURCES. Nowhere else in society could progressive ideals fall on such receptive ears. Nowhere else could a few ideas, a few new experiences be so revolutionary. In the incarcerated, we also find the most powerful opportunity for systematic and indirect improvement of society. A criminal turned father is one less future criminal. An inmate turned employee is a huge boon to the economy. A violent offender turned peaceful is ten people spared a beating. It's a perfect chance to not just do good, but make a PERMANENT IMPROVEMENT ON SOCIETY.

As a result, I have made a pledge to God and myself: to work towards the physical, mental and spiritual recovery of inmates through the dissemination of knowledge, culturing and spirituality, until I die.

While my personal victories against mental and spiritual oppression have been GREAT, and the continued pursuit of holiness is paramount to all success, and my various entrepreneurial endeavors are great, of far greater value is this aforementioned goal. I will devote much of my time and energy to the wholehearted pursuit of this goal.

May 2012
Mom,

As established repeatedly before, narcissism is the inevitable consequence of divergence from the norm. Look at my friend Ramon, for example. He's a very proud Mexican from Detroit, living in a prison in rural Louisiana. One could interpret his actions as narcissistic, but it's just a response to being different in an environment that devalues your strengths and constantly focuses on weaknesses. In the different person's mind, the "normal" people are simple idiots. Such is the thinking of many other cultures living in America or any foreign land. One could accuse Moroccan Moors as being narcissistic, an allegation reinforced by their complete diplomatic immunity to American law. You can say "they think they're better than everyone else". Personally, I DO think they're "better" than most people in most ways that count. This inevitably will offend people. Likewise, I think I AM better than many in many ways that count- and I'm willing to admit I'm inferior in a multitude of ways. I'm an outlier. A divergence from my local cultural norm in many ways. In some instances with some people/situations, I do not see a reasonable way to convey the value of my strengths and only see ways that they'll continue to see me as weak and inconsequential. It's these people who I DO write off because I know without this crucial understanding, they're all but worthless to me. It's very much like being in a foreign country 24-7. The only place I don't feel that way is Austin, Texas. I don't expect you or anyone else to understand. With all that said, I do need to try to overcome these inevitable misunderstandings and not offend people unnecessarily. It's just the same as any other foreigner's struggles acclimating.

May 7, 2012
Mom,

Thanks for your letters. I've not been writing as much partially because of a general reduction in writing (more distractions/ambient chaos in an open dorm) and partly because of the past few times I've tried I've gotten the "divine veto" after finishing a draft or entire letter, however seemingly innocuous. It's 5 AM. It's also the first night of what I plan to turn into a habit of semi-nocturnalism. Instead of 1 AM to 5 AM then 2 PM to 5 PM every day, 1 PM to 5 PM and 5:30 PM to 9 PM every day, cutting out the loudest part of the day in favor of the quietest. We have no restrictions here like Federal. We may walk around only in underwear 24-7. Sleep and wake and move about 24-7. Since everyone sleeps 1 AM to 11 AM, it only makes sense that I do all I can to capitalize on silence.

So last night I stayed up with my friend Eli. It turns out he has met you. You were passing out ESL cards near his apartment, and he spoke with you about his parents and himself. I don't remember where he lives, somewhere near your house. Anyways, I've been powering through the books you sent as quickly as possible. Want to make sure I read them now just in case. I must admit, I wasn't excited about reading more "Christian" books.

Oh yeah, *Addiction and Grace*[11] turned out to be a pretty good book. Nothing profound, yet it did do a great job defining psychological terms spiritually and proving the importance of grace. I've passed it along to a good steward (after notating the cover with my contact info for further support) of it- an ex-minister with a psychology degree who acts as one of the co-facilitators of the thrice daily prayer circles and the thrice weekly Bible study. He is enjoying it.

The book *Primal*[12] is very good. It was great at providing new ideas of ways to embody Christian ideals and painting a new, more hands-on picture of God and salvation. I took many notes, enjoyed it much, wrote in the cover (contact info) and passed it on. If I have time, I'd like to read it again. I got a whole page of great notes out of it and could have easily written three more. I especially liked George Washington Carvers' story. Also, I found the part on the heart very revealing.

Please, please read *A New Earth*[1] by Tolle. Have Dad read it as well. It's a great read.

May 13, 2012
Mom,

Hello, how are you? I hope all is well and you had a good Mother's Day. I'm doing well. Just hanging out waiting to be transferred, reading as much as I can.

I'm actually reading *A New Earth*[1], which is REALLY good. It's opening my eyes to certain truths in Christianity, despite itself not being a "Christian" book per se. It's explaining the symbology of Jesus' parables in ways that make SENSE, in a considerably (to me) different light than contemporary Christian interpretations. Of particular revelation, the clarification and reinterpretation (really just original meaning) of the terms: "poor in Spirit", sin ("to miss the mark/miss the point"), salvation, exclusivity of salvation. I feel the understanding of Jesus' flowering in such a way (in me) that will be far more transferrable to those who do not understand spirituality in general. Science and faith are coming together in a way that's NEW to me. I see the basis for my previous criticisms. I also know the fallibility of ALL human logic. "The wisdom of this world is folly to God." Knowledge can only point to the truth, and just as the moon is not the finger that points to the moon, so knowledge is not the truth. Truth is a state of awareness, not a set of beliefs, (paraphrased from *A New Earth*[1]). A big part of the things I'm learning have to do with "being present", that is living each millisecond with complete engagement- interacting with others as though each second were all we possess. With this mode of thinking, an understanding of the nature of the way God works has begun to grow, one that supersedes even time, which arguably does not truly exist. It's only a way for us to grasp the infinite with the finite (where we exist) understanding. Without going in too deep for the ramifications of this model, our prayers and actions TODAY actually shape what we think of as our PAST and our FUTURE.

Well, running out of time.
With love,
Cory

Chapter 3: Letters from San Diego Prison

At the end of May 2012, Cory was transferred via the Federal Transfer Center in Oklahoma City to MCC (Metropolitan Correctional Center) San Diego, which was the original place he did time before his revocation. This new prison was located in a high-rise building in downtown San Diego. I observed a distinct progression of exponential growth in the coming months in Cory's life.

Another interesting facet of this experience deals with Cory's handwriting, which 95% of these letters were hand-written. Cory, being a lefty, had previously always been challenged by tiny somewhat illegible handwriting. He much preferred to type for this reason. However at this time in his life, he wrote copiously by hand, since he seldom had access to type. And he gave it his best effort to make his writing legible. Around about August, I received one of his letters, and I was shocked when I opened it. The handwriting was so attractive and legible in stark contrast to his normal writing that I almost thought someone else wrote the letter! What happened is that overnight almost, the transformations that had been occurring in his life translated into his handwriting. It was such a beautiful manifestation of his growth and evolution.

Here are the next eight months of his letters:

May 24, 2012
Mom and Dad,

Hello, how are y'all? I'm doing reasonably well. As you probably know, I'm at the Federal Transfer Center inside the airport at Oklahoma City, Oklahoma. It's quite all right here. Nothing really "going on" per se, but I've gotten my hands on a stack of books I've resolved to put my best dent in. So far, I've downed two, both books y'all or at least Mom has read: Lee Strobel's *The Case for Christ*[1] and *In a Pit with a Lion on a Snowy Day*[2].

The Case for Christ[1] handily dispelled many refutations of salvation through Christ, an area that despite much study of the philosophy of, I'd previously lacked an understanding of the factual basis for. I was impressed, and many of the specific mechanisms of doubt (my personal doubt) were dismantled, even obliterated. It clearly demonstrated it's extremely likely a man named Jesus existed who was the "Messiah" the Old Testament speaks of and performed miracles, was empowered by God and resurrected on the "third" (technically the second) day.

Still, a few big questions linger: is even the Old Testament trustworthy? Just because God empowers something, a book or a religion, that doesn't mean it has a monopoly on God. We see evidence of this in Eastern religion as well as Islam and Judaism, which are to me clearly both empowered by God AND full of inaccuracies, even COHERENT inaccuracies. It's as though God intentionally created multiple roads to him, yet apparently, Jesus claims exclusivity, as do other religions. Perhaps the exclusivity he's referring to is symbolic- "except by my example"...Who knows?

Also, the language of some of the EXPERTS in that book who supposedly attest to Jesus' divinity describe him as a prophet and in language imply he's an ordinary man who was filled with God and free from sin. I don't know. I still have trouble accepting Jesus as God. If Jesus is God, how could he ever say, "Father, why have you forsaken me?" That makes no sense.

Also, even more personally, I've never felt overcome by any sort of sensation of "love" for this man. Even as a Christian, intellectually convinced, entirely willing (as I am now) to believe in Jesus, he's as foreign to my heart as the Pythagorean Theory. I've tried to care, but I've thus far been unsuccessful at believing a man could somehow make our misdirections all okay by dying on a cross. Perfect? Okay. Great example? Yeah. Revolutionary? Evidently. But atonement? Ehh...It's very difficult for me to even fathom the same God that created us, and our (sin) nature also judging us and condemning us. Aren't we his children? If he cares when a sparrow falls, how could he ever damn a person eternally? That's not forgiveness. That's not love. That's not correction or guidance. That's VENGEANCE. That's hatred. That's the worst thing anybody could do to anything, "damnation". So, my heart and mind remain open, but wholly unconvinced. Far though my mind may wander and waver, my heart is less suggestible.

40

The other book, *In a Pit with a Lion on a Snowy Day*[2] was very good as well, inspiring and encouraging. It affirmed many of the very traits and experiences with which I have at times been ashamed of from a non-God centered perspective, specifically: eccentricity and the "zaniness" of true worship and passion/enthusiasm. While I end up feeling silly for having been enthusiastic and passionate about things in the past, I still feel the things were of God, and I recall giving God the permission to make me look silly to accomplish His goals if necessary. Even if it means circumstances make me look flippant or fickle or flamboyant or immature or obsessive, whatever. If their basis is confirmedly from God, then so be it. That is not to say these things are in any way indicators of the sanctity of expression, simple likely symptoms.

It also affirmed a certain righteous feeling I always had when I acted this particular way. It's a way I believe I've described to you, Mom, perhaps not to Dad. I've always been this way but never understood why acting on it always felt beyond good or satisfying, but righteous: it is- the intentional pursuit of that which I fear. The biggest example I see is in the natural world- spiders, snakes, swamps, open saltwater (I'm actually terrified of the ocean), tumultuous seas. It's why I insisted on going out into the ocean during storms and getting tossed like a rag doll in the rapids without a tube. It's FEAR, and it demands to be confronted. More often than not, confrontation leads to the definition of fear. Sometimes not, but often so.

Anyways, I hope y'all are doing well and are not worried about me. Everything's going well. I've got a cell where I stay most of the day, reading as many of the books I found as possible before being shipped any day now. In fact, by the time y'all receive this letter, I may be in San Diego. Apparently, I'll have the opportunity (most likely) to do two months halfway house time in San Diego. So, that puts me out in January or February. I'm a bit disappointed I'm being shipped to MCC San Diego to do my time because it means I won't have access to a library or any other of the great resources most places have. I'll also not see the light of day. But I'm trying to stay positive about it and trust God has a reason for depriving me of "the good life" of camps and laws...really all "real" Federal prisons. MCC San Diego is actually not much better than West Baton Rouge Jail. Boring, bland, indoor cell living. I hope it's cell living. I'll really be disappointed if it's also bunk-style, dorm-style. The advantage to this is: the lack of resources and amenities means more time to focus on reading and writing.

41

One thing I've learned through incarceration: MUTUAL EXCLUSIVITIES EXIST. What we like will ALWAYS be an obstacle between us and what we love. The more enjoyment, the less fulfillment. The better life is, the weaker we become. The busier we are, the less we spend time with and for our loved ones.

We can minimize this effect but never reverse it. This sort of mutual exclusivity principle is crucial to my understanding of the execution of God's will. It stems from the limited nature of time and resources, a principle our human nature/sinful nature loves to ignore and deny. We all do it. Every time we participate in a healthy hobby or spend discretionary income, we're denying the limited nature of resources to some extent. Every time we spend two extra dollars on some frivolity, we deprive ourselves the opportunity to feed a person for two days (over half the world's populations average living expense). I often wonder what the world would be like if we had even a sliver of awareness God has about those in need. What if every time we went out to eat, we were required to eat next to a mother whose baby was about to die for want of a $.50 packet of zinc (real phenomena) and an Indian family who $2 could feed and grant one more day alive. Time too- I think of the times I've chosen something like exercise or eating healthy over spending time with God or reading, over writing some crucial revelations down for safe-keeping (good stewardship of knowledge, that is). Small differences in attractiveness of the alternative, even seemingly pure and beneficial motives distract us from doing the MOST GOOD. I'm very easily distracted. Hence why MCC San Diego may be a good place for me.

It's Wednesday, the 23rd, and obviously, I'm still here. It's been nice, actually. I kind of like it here. Yesterday, I realized I had a vision of this place in a dream about 13 months ago, exactly this place- the Oklahoma Transfer Center. I wish y'all could see the inside of it; it reminds me of a museum in its architecture, or perhaps a school. It's got a very clean, inspiring, almost academic feel to it. The food is the best I've had anywhere, plenty of fruit and veggies of all sorts, actually healthy food. Last night we had a tuna "casserole" with actual big chunks of tuna it (not cheap canned stuff). My celli mouthed off to a C.O., so I've got a private cell now, as well as a small stockpile of cookies, coffee, etc. he was forced to leave. I'm taking a lot of time reading, praying and analyzing the past and the future. I'm painfully aware of my hedonism and self-centeredness; even in my most altruistic acts, some sort of selfish motivation existed. I went so far as to accept this as a fact, and look for ways to be constantly benefitting myself while benefitting others. True selflessness was/is almost non-existent. Last night the question popped into my head: If God asked me to help ugly old people bathe as part of his will, and sacrifice any sort of material reward/success to accomplish his will, could I? If I'm honest, the answer is a resounding NO. I struggle with even letting go of little things like the right to sleep more than necessary.

Well, last minute...Love,
Cory

June 2012
Dad,

Hello! How are you? I'm well here, but pretty sick with some kind of throat parasite (I think). Things are going good. It's okay here. Nice to have access to a guitar, lots of good books (though of limited quality) and a great view of San Diego. I was just telling Mom I realized a friend of mine's condo is within view just a couple of blocks away- it's at the top of an old historic bank building (28-stories). Really cool place. It's a double-floor at the top, with huge windows facing this building. Small world...Three weeks before I got arrested, I was in that condo. This stay at MCC is going completely different from the last, so far. I sincerely believe it is a result of where I'm at spiritually. I think back to the accident, and I realized something explicitly/expressably that I was suspicious of from the start: we're spiritual beings capable of attracting either fortune or misfortune, in ways that transcend our understanding/ logic. Probability itself is ever changing, and our spiritual state can activate all sorts of improbability. The accident was improbable and quite strange in its occurrence. It was almost as if it were intentional. No reasonable explanation exists for why this woman drove this way. However, just a week or two before, I had undergone a spiritual change, a fall from grace. That day, I was sober and aware. However, it corresponded directly with a flare-up of pride. That morning I became the leader of the group, and I lead the group to an amazing place. Everyone loved it, etc. yadda, yadda. On the way back, we were so close to my home. We were above the very stream

43

where I essentially worshipped enjoyment in nature. It was as though my pride materialized this extremely unlikely accident. I can't fully explain/ describe just how unlikely this was, or just how improbable the situation, but for me it confirms an idea: things that happen happen because they fit into a bigger picture. Causation does not work in the linear, sequential way our mechanistic way of thinking suggests. Effect reaches out to cause; cause does not just hand down effect. Quantum physics demonstrates this phenomenon: particles somehow "know" which way to go. They can "sense" obstacles and avoid them. The end result manifesting itself in a way that defies ordinary sequential causation. What do you think? Have you ever seen phenomenon that defied normal causation?

Well, I gotta' go. It's late. With love,
Cory

June 3, 2012
Mom,

Hello, how are you? It's 10 PM, June 3rd, and I'm up writing by the light of an LED book lamp, not being able to sleep on account of both coffee and sleeping most of the day. I quit my "job" in the kitchen today. I'm sick right now; something I believe I caught doing 1,200 prisoners dishes, arms submerged in a solution of partially eaten food and saliva for hours on end. I specifically told Mrs. Martin, the woman who assigns jobs, I had a concern about getting sick from this type of exposure. That's when she told me essentially, "Get your lazy ass out of my office." So today, I am very sick with a very painful respiratory ailment of some sort. Now normally if sick, an inmate is free to refuse work and stay in bed. I decided to just stick it out and at least try. I told her I was sick. She said, "Well, just roll silverware, that's easy." So I did. It was kind of gross because I was coughing on everything. But I stayed. They fed us, and I ate. When lunch was over, she said, "The dishwasher is broken. Everybody do dishes." I told her, "But, I'm sick. I need to rest." She said, "Sick? You ate all that food. You're not sick." So I said, "So you don't eat when you've got a cold?" And she said, "Shut up and do the dishes." So, I said, "Ok, send me to the hole (solitary confinement)." So, she said, "Oh, you're going to the hole!" and got furious. She called her boss, the lieutenant, and he came down. I explained the situation, told him I was ready to go to the hole over working in this state. And

44

he was like, "Ok, it's obvious the real problem here is they gave you the wrong job. Just go to bed and we'll find you a new one." Viola, problem solved. It makes no sense for me to work a job that I don't want to when others DO want that job and there are plenty of other jobs. So, I'm very happy to have trumped these stupid C.O.s. I did everything I could to solve the problem/ prevent it diplomatically, and it took just finally standing up against an injustice to solve it. My ace in the hole is the fact I almost prefer solitary confinement. I know going there, though it prevents visits, phone calls, email, chess, guitar, socializing, etc., would help me progress towards my goals. I can bring books, and I can write letters, both of which have suffered somewhat since leaving West Baton Rouge. This thing, incarceration, has exposed the most peculiar phenomena, which part of my purpose here, my purpose for being in prison at all, is to describe: that is the inverse proportionality of stillness and movement. The paradox of emptiness and "fill-ability". Decrease of opportunity of diversions and increase of the quality of those that remain. Quantity vs. quality of conveyance. The way even tiny increases in quality of external affairs hurts quality of internal affairs. I do not think this phenomena is particular to me, but is the great ENIGMA OF HUMAN EXISTENCE. How to be human and spirit simultaneously. The answer to this contemplation is what everyone from Mohammed to Buddha to Mother Teresa to Jesus to Eckhart Tolle attempt to give. It's the reason "the love of money is the root of all evil." It's the reason it's almost impossible to be both rich and "saved". When I talk to people, I can clearly tell the difference in the soul of a man who is wealthy outside and one who's poor. The wealthy lack a certain maturity, an expanse of perspective, openness to the spiritual, as well as the spirits in others. Likewise, even the difference between having a good full rich diet and struggling to get nutrients/food makes a profound difference in the experience of spirituality, the "peace". Part of me is empowered by the awareness of this correlation. It means I know if I get to feeling "egocentric" or even afraid, in pain, angry, whatever, ultimately, I know (eventually) just being still will fix it, much like death, a form of stillness, will solve all sorts of problems and cause "ascension", assimilation with the One, whatever that might be. Practically speaking, prayer, fasting, various forms of separation/isolation (the modulation of the way time is spent so as to retreat and encourage stillness) can solve most problems. This line of "stillness" justification is the basis for the assertion, "Prison is a priceless opportunity." Even to the point it may be reasonable to intentionally go to prison. Yes, other sorts of retreats could work better, and I intend to take advantage of them, but prison is one of the best encouragers of stillness. It's clear to me we all should be intentionally constantly depriving ourselves of various forms of movement: eating, hobbies, sounds, sights, travel, money, etc. Fasting is VERY important, since it's the stilling of our very chemistry, one of the most powerful ways. The existence of biological phenomena, which rely on various forms of stillness, attests to its divinity. Starvation calorie deprivation repairs our DNA, activates natural resveratrol reserves that are the most potent antiaging hormones in our body (that we know of). Meditation, the stilling of the mind, has been shown to fix almost every imaginable ailment, and create/strengthen in us an "intuitive sense". The Bible specifically says, "Be still and know that I am God." The people who live longest eat the lowest calorie diets, a form of chemical stillness. The two biggest man-made form of movement: oil and money are implicated as the nuclei of evil in many people's world view. All this lines up very nicely and is very pleasant to think about, until we consider what it REALLY means: Sacrifice.

It's so hard to accept the full extent to which this is true. It's been the basis for most of my personal struggle with God, or my idea of him. I think it's a major part of everyone's struggle too. I choose to see it consciously, whereas most others live this conflict matter-of-factly. But either way, it is really troubling: I don't want to give up _____. Fill in the blank. Even things the world says are A-Okay fit in this blank, things we're called to let go of. Maybe they'll be given back, maybe not. The net effect will always be positive, but it's still something I doubt or have just enough doubt to substantiate reservation, and tighten my grip. "Hate your family." I've heard so many people try to reinterpret that scripture to make it more palatable. The rich man eye of the needle camel into heaven thing. It doesn't help that in our wealthy culture I've got almost NO examples of people sacrificing their security, hobbies, money or food for stillness. Especially in church. It's all commotion and rich people, comfortable people with full stomachs and nice clothes. It's a paradox when we look at it with even a little reason mixed with a little emotion. I want to help people, but I want to get rich first. I want to be a servant, but I nit-pick about the validity of my time spent. I want to stay frugal and modest, but I want to travel the world. I want to live simply, but I wonder why then do I have so many ideas, aspirations and goals? Is it possible to be both a capitalist and a man of God? I'm not so sure either way. It's a great paradox. Well, if I disappear on email, know I'll be popping back up in letters. I'm

46

probably just in solitary. I've felt myself sliding back into my skin. I need to come back out somehow. Perhaps I'll give up some kind of thing, chess, food, leaving my cell, for a week or so. Hopefully God will show me what.

Well, I'm very tired and off to bed.

June 2012
Dad,

Hello, how are you? How's the garden doing? Things are well here, just working in the kitchen, reading and writing. Perhaps it is sad, but I am happier here than I was in Baton Rouge any day. I am afraid most of my life will be spent at a great distance from my family. I love you all very much but there are reasons why living in this country is looking less and less likely. Also, I have many habits that will eventually land me in prison if either I or the law don't drastically change. So, I plan to do everything I can to change, but also simultaneously try to get a passport, set down roots elsewhere and also keep prepared to go back to prison. Even the crimes I've committed already can come back ten years later to get me. I intend no one evil and am not a thief or a cheat, but we live in a police state, run by people who can put people in prison for silly things. Even made-up things when they think you are a trouble-maker, which I am.

I am very sad that you and Mom disregard the concerns of myself and many about the malice of the American government. I know y'all think I'm crazy, but come on. You're an engineer. Can't you at least give building 47 research a cursory glance? Consider the testimony of structural engineers who attest to the impossibility of two planes bringing down three buildings the way they supposedly did.

It's not that they hate us. It's that they see us as cattle. Why care? For the same reason we get strange bumps on our skin diagnosed, even if it may (or may not) be a treatable form of carcinogenic melanoma. Live in fear? No. Act rashly? No. Be aware, practice due diligence and research something 40% of the population believes? Be mindful? Yes. It will if nothing else quiet my concerns if you can do even one hour of honest research into the possibility the twin towers were demolished. Remember visiting the Pentagon? Remember how one portion was closed off? The same section that

47

was hit! Dad, it's okay to not be afraid, but I feel very sad and guilty if I don't do what I can to open your eyes to the wolves around us. I'm not paranoid. I trust people and don't believe paranoid things. I've seen and researched very compelling evidence and have come to a conclusion. No voices in my head, no religious hogwash, just CONCENSUS. Seriously, start asking the smart curious people you know what they think of the 911 twin towers theory. This is a starting point to understand that no, the government isn't "evil", per se, just those at the top have no regard for human life and do anything to further goals.

June 2012
Mom,

Hello, how are you? I'm finally getting around to writing. Waking up early and going straight to work has been making it harder for me to focus on writing, etc. Things are going pretty well externally, getting used to everything. All the little things are okay, but I've been a bit troubled lately. Not really troubled but conflicted. I've spent the past month in a state of transition, all fine and dandy. But inside, it's like I'm losing some kind of focus or resolve. I still subscribe intellectually, but my being is more absorbed but what are, I suppose, distractions. I feel like a different person in some ways. I suppose this is normal. I'm constantly in flux by nature, but I miss the stillness of my first days in West Baton Rouge. Don't get me wrong. I'm pretty happy here, but there's a certain depth missing. I think a lot of it is the atmosphere. California is great, but it has a very superficial feel to it. There's less conflict, but also less drama, depth, even character. That's all okay. Part of what has made my life unique has been the constant moving between cultures and atmospheres, geography and philosophy. Here I feel more free to be myself, but who am I but a man, not a being. A person with likes and dislikes, an authority problem, a past, dreams, etc. I don't know. I know one thing: it's true you become like those you hang around. This used to bother me more than it does now. We were taught in church to "go against the flow," defy the world. I do, but only in certain ways: no TV, different diet, pursuit of godliness, wondering/contemplation. I don't know. The past month, traveling from place to place, transitory incarceration, has afforded me access to only two types of books. Christian "reform" books and fiction. I read almost no fiction, so I've read maybe 15 Christian reform books. I call them reform books because as a rule, all of

48

these Christian books are essentially about how the "the church today" is wrong, how their way is not right, and how amazing it is they're the only church that sees it. They all point to how wrong Christians are and some collection of anecdotes and potentialities of how we'd all become amazingly healthy, on-fire Christians if we just did X, Y and Z. I even read a book called, *Weird Christians I Have Met*[3] that portrays a variety of stereotypical Christians, each out of balance in our faith. It's pretty good. Backsliding Bill, End time Ed, Prosperity Pam, etc. His depictions, characters really are humorous, yet accurate. He suggests we should strive for more balance in our faith. Another I recently read but didn't finish is called *Radical*[4]. I wonder if you've heard of it. In *Radical* the essence of what all the other Christian books skirt around is this: a call to living for Christ in a radical way that's true to Christ's teachings and the "Scriptures", even when what they say doesn't make sense to us or calls for extreme sacrifice. I stopped reading when it moved on to talk about the actual hard truth biblical principle of exclusivity of the Cross for salvation. Everyone else- DAMNED. It was like waking up from a dream, the recollection of how much I hate the idea of Jesus, the REAL Jesus, not watered-down okay-with-mediocrity Jesus, came back like the real world after an intoxicating dream. I was reminded why I left the faith a decade ago. Some concepts taught by Jesus stand, but others just annoy me, even anger me. The fact is I've never felt a love for Jesus. Maybe the idea based on his teachings, maybe the people who followed him as God. Yet I love God. But this Jesus? Who is he to stand in front of and between me and God? Just because Jesus did some good things, even miraculous things and preached "love", which we know to be the purpose of life. Just because the Bible has accuracies, predicts the future accurately, has some wisdom, etc. does NOT mean it's God's book. Just because it's got a certain "living" aspect to it does not mean it's authentic. Many very profound books have a certain quality of having more and more meaning over time. Humans who live in this century can predict the future accurately, emanate powerful healing forces, have very potent love, even embody all the fruits of the spirit. Also, other religious texts have justifications and substantiations equally impactful than the Bible, yet we know them to be false. So, I'll keep praying to have God show me if Jesus is really God, and meanwhile, I really don't like the guy. There are far better people to listen to, people whose teachings actually make sense and are practical and have divine confirmations galore. Teachings considered "New Age" by the "Church" often have NONE of the markers of evil. I don't know. I'm confused, but still faithful to

49

God only. And even he, I'm not sure is a "being" we can "talk to" per se. I know he transcends time and space, loves us and wants us to love others. I believe many of the things the Bible says about him. I believe if he's not "in" all things, he is near all things/surrounds all things.

Anyways, the speed reading book has helped me tremendously, even in the past few days of practice. I STRONGLY RECOMMEND PRACTICING SOME OF ITS TECHNIQUES. It's not just about speed. It's actually about widening the portal through which knowledge (written) enters the mind. By learning to train your eyes and brain to read more proficiently, you can both read more and understand better/comprehend. I don't know why we weren't taught this in grade school.

You may be interested to hear the book on Sacred Geometry reminds me of the books Daddy Jim sent me on Fractals. I am quite sure he would have greatly appreciated it. I wish I would I have reached out to him before (he died). I suppose I was intimidated by his distance.

Oh, and I'm very sure I am NOT paranoid schizophrenic. Particularly for my "conspiratorial" convictions. I'm sure there's something very fishy about the 911 attacks. A few verifiable facts:

Trained firefighters who study structural integrity of large buildings under intense heat deemed it SAFE to proceed up the burning buildings. These experts DID not believe it could fall in the controlled manner that it did. They were ASTOUNDED to hear the building collapsed on itself because this kind of collapse is completely unprecedented, except in CONTROLLED DEMOLITIONS. A skyscraper in Russia was once hit by a plane and burned. The top section eventually began tilting, and eventually fell on its side, breaking where the plane hit, not collapsing from the ground. Also, Building 47, a third building, that sat near the two towers, but was in NO WAY DAMAGED by the debris or FIRE, which houses the Federal collection of records, Watergate, JFK assassination reports, also collapsed, inexplicably. The week prior, the building's owner DOUBLED HIS COVERAGE WITH THE INSURER. The Government report claims Building 47 collapsed due to "suction in underground tunnels." Are you even reading this? Humor me. Investigate. It was not two planes.

50

Remember when we visited DC? Remember how the ONE section was under construction? What are the chances that same section is the section that was hit by terrorists, 100% unoccupied? Furthermore, these "terrorists", who spent years getting flight training, didn't know it was unoccupied?

Oh yeah, the people at ground zero, as well as the tapes, have people commenting on "EXPLOSIONS" when the buildings came down. It does not make any sense in terms of physics. Many highly esteemed people from academia agree with this assessment. Why would they do this? To give them a reason to invade Afghanistan, get oil and opium, as well as an "Open Season" on "troublemakers"- people having nothing to do with terrorism, but the "Patriot Act" enabled the government to catch and imprison. It's not paranoia. If you did even a cursory amount of research, you'd see.

Why study this? Why care? To live in fear? No! To be a good steward of the priceless gift of life God's given. To diagnose a terminal illness and respond with prudence and awareness. We cannot do much now, but decisions will be made in the near future, which rely on being AWAKE AND AWARE! Paranoid? Fearful? No, but in denial, certainly not! God wants us to be hopeful, not hide our heads in the sand!

Oh yeah. Numbers. So the conflicting numbers in my head are: 1, unity, the notion God and creation are one, there is no real evil, etc.; 2, only God and creation exist, no Jesus; or 4, God, Jesus, Holy Spirit and creation...Who knows? The most troubling things have been the conflict between the number 1, the number 2 and the number 4.

June 2012
Mom,

Hello, I'm writing here at the end of the day. I guess I've been struggling with perfectionism and procrastination. I'm always looking for the perfect time to write and the perfect version of letters, poems and web page stuff. I am at least making progress, though entirely dissatisfied with the quality. Today was a very good day. My day off. I read two books, (one of them was 150 pages) in 45 minutes with speed reading. Speed reading works. It's not a good technique for things to study, but it's excellent for books on familiar subjects/written simply. Since learning some techniques and practicing, I also can see better. It's as though the words are larger, clearer and are recognized more quickly. The biggest perk is: when I slow down to normal speed (~400 wpm), my comprehension has indirectly increased, since recognition energy spent has decreased. I highly recommend it.

I've also got a successful enterprise going: a "tienda". I simply stock lots of lots of sweets, stolen vegetables from the kitchen, etc. and sell at a mark-up. So far it looks to have $80/month potential, if I create brownies like planned. I figured out how to make brownies from these free muffins we get using hot cocoa mix. So, I think I'll be able to sell those as well. I'm determined to stock my cell with great books. Very few other higher level readers are on this floor. Tomorrow, I'll go to the library and hopefully network with other inmates to get more books and info. Also, I've got a "Buddhist Meditation" call-out for two hours during which I get to skip work. Double win. Also, I find out if I get halfway house time tomorrow. Probably not, but I'll see. Supposedly, I am entitled to it by law, but who knows. Anyways, pressed for time,

Good night...
Cory

Poem written for a posting on "Lost Vault", which is a prison pen-pal program:

You, newfound friend, a mystery
What sort of tree comes of this seed
And who am I, of all could be?
For now just empty poetry.
Let you wonder this I'll say
And save the rest for later day
If you like travel or adventure
And understand and need no censor
Write to me a simple letter
Then stamp, lick, seal the little treasure
Though some would say "Writ's way old-fashioned"
Soon weaving words will become passion
This way we'll meet up despite lock:
Escaping nightly (in postman's box)
Let's correspond until we know
These tiny seeds become once sown...

June 8, 2012
Mom,

Hello, writing again. It's really late, and I'm tired but figured I'd write a little anyways. Life is good. I made very much progress on the website today. [Cory was trying to produce a website to help prisoners become more conscious and other practical assistance.]

I started a small store. I experimented with and created a recipe for brownies using cocoa mix and muffins that I think I'll make good money on. They're pretty good, and I can make them for less than $.10 and sell for $.40. Little ways I can afford to purchase stamps and email. I'm enjoying the company of my Russian/Bulgarian friend. It's amusing the kind of social situation prison presents. People who drive quarter of a million dollar cars and wear $5,000 suits sit with Cambodian cab drivers and Mexican paint huffers. We're all in this together. No distinctions can really be made on the basis of education or money; we all look the same in khaki. I've got people telling me how I should move to Laos, others who offer mansions for rent for $400/month on the beach in Mexico, others who offer to show me Europe, blah, blah…One thing's for sure- as SOON as I can travel abroad, I will. Also, enjoy the time you can spend with me. I'm always only an inch from being back in prison or vanquished entirely. It's just the way it is. It's okay. I'm not well-suited for American living, and I am well-suited for prison. So, any way it goes from here, abroad, Austin or back in prison- all will be good options. Freedom's mine. Just don't count on me being around until our regime changes, which is inevitable. I hope you can accept this. It's better than dead, which I'd be happy to be, though I do love life too. I'm okay with death. I'll try live but if for some reason that doesn't work out, I'm in a better place.

Well, just wanted to say hello. Everything's great. Talk to you later.

June 11, 2012
Mom,

Hello, I hope all is well over there. All is pretty good over here. It's my day off, so I'm going to take complete advantage of it. I have a few more books I'd like to order: *Science of Intention*[5], *Law of Attraction*[6], Balthazar Gracian's *Wisdom*[7], some book from antiquity called *The Biggest Secrets*[8], Plato's *Republic*[9]. Someone I met gave me a very cool book on yoga last night.

Have you considered reading *A New Earth* like I suggested?

I was thinking yesterday of how it's been almost 4 months. I'm almost a third done with my sentence. It reminded me how important it is to make progress towards my goals (website, book reading, Spanish, pen pals, etc.) So, I'm devoting this entire day off to making progress towards these ends.

I'm a bit disappointed about where I'm at, since I only have access to another 200 or so people, as opposed to a "real" prison where I'd be able to talk to 800+. It feels like I have less people who may benefit from the books I get sent. When I look at the issue objectively, only a small percentage of the prison population is ready to accept the notion that a sentence can be transmuted into something good. This realization is changing my approach, as it already has to some extent. Lead by example, and focus on using the website for this purpose. The written word is a lot more capable for conveying these ideas in their wholeness anyways. So, I'll keep doing what I'm doing and let it grow as it will. Like I said from the beginning, even if I only am helping a couple of people change perspective, and writing about it for another few to enjoy, it will be worth it. Actually, I guess if I think about it, the books we've sent in have been read by quite a few people. The books I left in West Baton Rouge were being read pretty regularly, and the books I've got here are fairly used. No drastic changes in perspective on the potential of the sentence or anything, but hey, one step at a time. I think before people get to prison or at the beginning of a sentence is the best time to resolve to make the most of this.

Anyways, I'll talk to you soon. With love,
Cory

June 19, 2012
Mom,

Hello. It's 4:30 PM on June 19th, a nice relaxing Tuesday, my 3rd day off of work, one scheduled, the other two manipulated out by participating in Buddhist meditation and photo-taking. This makes me very happy because I don't like this job, and meditation is a sustainable practice. I can get out of work two extra days by simply doing things I already want to do. Things are going well. I've been keeping myself very busy with various things: reading *4-Hour Work Week*[10], an excellent book on escaping the "deferred living plan", which is working 9-5, 50 weeks a year for 30+ years to one day live your dream life (retirement) and replacing it with a dream life of traveling, periodic entrepreneurial creations, which create residual income to travel more. It's been both reaffirming and informative, since many of the concepts contained inside are concepts I already live by: minimize "work"/time spent on work, minimize expenses, maximize income/hour, use "business" geography, different economies and opportunities to maximize quality of life without having to increase income expenditures. It's a very empowering book, full of examples of how to achieve your wildest dreams-career, travel, experiences. It's written by an American named Timothy Ferris who has learned six languages, most in 3-6 months. He's the only American to hold a world tango championship record, Chinese kickboxing champion, breakdancing champion, leading expert on entrepreneurialism. Great guy. If you get a chance, print as much of his website in mobile format with the tiniest text possible.

When I get out, I'd like to start a paid remote research service for inmates. Also, I'm thinking of specifically gearing the website for educated people who serve prison sentences: the conscious prisoner, the educated prisoner, "the smart way to do time."

I'm sad to say I've been getting distracted. I think it has to do with my store. I spend a lot of time dealing with people, taking inventory, collecting debts, etc. all to earn 20% mark-up (a few cents/transaction). It's a lot of work and only maybe $10/week profit, but enough to eliminate my expenses and perhaps eventually pay for one book per week. So for that, it's worth it. It's against the rules. But I will be glad to get sent to solitary confinement. I could use some time to collect my thoughts and develop writings, website, letters without distraction.

I began studying Sacred Geometry, which is part art and part science, really the place where the abstract and the material come together. A lot of it has to do with the analysis of common geometric forms and symbols in nature: spiral, circle, square, various numbers and what they symbolize. Many have said, "God is in the numbers and his fingerprint in mathematics." It's becoming clear his very voice is in the geometry of the universe once we understand it. For example, the number 12 symbolizes the conception of the abstract into the material- 5 (man) and 7 (God), at the same time 6 (material) and 6 (material) the womb, etc. The chlorophyll molecule is a 12-petal molecule resembling a daisy in shape, which converts light into matter, hence the abstract into the material. The twelve disciples, the twelve tribes, etc. When we look at the design and shape of very many things, we see the symbolism of shapes and numbers and grasp a deeper understanding of God's design. I've often noticed this in nature, things good for the heart- tomatoes, are red and have four chamber sections, like our heart. A certain variety of sage that's particularly good at assisting breathing (almost like vapor-rub) has hairs reminiscent of alveoli of lungs and are somewhat lung-shaped. This symbolism, found both in shape and number, has been used by religions mainly in "secret" (though often not really secret, just not understood enough to spread) as well as secret societies who claim to use knowledge from this study to bridge between the abstract and material worlds- by extension, metaphysical and physical. Much promising recent science has been giving real life proofs of this. Anyways, all churches, political buildings, great cities, famous landmarks, follow these rules, patterns of arrangement; their builders all had an understanding of this art. Furthermore, there's evidence (as well as testimony dating back to antiquity) that drawing these designs actually synchronizes your brain frequencies and promotes unification with the Divine. It's actually quite mesmerizing, even just to look at some of the designs. Anyways, there are a great many promising technologies, not even technologies but awarenesses on the horizon these days- we're on the verge of entering into a new level of awareness. It will not be long before things we now consider only possible by Divine intervention, the manipulation of space and time in ways beyond science, will become reality. This is nothing evil or even bizarre, only entering into a deeper awareness of the existing (and antiquated) techniques God provided for us to help ourselves. They will be used for both very good and very evil purposes, though in and of themselves, they are neither. I am talking about the purification of water, the healing of illnesses, mental and physical, new ways of communicating; we'll begin to see energy as plainly as we see plants and trees (space and time travel, "psychic abilities"). It's already begun, but only in part. You'll see as time goes on. THIS IS A VERY GOOD TIME TO BE ALIVE. And I'm very rapidly becoming more aware of the full extent of reasons why I just read your response to my email about halfway house possibilities, and I was tempted to be more angry about you seeing a more limited perspective on the possibilities I've got in front of me. Then I remembered it's normal for people to limit others in their perceptions. So, I understand you want what's right and safe for me. But I don't ever want "safety" (stagnation). I want to live outside my comfort zone. I want to establish a lifestyle, not just a way to make a living. I want to emulate those I admire who have minimized their responsibility to income ratio in order to pursue dreams that have no direct correlation with income: the things we dream of, helping others, participating in events, riding a bike around, camping out for months on end, etc. A very low commitment/income ratio is achievable, and I intend to shoot for it 100%. I want to be free to live abroad and start schools in Cambodia and communities in Mexico. Participate in ceremonies in Guatemala and swim with sharks in Australia. There's no reason I can't live a dream life, as long as I can get my inner problems under some level of control. I already have started to live a dream life in Austin. The only thing between me and the full realization of this life: a passport, more focus and money on ideas I've been given/collaboration opportunities I've found while locked up. Living abroad is actually cheaper than living here in the long run. Well, I can't fully explain what I mean and don't expect you to understand, but just WATCH. If I can even half manage to stay clear-headed for six months, money and travel will become a non-issue. The law and risk of prison will always be an issue, as will risk of relapse or catastrophe, but money, money will not be, nor will travel, a limiting factor. I've got everything I need to live well without committing to live in one place and work a "job". I can make money, plenty of money living free. I'll not give that up for nothing.

Please watch the documentary "What the Bleep Do We Know" with Dad.

Anyways, gotta go.

Later on June 20: What I need is support to chase dreams. Give me that, and I'll give you a small village of grandchildren, (though you may have to travel the world to see them all.)

June 2012
Mom,

Concerning your last letter, in retrospect, one of the finer points of my upbringing when I talk to others about it was our daily home-cooked dinners. It did not go unnoticed. I mention it as a point of privilege and nostalgia very frequently. I think we all recognize the value of this experience which you have enabled, though amongst ourselves never thought to speak of it. I'm sure Bethany and Landon also speak of regular homemade dinners during our upbringing and contrast it with the normal American way of independently eating, so it's kind of funny you'd think we don't remember or appreciate it. Perhaps we didn't then, but I'm pretty sure I'm not the only one who sees its value now. I always thought it was strange that you didn't "repurpose" meals/cook in bulk instead of daily "just sufficient" quantities, which require more work and expense. I remember constantly suggesting: cook two times as much, freeze some, have more left-overs. Some people cook everything for a month in two to three days! For a family of five! Freeze it all, prep veggies for multipurpose use, etc. Anyways, it laid a good foundation for a valuation of communal eating/ good eating habits.

Also in response to your last letter, the minimization of resentment and the time dealing with that process is called "presence" and "awareness" and is exactly the basis for Tolle's teachings, also taught in Buddhism and all meditative practices. The concept is simply: no longer being your thoughts, resentments, ego, "id". Being the awareness which observes these thoughts and emotions.

Inside our brains, we actually have a tiny structure called the pineal, which is like a brain inside a brain. This is what we use to observe ourselves, and it has been called the "seat of the soul". Enlightenment has to do with expanding your awareness in such a way that your attention is focused intently on this present moment, which is the way to address "resentments" and adverse emotions rapidly. "Pain cannot live with joy."

With regard to your statements about feeling disconnected from what you have known all your life to be "God", I have felt the same way over the past year. I knew he was real, but didn't think he would respond to my prayers. I still recognize it's only by grace that we are able to live, let alone avoid adversity. I've been granted grace for now. Who knows what the future holds?

When you speak of the situation where you don't want to "hurt anyone's feelings" while still addressing the issue, I do not feel it is necessary to deal with people with "kid gloves". What's important to me is keeping the heart's intentions pure towards others despite tendency to get angry. However, I do find there is a time and place

58

for responding in a way that hurts the other person; just as when we touch a hot stove, it hurts, if a person oversteps boundaries, it is at times appropriate to respond forcefully, as long as we keep the heart pure. For example, there was a guy in our tank in West Baton Rouge that disrespected a Muslim brother during his prayer. Without getting into all the details, he got badly beaten by some very easy-going God-fearing guys. What needed to happen, happened. He asked for it. He was the aggressor and got his fair consequences. Also, when guards talk disrespectfully to me, I sometimes just brush it off. I sometimes "flip the script" on them and expose the banality of their rudeness with some sort of improvisation. It actually gets the job done sometimes, makes them realize how stupid they are being and how their notion of superiority is unprecedented. What's important is lack of malice/ fostering a genuine care for the individual, even if I don't respect what they're doing. Even if I must hurt them. I don't prefer to, but sometimes passivism just doesn't suffice.

On another point you discussed, what you're saying is a powerful truth: "No one can make us feel anything." However those who we engage with have the ability to build us or destroy us with words and thoughts. I liken it to playing music with others because this analogy is almost exactly what it is, except instead of audible sounds, it is brain frequencies. When we play music together, say at a drum circle, everyone's playing drums in a tribal sort of beat. Now a guy comes along with an electric guitar and starts overlapping Metallica songs with the drum beat. Okay, it may sound cool, but it TOTALLY CHANGES the vibe. Same with guitar. I can be playing some melodic type of music and another person can come in and "play along" but with a more rock and roll lead guitar edge, totally changing the tranquil vibe of my song. Did this person ruin my song? No. Did they prevent me from just ignoring them? Not really, I could just ignore them and just keep on with what I was doing. But it DOES change the vibe. The best thing I can do is either walk away or play along empathetically. Same with kids and people not familiar with improvisation. The only thing to do when they start playing music with you and kind of ruin the vibe, is either walk away or do your best to play along. This is the reason I found sounding and dance so profound. They made the essence of human interaction CRYSTAL CLEAR. No, people can't make you feel things. They CAN interject various frequencies, thoughts, criticisms, etc. that may detract from our idea of beauty. But the best we can do is improvise. Play along or walk away, play somewhere else. But they are very

59

real things they project. That's why we get so emotional when people say and do them.

And finally about your last comments, I recognize this constant questioning, peace and "shaking up" of belief will likely continue on for this life. For now, the rejection of the doctrine of salvation through "Christ" seems to serve me well. I'm not wondering/ in conflict anymore. I just believe in God and see my own manifestations of him here and there. I believe God's omnipresent, so we are fragments of God. Everything we perceive as various pieces of God's voice, echoes his creative dictations billions of years ago. Some wrap into balls, creating matter. Some flow- light. I don't know, but I am not troubled by Christ anymore.

June 30, 2012
Mom,

How are things coming along? I've come to terms with the kitchen job, helped in large part by the absence of a certain guard I find disagreeable. The guard who is in charge is a stark contrast: the one is micromanaging, negative and hypercritical, while the new one is a huge cheery Hawaiian guy who does little else than walk around and joke with us all shift. Things go even more smoothly this way, and he almost never gives any directives. He's a pretty interesting guy. He was talking about getting ambushed by Muslims who detonated IEDs on him in Iraq on THREE separate occasions. His wife was recently blown up (she survived) as well by an IED. I say all this about him being a great guy, and he is, but this same guy told us about how he once threw a grenade for no reason in a crowd of small children that gathered around while they gave out water.

The soldiers I meet in this system are REALLY messed up. I'm not talking about the guards, the inmates as well. This system is creating a subculture of complete psychopaths through our military action abroad. When I say psychopaths, I mean it in the truest sense. These are people who one would NEVER know they were mass rapists and killers in certain situations, unless you really got to talking with them about their stories. They'll be the best, most easy-going pleasant disciplined people you've ever met (in this case a cheery Hawaiian guy), but then I'll get to talking to them, and they kill women and children, often just for fun or vengeance. There's really NOTHING to indicate that they are capable of these crimes in

60

one's interaction with them, which confirms for me a theory I've long held that anyone is capable of any crime given proper conditioning and enough time. Some closer, some further, but all human and as such all susceptible to being shaped into torturers, murderers, rapists, criminals. I think many of these guards see that and offer us respect because they realize that we're no different from them, just happened to get charged with a felony.

Anyways, going back to positive things: People are eating up the quality literature I've got, confirming my theory that any good books I get sent in will find a perpetual and receptive audience here. Less people than I thought would be are interested in bettering themselves or open to looking at the situation optimistically. But there are a great number of people, so there is no shortage of people who ARE. The best I can do is listen for any openness or optimism in people I meet describing their circumstances and try to use inquisition to encourage them to expand their perspective.

July 13, 2012
Mom,

Hello, how was your trip? Things are much the same here, going well. Every day is busy, interesting and fun. I am working late at night (11 PM to 2 AM) cleaning administrative offices and various parts of the building. It's a very easy job, and it's ten times better than the kitchen. The only bad thing is it interferes with my sleep schedule. Not being able to be awake early changes the tone of the days, makes them less productive. Anyways, I kind of missing the stillness of the beginning of my sentence, but not sure if it's possible or desirable to get back there. I know going to the "hole" (solitary confinement) will accomplish it, but I'm not sure it's worth going to the hole just to get some peace. I've got a new celli, Jeremy. He's a 30-something white guy from San Bernardino who's also here for alien smuggling. Good guy, he's got a kid; he lives for her- a 10-year old girl. He told me some funny but sad stories about being raised by two addicts. He says he wants to start some kind of service organization to help children with insufficient parental supervision, a sort of YMCA or something. We pass time talking about it.

I've gotten better at guitar and found a guy who's pretty good to jam with. We have a great time jamming. I have finally passed a certain threshold and now consider myself a "proficient" player, since I can play along with almost anything and emulate most modern difficult songs after only a few seconds of demonstration. This to me is a satisfaction.

I've been pondering the 16 hells described by Buddhists and decided I'm prepared for all of them if that's where I end up. Fortunately, the Buddhists say they're temporary. Who knows?

I've been steadily studying, especially Tolle's book *Power of Now*[11]. It's given me certain techniques to "dissolve" my mind/ego. It's like having an endless supply of pills that put a person at 100% peace, 100% ease, increase energy, multiply creativity, diffuse animosity, or at least the acute passion and emotion associated with it. It's great. Yet another goal of this sentence accomplished: find a technique(s) to arrest/deflate/decelerate thought- that is, still the mind. Silence the chatterbox. "Be still and know that I AM." The technique is very simple- divert attention to the body intensely. Focus intently on either breath or center of gravity or heartbeat, whatever. If you try it, it will stop all thoughts until you release the focus. Now it seems obvious there are varying levels of stillness, as there are varying levels of consciousness. Even if I become "still" in the mind, stop the chatterbox, I may still have some unwanted, parasitic movement in my mind/body. So, it is not a complete fix. Desires and emotions often persist despite this technique, but are always muted or their resultant, self-perpetuated aspects are removed so they begin to fade more rapidly. Still, intense anger, unease or bad moods sometimes persist. I have been amazed how capable purely mental techniques are at remediating digestive/general funk in my gut that's emotive, metabolic and mental, simultaneously. I believe we all experience this, but only some notice it. Most in our culture have very little perception, if any, between diet, mood, energy, spirituality. This is evidenced by people being completely unwilling to alter diet for anything other than outward appearance (of themselves). If/when I get in a funk, cutting back on my meat intake almost always fixes it. But simple "re-centering" techniques, even for ten seconds, works wonders. It's a very close parallel to the merits and motivation for using drugs. Drugs assist stillness in various ways, connecting one with Being/God, although in a perhaps undesirable and temporary way. Anyways, gotta go to work.

Love,
Cory

July 2012
Dad,

Greetings! How are you? I write to you from the "hole"- jail inside of jail, where I sit for helping a young man call his mother using my telephone account. It's a great blessing, this opportunity for solitude. (I have a cellmate, but he's an orderly. So, I'm home alone most of the time and only leave the cell for shower and "rec".) I don't envy these people for having to try to punish me, for it's not easy to do so. I've been very respectful to the staff. I just haven't followed enough rules or have attracted too much attention (every guard seems to know who I am). No word on how long I'll be here, but maybe until January. This I think will do wonders for my studies. All there is to do is read, write, sleep, talk to my celli and "shoot lines". Shooting lines is sort of like fly-fishing meets prison tech. It's the art of using a small projectile to slide a line across the floor. Some can even slide it across the wall and down stairwells, where another person shoots a similar contraption to snag it, creating a linkage between cells. Now food (mashed thin enough to fit under the door), notes, coffee, clothes, etc. can be passed, and the prison economy can go on. It's really something to see a guard leave a magazine on the floor of the pod, and suddenly after they walk away, three or four bars of soap and toothpaste tubes shoot out of three or four cells like lizards' tongues, hoping to snag the magazine and reel it back in for reading. It takes both peace and ingenuity to do confinement without breaking, I think. Fortunately, by this time, I have both. Gotta go. Love you,
Cory

Garden Analogy

Now that the soil of your "spirit garden" has been thoroughly "scorched" by adversity, composted by uprooted occupations, fertilized by copious amounts of time and broken up from its hardened state by humiliation, the soil of your "spirit garden" has become soft soil, ideal for fertile harvest. Thus the very adversity that proved so trying was/is the mechanism that prepares you for growth. The time is now to plan your "garden", which is your "program", the way you'll spend your time, day by day. Whether the cash crops of learning a new trade or way to make money, a beautiful prayer garden of spiritual practices, a rose garden of renewed romance or all of the above. You may now draw up a plan for how to USE not waste your time. Beware! If you do not create a

63

program, the weeds of distraction, wasting time will take over: idle pointless conversation, playing cards, sleeping excessively, fretting, overeating, etc. The point is: if you don't do time, it will do you. "As if you could kill time without injuring eternity."- Thoreau. Don't be the guy who does a few years with nothing to show for it but 20,000 hours experience playing dominoes. You must be vigilant about pruning and weeding these sort of wastes. Reflect on your day. Review where your time went. This is not to say recreation is bad, just that the direction should be towards productivity. Don't waste precious water on weeds.

At the beginning of the day, set the tone for the day with gratitude for the opportunity and a resolution to use the day for a purpose. Throughout the day ask: am I doing what I should to achieve my purpose? When you find yourself faced with an option of what to do, pause, re-center, then decide. At the end of the day, reflect, write, consider: what did I do today? How did I spend my time? Re-center. "If you don't measure, you don't manage."

Now days have passed. You will very soon experience a bountiful harvest. Letters will come in. Your practical skill will grow. You will finish books, come to realizations, see a change. Your little seeds have begun to grow. Harvest comes. Now share it. Look to lend books, share knowledge, express optimism to others.

Your criminal proceedings are just like any other disaster- there is a certain amount of loss inherent. The question is: will you be one of those few who uses it to your advantage and replant quickly? Or will you just let weeds grow?

Here is a list of books/ information Cory wanted me to send to him:
Practicing Presence[12] by Eckhart Tolle
The Intention Experiment[6] by Lynne Taggert
The Secret[13] by Rhonda Byrne
Deepak Chopra's most popular two books
Stillness Speaks[14] by Eckhart Tolle
Most popular books on Thoreau, Ralph Waldo Emerson and Seneca
Books by Timothy Ferris
Information about Sacred Geometry
Stuff from Khan Academy
Michael Santos' blog

Anatomy of a Conscious Inmate

Self Aware. Open minds eye. Open mindedness. Present. Accepts what "is". Non-judgmental. Does not complain.

Perception: Sees only opportunity and possibilities. Reads and writes regularly. Self-aware- "Watches" self. Direct eye contact with compassion that knows all brothers and does not focus on differences.

Avoids: TV, vain magazines, newspaper (as they drain spiritual energy, condition us to be drones and desensitize us).

Uses nose for deep inhalation during meditation.

Heart: Keeps the heart pure. Does not harbor resentments. Does not harbor anger more than a day. Is aware of emotions, focuses on feeling them without thought, about why he feels them. Lets feelings dissolve before acting. Saves reprisal for a time when passion and judgment is clear. (This also helps because it will be unexpected.) Only harms another when necessary and from a place of peace. Keeps deep gratitude and compassion at the forefront of re-centering exercises and meditations.

Stomach: Avoids eating excessive junk. Watches what he eats and takes note of how it affects his energy. Meat is the most toxic thing, so discerns which meats to eat. Fasts.

Mouth: Does not complain, gossip (true or untrue), idle chatter. Reserves expression to manage perception. "Don't spill it all at once." Inspires curiosity with brevity. Minimizes profanity. Blesses others with optimistic assessments/ compliments. Speaks as a god, to create possibilities. Makes people feel important with respectful speech. Avoids making self seem simple with stories from past. Keeps people guessing. Conceals intentions. Avoids talking to negative people. Does not reveal plans completely. Does not prematurely commit to anyone. No victim mentality talk.

Avoids sexuality altogether. Sexual focuses will provoke imbalances and frustration. They're best simply forgotten for now, or least not pursued (porn, TV, masturbation). Otherwise, they will drain spiritual energy.

Uses wise positioning: Avoids negative people. Avoids places of gambling, TV, distractions, etc. Seeks quietude and solitude or company with good positive people from whom something may be gained.

Re-centering Practices

"We must die before we die if we are to achieve salvation."

The purpose of life is to ultimately return to a state of "oneness" with "God". While we are alive, the closest we can come to this state of being is stillness- being "present", for it is only through the narrow gate of stillness in the present that we may enter the eternal-commune with God. For Buddhists, that is meditation. For Christians, listening to that "still small voice". The destination is always the same, as are the majority of steps. Here are a few examples:

- Gratitude lists
- "Presence" techniques
- Fasting
- Environment change
- Retreat

Gratitude Lists:

"All blessings come from gratitude." Gratitude lists are a quick re-centering exercise I first learned of in Narcotics Anonymous but soon discovered they were touted implicitly and explicitly in all religious systems. Simply, they are listing and focusing on the things you have to be grateful for. These can be anything. Many will be things you had forgotten that you had, obvious things you didn't notice until they are taken from you or you see somebody without them (life, family, health, youth, etc.). Making and contemplating a gratitude list is one of the best ways to "reset" perspective, a simple act that can in its own right cure the blues and evaporate self-pity. (Perhaps this is why a person who is a paraplegic has "a greater chance of making a person happy than winning the lottery.") Here is an example of one of my gratitude lists:

I am grateful for: life, three meals a day, learning practices, opportunity in my sentence, family, health, friends, my "program".

Since true gratitude is always expressed with action, I've created a more in-depth version of my gratitude lists that connects gratitudes with actions and concrete "to do" lists (resolutions):

Grateful for:	Show it by:	Specific To Do:
Life	Living it fully	Waste less time today
Mom	Being the best son I can	Write a poem for her
Health	Stay healthy	Exercise routine
Today	Re-center/Be present	(Not all have To-Dos)
Sacred	Read more on it	
Geometry		

At the end of the day, I circle the "To-Dos" I did, and don't feel bad about the ones I didn't. "To-Dos" are always possibilities, not expectations. "Plans are nothing. Planning is everything." – Winston Churchill.

"Presence" techniques- It's impossible to both think and focus intently on the body. This is the basis for Yogic meditation, as well as the simplest methods for achieving stillness:

- Focus on breathing or heartbeat intently
- Hear, See, Smell, Feel every cell in your body simultaneously
- Feel any imbalances in your head, stomach, back and allow them to be. Release tension.
- Just focus on the sensation of being alive.

Fasting- Fasting is invoking stillness at the deepest level possible, metabolically. From metabolic stillness, all other forms of stillness follow. This way our very molecular structure enters the Now, and the Divine flows through. This is why every major religious leader fasted. During a fast, we slow down and become keenly aware of a new level of communion with the Divine. Synchronicities and omens abound, and our prayers and intentions are of multiplied effect.

Dietary technique- "As within, so without." Through the modulation of our diets, we become aware of unwanted movements within our being. If one eats everything he's given, inevitably he has tremendous room for improvement in this regard, since prison food is often of the lowest grade, downright poison, passed off as food regularly. The effects of substandard nutrition are: aggressiveness, lethargy, decreased contentment, depression, indigestion, decreased presence and hunger.

Once a person demonstrates to themselves the CAN go days/weeks without food, it becomes apparent: it's better to be hungry and spiritually well than to eat and be cut-off.

A bit of experimentation- a variety of experimentally imposed fasts from various potential toxins in the diet is in order, as is intentional "shifting" from one item to another. For example, stashing others' bread rolls in the morning and making yogurt from collected milks, then later foregoing a pork chop in favor of a double portion of rice. Other meals can be sold or traded for a healthier item. Ninety to ninety-nine percent of people have no clue about how much of a difference diet makes on well-being, not just obesity, but psychologically and spiritually too.

Environment change- Often we have a decision about what sort of environment we chose to do our time in, whether we recognize it or not. If nothing else, we may choose solitary confinement/the hole for any number of reasons. Solitary confinement is often the best option for he who seeks spiritual growth, since it's a place free from distractions where we can practice more freely. Cell living is always preferable to dorm living, as with cell living, one may achieve some degree of separation.

July 2012
Mom,

Hello. I write to you from the C-unit, also known as the Special Housing Unit, also known as "the Hole". Around the same time I was caught for taking the cheese, etc. from the kitchen, I let someone use my phone to call their mother, since they had no money on their account. Two days after my explanation to you about the outcome of the kitchen incident, I received the write-up for the phone incident. So here I am. I'm waiting to see if the man in charge will stick to his promise to put me in the hole for 5 ½ months for my next write-up or if the fact it was already committed and wouldn't make a difference if I heeded his warning as to whether I would receive it or not. So we'll see. Either way, it's actually a great outcome; if I'm kept here until January, I'll have an excellent productive stay- plenty of reading and writing. If not, I'll still have a very productive month of solitude followed by a few more of guitar playing and chess. Honestly, the first sounds even better. Five months of study would be very productive. Anyhow, all is well, and increasingly better as time passes and inertia develops. I am patiently awaiting your letter.

This was all well-timed. I think I had been procrastinating productivity in favor of recreation for long enough. There are so many letters to write, books to be read, website stuff to be worked on, this time will give me a great chance to do so.

Anyway, I have been sleeping the past two days for no particular reason. It's just nice every now and then to sleep a solid day. The view here is not as good per se as it was up on the 9th floor, but I'm very close to the street, so it's easy to people watch. Today there must be some kind of convention. I see people walking around in medieval costumes.

Remember how I told you my celli punched my best friend, Carlos, and they both got sent to the hole? Well, here I'm two cells down from Carlos, so that's a big plus. We can talk at will. There's also a large gap in the wall at the corner through which I can talk to my neighbor and pass notes, food, etc. The way people communicate and pass things here is (other than just yelling really loud, "Hey, So and so" so they can hear all the way across the floor) with "kites", which are contraptions using a bar of soap, a string-thread really and an envelope. A variety of incredibly accurate techniques are employed to propel the soap to an adjacent or perpendicular cell, through the crack under the door, tied to which is the thread. Then the envelope is stuffed with whatever the cargo is: coffee powder, stamps, mashed up food, notes, etc. and the recipient pulls the envelope in. Sometimes "trains" are passed, which are long strings of envelopes with lots of cargo. I've seen everything from cake to lit rolls of toilet paper (for lighting contraband/drugs) passed this way. Some really ingenious stuff.

Though I miss my friends somewhat, I've learned scarcity increases value, and the same applies to human interaction- a person's availability is somewhat inversely proportional to the value people hold for that person's presence. This is why it's no good to have a friend be your roommate and why someone seen daily, once removed, becomes precious and missed. So I know my distance will only be beneficial.

July 15, 2012

Good morning, it's Sunday, day 3 of my time in "the hole", and I'm enjoying my time. I've been reading the *Law of Attraction*[6]- one of the versions I did not actually want, which is something about a man who "uses" his wife to channel some entity or group of entities and get advice from them on his concept called the "Law of Attraction". The premise is rather silly, but the "teachings" themselves are somewhat interesting. They speak of a way of looking at our thoughts and words and how they create our realities. This is accomplished by the Law of Attraction, which has been the subject of a great many "New Age" teachings. It's essentially a deeper look at how "faith can move mountains" and how we can harness this power. It is similar-type thinking that is the basis for "vision boarding" and other visualization creation techniques. Even if you cannot accept all the claims that are made about the power of our minds to actually reshape matter, I think these techniques are of a priceless value to creativity. It's pretty simple: just envisioning the life of things and way of being you want and "pre-experiencing" them, being there with all the senses. Articulating the various aspects and diving into the experience of being there deeply. Just another form of "praying" if you will. Examples:

I am seeing myself accomplish great things.
I am meeting with investors. I feel the grip of their handshake.
I see the condominium complex I'm developing.
I hear the cranes and contractors creating it.
I see the clouds of dust as it rises to completion.
I smell the new paint drying.
I see myself donating to charity. I feel the sacrifice.

July 26, 2012
Mom,

I have read and reread your letter and notes on *A New Earth*. It makes me very glad you seem to have taken quite as much as I from it and can join me in this understanding. This book I think has some of the greatest potential of all books I've read to liberate people from the mental cancer that is so pervasive in our society today- particularly with western culture. Identification with FORM, EGO, COMPLEX STRUCTURES, constantly creating, opposing, cluttering systems of differentiation. It is inevitable these systems must go or else reach a critical mass and cause a nuclear meltdown quite literally.

The trick of Tolle's writings is finding balance. Ok, so presence, great but for example, consider the quote, "Plans are nothing. Planning is everything." – Winston Churchill. One of my favorite things to do right now is "catalogue possibilities". That is, plan. I know they're just ideas- nothing. I know they're not to be attached to, but is it really being present? No, not totally. Also, a friend of mine was telling me how a POW in Vietnam would survive is by recalling systematically everything he could remember, replaying his whole life over and over. This isn't presence. So is presence better? Also the principle of "Unity", presence and non-attachment is still perplexing. It seems almost impossible to survive without concerted efforts based in desire. We think we're detached until we lose more. This is what the accident was like. [Cory experienced a bicycle-car collision in 2010 where his head impacted full force into the passenger window of a vehicle while riding at 30 mph.] I thought I was detached until I realized how much I valued my mental and physical wellbeing. Not having mental clarity was a crushing blow, evidence of deep attachment to mental dexterity. How to detach? Beats me. Anyways, I'm experimenting with it daily, taking moments regularly to simultaneously experience the essential message every cell of my body is expressing in its electric music, dissolving the illusion of reality in the wind being sucked through my nostrils- all the while measuring presence and the success of my technique by the degree of peace and unity felt. The results have been excellent. It is a form of interdimensional travel. That is, shifting your way through similar realities, into the realities in which our lives progress with a greater degree of grace, perceptible coherency. This of course, like any expressible notion, is not truth, only a pointer at truth. The notion that as humans it's impossible to truly "grasp" truth, arrive at any spiritual objective through manipulation, collection of proper alignment of ideas, only to assist in the approach thereof as a belief, has also been extremely liberating (though in its own right, it too is not truth, merely a pointer at truth). It neatly answers and clarifies all sorts of conflicting ideas in religion from the notion of people who never had the opportunity to be exposed to certain beliefs being "judged" to an ocean of seemingly unrectifiable contradiction in truth. Just as a fractal can never be accurately depicted by any physical portrayal, for it is of unlimited degree of complexity, so is the nature of God and how we approach "him". So

71

it seems to me. This is relativism and looked down on in Christian circles, but it seems to work well for me.

The book *Sacred Geometry*[15] you sent is proving daily INCREDIBLE, INSPIRING AND REVEALING. It's done what I'm amazed I see as so rare in our society in a few short pages and a handful of exercises, which is demonstrate the immutable forms in our reality, the connection between God and reality as expressible in mathematics and design. It's something I do not feel capable of explaining because it's so far from our modern idea of God in math or science, yet so close that it's just something one must not only read, but practice to understand. In a few short hours, understanding is opened up to see the way in which the divine traverses into the material, and by extension, the way we traverse back. I highly recommend you, as an artist, make some study of this art. It's fairly simple to do. The basic idea is that we live in a culture that is empirical and disconnected from even the most basic understanding of creative principles, something even the ancients (even 1700 era) had a much better grasp on. It's very beautiful once you begin to understand. I'll demonstrate one simple example. Simply forming a circle, then forming another using the same radius but alternating the centers yields "the seed", the versica pisci, which is the symbol of Jesus Christ. The depth of this symbology is too extensive to explain in full here, but let it suffice to say, the early Christians used a fish for a reason. The symbol signifies and forms the basis for the divine entering the material, and using the concepts of sacred geometry, we can see just how. This progression actually forms the basis for EVERY STABLE SHAPE, from equilateral triangle to square, pentagon, hexagon, octagon, n-gon, etc. It's an incredibly clear demonstration of complexity arising from the most basic simplicity, design emerging from chaos. Sacred geometry was practiced by Jesus' original followers, all major religions, is the basis for all architecture and all nature. It perplexes me why we're not taught it as children. It has been said that by actually drawing and contemplating the concepts behind the various sacred designs, we actually enter into a new world of communion and

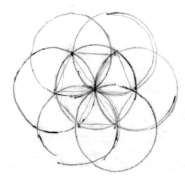

understanding of the divine. That it reshapes our subconscious mind and evaporates the blockages associated with human perception- a therapy of sorts. I highly recommend you study it and experiment with some of the basic principles. All that is required is: a straight edge (I use folded paper), a writing implement and a compass (I use a piece of paper folded over 4 times with holes in it at intervals as a compass). All that's needed is the ability to swing an arc or full circle at various lengths. If you would, send me as much about this study as you can find.

Anyways, externally things are well. It's quite a challenge to co-exist 24/7 with this Boston guy. He's an old state prison con-man who's got a very violent past. I can see through it to his "inner child", but the problem is he's constantly grunting, cursing, expressing paranoia, hate, murder, etc. I do what I can to let it just dissolve and am trying to see it as an opportunity to tap into stillness despite negative stimuli. In that respect, it's an IDEAL situation. It's going better than I would have thought possible in the past, and we generally get along. As I think about it, it is a considerable feat. Living with even fairly normal people has proven/proves challenging in general, let alone 24/7- literally are we rarely more than 5 feet apart. So, it's something good to be able to maintain patience despite every imaginable negative stimuli. It's almost as though this guy was designed to test my patience- or perhaps we each others'. Even his farts sound like explosive rage. The simplest setback (dropping a pencil) results in a train of expletives that seems to never end. It inevitably rubs off. Grinds teeth, grunts and moans every 15 seconds…It's almost like an act, a practical joke of sorts. I say all this not to complain, but to observe the perfection of opportunity, in its full expression.

I have been making various dairy products for about two months now. I came up with everything from like a kefir-like product to a ricotta cheese-like product (except with a strong parmesan-type smell). It's a godsend, really, because I cannot digest the milk, and the food here in the hole is just shy of enough without that daily snack. It really improves a bland meal to have some flavorful, fresh cheese to add. The food has actually been very good lately. It coincides with an improvement of perception. But I maintain that perception has incredibly potent effects on objective reality, not just perceived. This is what the book *Biology of Belief*[16] is all about. He shows how science is proving what esoteric healers have been saying all along: beliefs aren't just influential, but CAUSATIVE. An

73

array of energy that extends beyond our current scientific understanding is behind all reality, especially biology. It is exciting because it offers us a CURE for the rationalism that's taken our collective mindset. We truly are approaching a new era in human existence- one that promises to offer us a far more colorful, vibrant, divine experience than history has ever known. I am very grateful to know we can be a part of ushering it in. That's all for now.

Book Wishlist:
Biology of Belief[16]
The Undiscovered Self[17] - Jung
Oprah Book List (with descriptions)
Timothy Ferris book recommendations
Collection of Sacred Geometry Designs
The Silent Mind[18]
A book on the art of writing letters

July 26, 2012
Dad,

Sorry the tomatoes didn't make it. I have been thinking about gardening and how it's got such a correlation with wellbeing- even longevity. The depth of causality related to interacting with nature- particularly the transmutation of light into substance- is of supreme beauty.

Lately I've been studying Sacred Geometry. It talks about how the chlorophyll molecule is a 12-sided molecule that looks like a flower. That 12 represents the "womb" in which the divine or abstract enters reality. It's a very exciting field, sacred geometry. Its premise is divine order permeates all things, and that simple geometric mathematic concepts symbolize, correspond with, and help us understand and harness the metaphysical. That through basic exercises, we understand to interact with the world in profound ways. It's truly amazing how far reaching the concepts presented are. They show how complex-manifest reality springs from very simple designs. I highly recommend you check it out. It's very revealing.

I was blessed to come across a book by the Dalai Lama in here: *How to See Yourself as You Really Are*[19]. This title is misleading. It's basically a rundown of the essential practice and perspective of the Buddhist and philosophy thereof: detachment, "emptiness" (similar to the concepts of interconnectedness and temporality), meditation, altruism.

Indeed it is wonderful to have my faculties back. It's somewhat perplexing how it's possible for them to stray so, but I'm rapidly growing in insight to the nature of peace, balance, completeness. So it's impossible to suffer the same. Anyways,

Gtg, Love,
Cory

July 2012
Mom,

I've been having to learn some patience, living with this guy, my celli here in the hole. My intention is to build him up and make him feel respected and esteemed, but there's not much to go on. He's an old very violent jailbird from Boston, very negative and doesn't seem to be giving me much to admire or latch onto and build on. I'm constantly having to convince myself there's a good guy under there. It's valuable in one way- helping me recognize my own egocentrism and negativity. But gosh I struggle with keeping my mind from further damaging this already very fragmented guy. I believe we co-create each other's experience and even personality through perception. So, I must find a way to create better not worse.

Speaking of, thank you for helping re-cocreate me when I lost track. It took incredible patience and discernment and set an excellent example for me to follow. Anyways, Good night,

With love,
Cory

July 2012
Mom,

Thank you for the thoughtful letter. Yes, I received both letter and book, both of which I lent to my good friend Carlos after reading and rereading. Thank you.

I imagine you're glad to have Landon a bit closer now. I know I am. Having them so close is making me second guess my original plan to leave the U.S. soon after the halfway house. I am feeling more drawn towards Austin and Houston where I can be around to see my nephew, at least for a few months. Who knows? I recognized that the "uncentering" was a result of the excitement of expectations- inherently deceptive and wasteful of energy since they don't exist, and also sabotage the enjoyment we get from their manifestation. Essentially the excitement of travel, money, opportunities for entrepreneurism, promise of growth of identity, all these things of which I have been deprived of being returned to me, which all exist in the future. And their manifestation in the Now is ONLY the loss of attention and imbalance they create. The imbalance manifests itself as constant desirousness of recreation and food, the loss of attention (closely-related) results in not doing the things I should be. *How to See Yourself as You Really Are*[19] by the Dalai Lama helped me see this. So the remedy, aside from simply recognizing the futility and danger of being excited, is to begin to train my mind to associate these detractors with their downsides, heavy weights and lowness. I have been amazed at the efficacy of these techniques. Since I have been incarcerated and read *From Poverty to Power* and read about "detachment" and dying before death, denying self, I had been very apprehensive, skeptical, even unnerved by this concept of the goal being detachment- freedom from desire. Do you understand what this really means? I desire to see family. I desire to prosper. I desire to enjoy life. In detachment, I may or may not do all of those things, but if I do, my motivation is exclusively selfless. This is a bit unnerving. I only have met a few people who seem truly detached and read of a few more. Their lives do not seem desirable to me, but what I am beginning to realize is the benefits of this pursuit are merely harder to see. Yet I was sitting in the cell yesterday by myself (when I got my disciplinary sentence of 15 days in SHOE/hole, they moved me out of Boston Bob's cell), and I have been fasting and thinking and meditating on this, and the space around took on a certain iridescence, much like a mist of diamonds that formed a web of rainbows. I became aware that it is impossible to ascertain the pleasantries of any other lifestyle than the one we're living. And just as the rich often struggle with depression and unhappiness, and the paraplegic finds great joy in life, it's simply impossible to discount a pursuit because we cannot comprehend the experience from afar. It's like looking at a man on a tall mountain. We can say, "Man, he looks lonely up there. He's so far from the streams and meadows. He must be cold." But until we see the spectacular view, it's all

76

meaningless. Besides that, some of the most wonderful experiences I've had were very mundane, seemingly inconsequential. So I cannot say where I will end up, but I can say I've made a major step towards being willing to go farther down the path, recognizing desire as deception and unwanted. It's impossible to completely prevent or counteract attachment, but we can let go and focus on nearby things that essentially weaken them. So, that's what I'll do for now. Meditate on altruism and the illusions inherent in the human experience. It seems to me the Buddhists have a lot to offer ANY being experiencing humanity. It's really a no-nonsense practical pursuit. Just my take. What do you think?

Anyways, all is well.
Love,
Cory

July 23, 2012
Dad,

I was just telling Mom it's really something when you think about it- the degree of ease with which we manage to cohabitate in prison. Whereas on the "outs", it's common to not be able to stand a fairly sane person who you are only around for a few hours (roommate); in prison we're forced to live within 5 feet of another person 24/7, and we actually find a way to do so relatively peaceably. My celli in the "hole" (95% of the week or more) is a 50-something hardened state prison white supremacist super violent killer-type who's about as loud and obnoxious by empirical standards as they come. But we get along fine. Rarely do we get at odds or really any more than superficially annoyed with each other, despite what most would consider an ocean of basis for annoyance. It's as though the knowledge of anything less than 100% patience and forgiveness of annoyances will result in both of us losing our lives (one to being killed, the other to a life sentence for killing) is sufficient to result in a very high degree of co-habitability. I've had 7 cellis so far, and this has been true for all. It just flies in the face of the experience of incompatibility I've observed in the outside world with myself and others. Anyhow, life is good. Hope to hear from you soon.

Love,
Cory

August 6, 2012
Mom,

Great to hear from you! Very good about the books you ordered! I'm excited to read them. A sizeable pile of books is accumulating here in the corner of my little cell. Twenty-six to be exact and many more in my property box. I'm going to have to manage the very real risk of being charged with "Excessive Reading Material" (not kidding), a low to moderate severity infraction. The good news is the solution is to lend out (also an infraction) as many of them as possible, simply continuing to order more books as though it were not. I see virtually no limit to the quantity of time and money I am willing to devote to this end, since in my estimation, I'm getting a 100 times better return on my investment by self-directed education than college could ever offer. So if college is at all a worthwhile investment, this investment is for the better. This justification does not even take into account the even GREATER effect this literature will have on others, many of whom otherwise would not read at all. For these reasons, I hope Father will be willing to extend more credit in the event the settlement [from his bike accident] is not completed expeditiously. To me, the biggest tragedy would be to not seize this opportunity in full, which is to say, come anywhere close to not having plenty of opportunity to learn and study while the time is the ripest possible. And can see no more optimal circumstance for education and guided contemplation than a prison sentence.

Speaking of enjoyment of life, the past few days have been sublime. You know that Netflix commercial? The one where the old man asks the cartoon animals, "Is this gonna make me cry?" to which a little fluffy bunny says, "Only if you believe in the power of friendship." The past few days have been reminding me of that. It's "reality" but conceptualized and almost like a cartoon- wildly vibrant colors, birds singing, interlocking double rainbows with psychedelic Buddhas singing about good fortune. The superficiality of their façade called reality almost as comical as the symbology my subconscious is superimposing. It feels as though at any moment I'll discover a little rip somewhere. I'll look over and see a beam of neon magenta light poking out. I'll walk over and rip the tear a little wider. Then with one light tug, all of reality will rip off like cheap wallpaper, a Jim Carey "Truman Show" moment when I realize it's all 100% contrived. In one hand I'll be holding a crumpled reality, like a sheet, and I'll be floating in an iridescent harmony, watching the spirals of energy, which compose my being untangle back into rays of light, or sound, which I'll no longer be able to differentiate, since my very eyes and ears will have become energy. But no such rip has appeared. So I just sit here and laugh at it sliding through the molecules. Yes, if it all weren't so uncommonly SANE, I would have to admit insanity.

You really should get yourself a copy of *Creative Visualization*[20]. It's an excellent book of visualization techniques. I received two books from the "Human Kindness Foundation", one called *We're All Doing Time*[21] and another called *Lineage*[22], a book of short stories. It turns out, Bo Lozoff is doing almost exactly what I had envisioned: providing a book of techniques, spiritual writings, letters, artwork, quotes selected especially for the prisoner. It's such a beautiful book. It actually brought me to tears. I read them both almost cover to cover the same night I got them. Very powerful books. In fact, even the Dalai Lama himself wrote its foreword. The entire book is essentially about achieving stillness and devotion to compassion. It's so profound. And it's written so gracefully, so gently. It speaks the truth in a way that's personable, yet venerable. Explicit yet contradictory. I've never seen a work thread a needle so tactfully concerning spirituality. He uses techniques from the East. I used to tread very lightly around anything remotely Eastern, but now I see it's not really about one person's perception or some vague notion of anything we don't understand being "evil". It's just a thing. There is no religion in heaven. Buddhism gives us the most practical way to "commune with God", so who cares what else. God said, "Be still and know that I am God." This is all meditation is. I no longer believe spirituality is a battle. Jesus only fought the establishment. Jesus was a Buddhist! Either way, I'm so grateful for all the awareness.

There is a principle in Buddhism that the journey is to reach enlightenment, but once a soul reaches enlightenment, then it is reincarnated in the lowest form so it can demonstrate to others the way. This is exactly like all other pursuits: for example, when I learned to play guitar, I learned the scales etc. They helped me immensely to improve. But after a while, I reached a point when scales only limited me. I had to try hard to forget all I knew in order to move on. All perfection is CYCLICAL. The whole of existence is made up of waves of God's voice. It all returns to "imperfection", which is really our own idea.

Anyways, all is well. Oh yeah, Today the lieutenant came around looking in cells asking inmates how we are. (They constantly check to make sure we're not killing ourselves.) I feel like I'm an exhibit at the zoo sometimes. Probably 20 different people come ask, "How are you doing?" sometimes 5 times a day. Psychologists, wardens, guards, researchers, lieutenants, food service workers. I'll be sleeping and wake up and a line of 5-6 officials will take turns peeking into my cell to look at me. Ask me if I'm okay. So today the lieutenant (woman) came by and asked, "How are you?" Me: "Excellent!" Her: "Excellent! You can't be excellent. You're in jail!" Me: "So are you!" Her: "Yeah well...I get to go home." Me: "So do I!" Haha

Well, I'm going to take a break. I'll write you in a couple of days.

With respect and love,
Your son,
Cory

August 6, 2012
Bethany,

How's it going? Life here has been nothing short of AMAZING. You know the YouTube video "double rainbow"? I am on the same wavelength as that guy. Maybe I'm not as hysterical, but the experience of life is just so rich, so surreal right now. I feel like I can see atoms, and they're suspended in a diamond mist inside my cell. The blank white walls scream with color, an iridescence, really. The mundane silence sounds like a symphony orchestra, no, an angelic choir. I'm not kidding. I'm not going crazy either. This I'm realizing is the true nature of living. This is why the blind and deaf paraplegics find happiness closer than most wealthy. There are thousands, millions of layers of perception we go through life simply missing. It's like the people you meet in other countries, almost completely unaware of the paradise around them. Our minds are like a plot of land. Left to its own, it will grow a fine array of plants and animals. But if we tend to it, we can make a spectacular garden from it, full of tropical flowers and delicious fruit. I've been sitting in the same spot for 95% of the past week just meditating, reading, writing, and yet, I am on the verge of tears at the beauty of it all. Even in the smell in my nose right now is more beautiful than the best perfume I've ever smelled. It's beyond just perception. We're born with the God-like ability to create! I've dabbled, but this is a whole new level. Every second is so full of life. It seems like the deeper I dive in, the deeper

80

it gets. I wish I could let every person experience this. I don't think it's possible to explain, but I know it's possible for all to experience. If everyone knew what it was like, everyone would pursue it. Anyways, I wish you well.

Cory

August 14, 2012
Father,

I was just sitting here thinking of you and figured I would say "hello!" Have you ever taken a day to just BE? What about fasting, have you ever fasted? I am curious what led you to begin sending the Dalai Lama quotes. I ended up finding one of his books, *How to See Yourself as You Really Are*[19] here in the "hole". It was very revealing. It talks about how the untrained mind is like a waterfall of thoughts. It simply never stops and is too violent and turbulent to be of any use for achieving peace and how regular practice is required to tame it. The idea is, unless we become skilled at shutting off the mind, we cannot ever be truly content. We may catch fleeting glimpses, but that's all. Upon experimentation, this has proven true for me. It's next to impossible to silence my mind. The suggestion was regular practice, like anything else. It must be worked at. It's been only two weeks, and already I'm seeing HUGE progress. I've actually been able to have a few "thoughtless" sessions. What's been more of a blessing has been the change in the quality of my awareness. You know that crystal clear, precise feeling that develops over time when we learn a new skill or sport? Well now I feel that way most of the day. My notes come out very organized. My cell went from disaster to tidy. Most of all, the sensation of awareness has just generally become BRIGHTER, CRISPER, CLEANER. It's very nice, I must say. So, for now I'll stick with it.

Well, I look forward to hearing from you.

Best Wishes,
Love,
Cory

81

August 14, 2012
Mom,

Thanks for the thoughtful letter. I received Meimie's letter. I must admit, it's difficult for me not to feel a variety of negative emotions about her not being able to come visit me before she leaves. I will just have to try to visit her soon. I don't get off visit restriction until September (not sure). I've been in a solitary cell for a week now, and I think I actually like it most out of all. I can't say living with Boston Bob was exactly a perfect example of compassion. It's very difficult to overcome a person's own negative impressions of themselves. I felt bad for not offering more active affirmation. I often ignored him completely even when he was talking to me, just so I wouldn't encourage him to keep talking. I tried. But I also believe it's impossible not to co-create negativity in a person's life through mere perception if it all resonates with perspective. And unfortunately, it did. Well live, learn, purify, perfect. Right?

Over here the dynamics have been A LOT different. Carlos and I sent big stacks of notes back and forth down the hall using our "fishing lines". There's this "chick" named Evelyn that's like Mrs. Attention. All the Mexican guys flirt with him all day. And he's constantly singing and talking to the guys. It's like being in the Evelyn Show most of the day. Oddly enough, he looks a lot like a skinnier version of Bethany except with a slightly different nose. Then there's "Diego" who is another case in and of himself. He's like 35 and just got out of a 16-year prison sentence (was out of 4 months, got a girl pregnant and came back looking at 3-5 years.) I can't help but feel guilty at my contempt for some of these people, but I suppose anyone in a small box 24/7 that has to hear another person 24/7 will get annoyed with them sometimes. One thing about Mexicans, they've got a different perception about what's reasonable in terms of noise pollution. Then there's Bobby (cell 5, Carlos; cell 4, Evelyn; cell 3, Diego; cell 2, Bobby; cell 1, me). Bobby is a 22-year-old white guy from a family of 14, the eldest of 12 kids. Yeah, his mom had 12. Same woman. He's got NO criminal record, had a good job working for his dad's big electrical contracting company and took some psych-pill and decided to rob a bank while he was high. He barely even remembers it. I feel really bad for the guy. He's probably going to do 5-10 years. We spent a lot of time talking about different things.

I spend most of my day doing creative meditation visualization when I'm not reading or writing letters. Just playing with possibilities. Shakti Gawain talks about creating a "sanctuary"- visualizing a place that will act as a creative workshop for visualization. So I created a sort of limestone temple made on a big circular platform in the sky. I see myself up there made of various shapes and patterns- a "polygon" Cory- the idealized energy version of me, a sort of reflection except amorphous. I go up there and work on myself like a sculptor working on an art piece. Then I look out and each of you all, Dad, you, Bethany, Landon and Amanda have their own temples floating nearby. And y'all are like "Hey, What's up? We've all been here wondering where you were at." Amanda comes out and she's pregnant. And she somehow pulls the baby out and shows me and is like, "Look what we've been working on." It's all rather silly but profound and sensible all at the same time. What do you think?

So I discovered milk bags (little sealed plastic bags of milk we get daily) turn into various tasty dairy products over time when simply let alone. First they turn nasty, that slimy sour milk stage (3 days). Then they separate and all the sliminess goes away. At this stage they're great with juice as a yogurt smoothie. Tastes exactly like yogurt. Then they go further, gets firmer, and it becomes like sour cream/cottage cheese. Mixed with sugar and cake, DELICIOUS! Who knew? If I strain it out and mix in salt, it's a tasty sour cream thing. But we get this low grade cake stuff every day, so I put it on that and mix it up. It's like cheesecake pudding. It's so good! I can't digest milk well anyways. So now I just allow all of these to age and rotate- so good! It starts becoming cheese-like on day 7 or so. I wonder what 3 weeks would do. So far, not once has a bag come out wrong, off or upsetting to the stomach. I tried a carton milk and it became DISGUSTING. I'd like to continue when I get out. I've got a friend who makes kefir. It's very simple. You should consider doing it. It requires almost no effort and digests better than milk and more nutritious.

Anyways, I'm off to bed. Much love, thank you for your constant devotion, diligence, patience,

Your Son,
Cory

August 21, 2012
Mom,

Greetings! I'm over here in the "Embassy", the joke of a name Dimitrov has given our cell: it's a place of diplomatic immunity and cultural exchange, really more like instruction. (He does not allow stupid Americans in.) He talks and talks about everything from world history to the very comprehensive recent history of organized crime in Bulgaria, how stupid and contemptible Americans are, kidnapping people, being kidnapped, etc. I just listen intently. It seems to make him happy to think of something other than lethal revenge, so I just listen all day. Do you have any older friends you just listen to, as opposed to actual conversation?

I've been "taking it easy" lately, no longer running a store and busying myself with things. My focus has shifted somewhat from doing to being, leaving my top priorities developing deep mindful concentration and pure interactions with others. Moving towards LESS IS MORE of Karma. I'm greatly enjoying learning from so-called "Buddhists". We tend to write it off as "religion", pantheism, etc., but it's really just a collection of ideas passed on by people who listen and seek. Its premise is simple and being rapidly confirmed by science- "God" permeates and comprises all, an ocean of energy and potential that connects us all. As we grow and begin thinking, we get out of harmony with the energy. By silencing our minds and purifying karma (speech, thoughts, actions) we REUNITE/ HARMONIZE with this Unity and achieve the ULTIMATE GOAL, which is the End of Suffering, "Enlightenment", which is a crystallization of consciousness. Apparently this crystallization actually takes on physical form- SHARIRA. Would you look up and print out a Wikipedia article on this for me? [Note to reader: "Sharira" refers to actual relics, rock-like crystals, found in the cremated remains of enlightened souls. I found many in Cory's ashes.]

Anyhow, the ability to "listen" to "God", something I have always wanted to be able to do, is a great joy. We really never stop listening to "God" but by silencing our cancerous mind/thoughts, it becomes a much more efficient process. I always used to fret, "Why doesn't God say anything?" Now I see the answer "because God is saying EVERYTHING at once", singing it really. And I prefer not to personify "Him" anymore. It's just too VAST for piddly ideas like being human. There is nothing that is not comprised 100% of "God". Only perception is even capable of differentiating. Anyways, the "proof is in the pudding", and it is delicious. I have taken time to review life, spiritual progress, etc. And the verdict is clear- this is no passing phase or house of cards belief system. I've tapped into something even deeper than the SERENITY of 2009-2010. In this lifetime, I will always have a way to "God". This is not to say more trying times will not come. They WILL. The cyclical nature of my spirituality and well-being used to trouble me. But now I see- this is the TRUE nature of life. We all go through it. I'm just going through the cycles very rapidly in life, as I am getting nearer to crystallization. So I accept the "hell phases" and even that to others my path will seem failure after failure until a certain point. This is the life I chose before I was born. So drugs, depression, even death are all OK. Though life may go "NORMAL" for me (kids, job) at some point, I wouldn't count on it. My priority is Saturation and Crystallization of Consciousness, as it has been all my life, moment by moment. Whatever that entails (maybe it does entail wife and kids). But for now, those seem like distractions. How would it even be possible to find a girl who's even near where I am spiritually? I've only met one IN MY LIFE. A far more likely outcome is polygamy, as culturally taboo as it is in our confused, broken culture, it's the only possibility of spending the rest of this lifetime that would seem to fit. And it IS a very practical, workable possibility, even if not one for this country/culture. Well, life is good. I'm thinking of you, and hope to hear your response to these ideas soon.

With love,
Cory

P.S. HIGHLY RECOMMEND reading *The Intention Experiment*[6] or at least checking out the website.

August 21, 2012
Dad,

Greetings, thanks for the letter. One of my two main friends right now is a 60-something market analyst for nuclear power plants world-wide. He specializes in "competitive strategy" and has given presentations even to the U.N. on certain European plants. He won't tell me what he did, but Dimitrov had his researchers look and found that he got drunk and drove, ended up paralyzing a guy on a military base here. Really good guy. He's got daughters my age. Dimitrov, the Bulgarian, keeps the excellent stories of the Eastern European underworld going- the degree of power he and others have/had in that part of the world makes even mob bosses on this side seem like petty criminals. It's very entertaining, stories full of assassinations, shipping containers full of counterfeit bills, fly here, there, this, that... Perhaps it is exaggeration, but the newspaper and law computer here have done nothing but confirm, even expand on what he's told me. So the spy and gangster movies turn out to be surprisingly true to life, even watered down.

Still meditating regularly. Life is very good and rapidly improving. Anyways, hope to hear from you soon. Tired now. Good night!

Love,
Cory

August 22, 2012
Dad,

Thanks for your thoughtful letter. I appreciate it. I'm going to follow your example and speak to each point sequentially.

I can understand not having the inclination to read after a day of intensive work. Outside, just about all I read is research online. Since I've been in, I've realized perhaps the hard way, it's not easy to identify which books are truly worth their time. *Pillars of the Earth*[23] was an excellent suggestion by Bethany and Mom. Something about the organic simplicity of the culture the story represents I found cathartic to read about. Especially the integration of church and society. The notion of the church spearheading public service, from entertainment to commerce is a good one. It reminds me of something else I was reading that spoke of the many unintended consequences of our government-based welfare system: the lessening of person-to-person giving. We've begun to see the need of others as the responsibility of the government, not ours or the much better suited- church. Anyhow, I really enjoyed it, for fiction. As you may know, I prefer non-fiction, seeking the perfection of reality over fantasy, even if historically-based or uplifting. The thing about non-fiction though is since we're all at such different levels of understanding, it can be very difficult to select helpful books. Suggestions by far have yielded the best results. I can say with certainty, the books I've read that others have suggested have and will continue to rewrite my destiny in a plurality of golden ways. Allow me to share a few if you will. Perhaps you will find time to read or listen to it as an audiobook.

To you, I most recommend:
Biology of Belief[16] and/or *The Intention Experiment*[6]. Both books deal with a similar concept, one that understanding it is a key purpose in my life to convey, that is:

"Quantum Entanglement" as a spiritual principle refers to "Unity" and the "illusory nature of reality". The concept is simple yet profound, and though it flies in the face of modern conceptions of science, it's familiar to the mystics of all religions as well as the recently confirmed suggestions of quantum physics:

Everything we perceive is God's voice coiled up into various shapes that appear constant and rigid, but are actually deeply dependent on each other. Cause and effect are not the linear progression they so appear, and the mind is capable of altering time and space in ways that are without limit. As days progress, we are becoming more and more aware of how to create and restore the world around us quicker and easier than ever thought possible. What was once considered miraculous or impossible is now proven science. The limits and constraints of Newtonian physics, as well as Western medicine, are and will continue to crumble, replaced with a power that can not only move mountains, but rewrite history. It turns out virtually every "super-power" is not confined to the realm of comic books but is demonstrable by ORDINARY people with very little or no training: telepathy, healing, telekinesis, time travel, withstanding extremes of heat and cold, repairing psychological matters both individual and collective, all not just possible, but DEMONSTRABLE.

Biology of Belief shows how our bodies are actually colonies of cells, all communicating and responding to a variety of electromagnetic and emotional cues. Placebo has proven often MORE effective than real drugs. We can stop cancer with thoughts. Genetics are almost inconsequential, and we are literally as we perceive we are. Even muscle growth can be "believed into effect" almost as effectively as traditional workouts. What's more is new techniques exist to observe and rewrite our beliefs rapidly so as to implement all sorts of changes in living things, virtually without limit. Personally, I've

87

found a well-spring of energy, vitality, sleep and general clarity. I look forward to the opportunity to apply this knowledge and techniques to running, cycling and recovery, when I do fall ill.

The Intention Experiment[6] looks at the mind-blowing examples of consciousness affecting reality. It moves understanding of prayerfulness and "intentionality" from CURIOSITY to TECHNIQUE, explaining and solidifying previously vague notions of how to go from thought to effect. It's really cool stuff. All living cells communicating through light waves, bacteria, plants, human tissue are constantly communicating in an incredibly precise way. Plants can detect and seem to instantly "know" when other cells are being stressed or killed, even from a distance. They also seem to be able to READ OUR THOUGHTS, effecting detectable and instantaneous electrostatic changes based on simple INTENTIONS, be they benevolent or detrimental. For example, plants can become very stressed when people even considered burning their leaves. Instantly, there's a large body of evidence our cells all communicate very coherent specific messages to each other and other living organisms, not just chemically but through a combination of light, electromagnetics, electrostatics, as well as forms of information exchange called "quantum entanglement", which travel faster than light, and seem also to be able to travel BACKWARDS in time. (Thus you and your garden's cells are literally conversing about how best to serve each other's needs at all times!) Husbands and wives at a considerable distance were demonstrated not just to share/transmit physiological responses to stimuli, but actually PRECONCEIVED EFFECTS of a stimuli. These seem not to be exceptions at all, but the norm. Thus two minds literally become one, even at a distance and even before the other partner experiences a stimuli. Even strangers who were introduced exhibited an astonishing capacity to "synchronize" thoughts and physiology when intended. Simply talking kindly, even one compassionate word seems to be able to alter water's crystalline composition, tending it towards coherency, whereas vulgarities were shown to disrupt the lattices. Groups of meditators were able to cut the crime rates in major cities by 25-50%. Just bizarre stuff. Anyways, she, the author, explains and compiles all of the most informative and scientifically confirmed evidence of intentionality in her book *The Intention Experiment*[6]. It really is a POWERFUL case for devotion to "God", introspection, faith and meditation. It's particularly compelling because she limits her exposition to only the most widely accepted, reproduced and confirmed effects, as published in major scientific journals. Most of the book she even limits her speculation, sticking to the most direct implications, leaving speculation to the reader. Anyways, it's worth its weight in gold; both the informative and entertaining aspects would independently justify the reading of this book, were they inseparable. I foresee some profound changes in our culture and the range of possibilities in life. We are on the verge of a New Age, and it is becoming more and more obvious.

About the work ethic comments: One thing I've been increasingly aware of over the past few months is the variety of paths to "success", the expression of purpose. (There are certain purposes not easily monetized.) The worthiness of a pursuit (vocation) cannot be evaluated by its lucrativity, much less its demands (hard work/ long work) but instead only to the degree to which it matches our respective proclivities as determined by the net effect or overall happiness it has on the world. So, a job that's most lucrative nor a job that's most demanding nor a job that's the most idealistic are optimal. For me, I believe my proclivities don't lend themselves to monetization. I feel my financial needs can and will be taken care of through a low time/energy input to high yield output (< 10 hours/week) pursuit, leaving 90% of my time to commit to non-profit work. I have met very many people who live this way, making almost all of their income without much effort, devoting their time/energy to art or service. This experience has proven a very good example of such; in order to cover my own expenditures, I simply opened a "store". I made an initial $150 investment and have been living off the 12% return. This is how I intend to live: by buying and selling. I believe I can live a very good, productive, financially successful life by trading various non-perishable goods internationally: cars to Asia, electronics from Asia to South America, used clothing and housewares to Mexico. Through application and some basic principles, I can make money and live well.

In five years? I see myself with a few homes around the world, traveling around, participating in and demonstrating practices that usher in the new consciousness. Perhaps I'll have a wife and kids. This is actually more of a 1-2 year outlook; 5-10 years is simply too long for me to tell. Perhaps I will not do this and just travel around W.O.O.F-ing (World-Wide Opportunities on Organic Farms) and meditating all day- the life of an itinerant monk. But for now I've got a catalogue of very specific plans, things I've absorbed through persistent "interrogation" of people I meet in prison. Combined with study of all the most esteemable role models I can find, along with the principles they promote, whether spiritual, political, entrepreneurial or practical in nature. The notebooks I keep are full of introspective, contemplative and theoretical ideas for life from the broadest spiritual maxims to the most specific step-by-step business plans.

Anyways, I am rambling.

Perhaps it would be more helpful to simply share the principles themselves that I am subscribing to:

1. Most important thing to do- Meditate twice daily. All else will flow from the union with Unity (God) this represents.
2. Follow Chopra's *7 Spiritual Laws for Spiritual Success*[24]- these represent a very good, simple summary of all the rest. Great read- only < 100 pages. Maybe 30-minute read.
3. Follow Gracian's 300, *The Art of Worldly Wisdom*[7]- no time to explain all. A few good ones:
   - Be esteemable in all things.
   - Act, but also seem (great).
   - Stand on the shoulders of giants- pursue great people's company as I have done most of my adult life, spending most of my time with people three times older than I- professors, artists, entrepreneurs, etc. As I am doing here- my friends all embody esteemable traits, successful presentable people I can gather something from. All the times in my life I've suffered or failed has been while around suffering, failing people- likewise the converse has been true. So now I recognize the comradery of the unfortunate is not worth the contagion- misfortune. Better be servant to the great than a master of fools. I've been repeatedly blessed with optimal cell assignments in this regard. It seems as though "God" has seen fit to only pair me with the most virtuous and accomplished cellmates in the population. Truly the trend defies chance. For whatever reason, the most educated, cultured, powerful and connected person I have met thus far in prison has taken a liking to me, and then- after getting sent to the hole- an experience which in itself was full of chance- defying synchronicities of proximity to the great- I somehow by chance was assigned to his cell. He was very happy, as was I; while I disregard all the techniques which involve

murdering, kidnapping and conning one's way to millions, the positive things I can learn from this man are priceless. Perhaps he, here in the last years of his life as a wealthy global kingpin can learn some forgiveness from me (which would save at least two people who have wronged his life.) I must admit I am honored such a hardened and experienced person would open up to me as he has. As a bonus, our cell has an EXCELLENT sunset view. I get to watch the sun set over the Coronado Island every day.

4. Help those who suffer similar experiences to what I have:
   - Homeless people- feed and shelter, pay for haircuts and clothes
   - Prisoners who read- send books and info
   - Kids who are hungry for knowledge- mentor, tutor or give books
   - Drug addicts- direct to N.A or country where it's easier/safer
   - People fed-up with broken belief systems- direct to simplicity

5. Delegate- Use outsourcing for all information/administrative processes and to automate.
6. Travel, network and research regularly.
7. Watch for "red flags" in life daily, weekly, monthly.

Anyways, thanks again, and sorry if I rambled too much.

With love,
Cory

August 27, 2012
Greetings,

I write from the 5th floor, where an incident involving getting a bag of laundry out of a guard's office landed me back in the "hole". I don't know why I find it so easy to get myself into trouble. In my own head, I'm conducting a very considerate, simple, quiet life, yet I find myself in deep trouble with the Federal Government at every turn. All I can think is it's a result of what's left of a belief system that's dying- specifically the belief of a life of 100% honesty cannot provide as well as one of 99% honesty. The matters in question are so trivial in actual malicious intent, but unfortunately not so trivial in the sense of the punitive consequences they incur. In this case, I tried to retrieve a bag of new laundry left by another inmate who left from the guard's office while he was away. Ninety-five percent of inmates have excess/"illegally" apportioned garments and opportunities to simply "inherit" such garments abound. The net effect of "stealing" these "new" garments is only this: I wear new clothes instead of the other inmates who work in the laundry room, and those they sell all new clothes to. (They steal it when sent out for laundry anyways.) So really it was so trivial, yet for some reason I snuck into the guard's office and "stole" it- resulting in two "offenses", probably the loss of some halfway house time and definitely more "hole" and visit-less, email-less time. I am somewhat relieved since I feel the most productive way I can spend this sentence is alone. But I also feel very bad about the disconnect from those I love (seeing Landon's baby later, no visit from y'all, etc.) and those I might help in the general population. There are also some selfish losses- any income I would have made while at the halfway house and the chance to become a guitar virtuoso through the five months of practice, the chance to learn law and "real world" Latin from the law computers, etc., good food and extra servings, meeting people, my sunset view, contact with Dimitrov and Mark, etc.

There's also the fear-invoking precedent: will I perpetually be subjecting myself to penalization for such trivial offenses, as I have so many times in my life? (As you will recall, I was always in trouble for the most stupid things.) Ironically the same guard who caught me for this and the kitchen incident is a guard who by misrepresenting his "active-duty" status in the National Guard, defrauded the BOP out of hundreds, if not thousands in bonus pay. I was at the time actually priding myself in my respectfulness and adherence to rules. I do believe everything happens for a reason and will not get into the very promising aspects of the possibility of doing the next 5-6 months in confinement. I also accept, if it is, but make no judgement about the possibility incarceration is and will play a recurring role in my life. "The only thing we have to fear is fear itself." I contend that the normally prescribed fear, even abhorrence of "institutionalization"/recidivism IS recidivism. That transcendence from the cycle lies in acceptance, even of it as a possibility, for fear only serves to manifest its own outcomes. The disapproval inherent in modern mindsets of evaluation discounts God's own provision. That is- anything less than acceptance is to doubt God. Acceptance does not contribute to a pattern, instead it severs the stream of energy emotion represents, regardless whether positive (desire) or negative (fear). Our focus contributes to the likelihood of an outcome, so ACCEPTANCE becomes the first step to redirecting our energy, our creative power from negative to positive. Instead of fighting an outcome (relapse or recidivism), we merely focus on the exertion of DUE DILLIGENCE; in this case, to be satisfied with provision, that grace, ease and abundance might flow despite me. It raises other topics I consider as well:

CYCLES OF LIGHT AND DARKNESS: I used to be embarrassed by both remissions into "darkness" (confusion, disconnectedness, non-spirituality, relapse, active addiction) and questionably complete ascensions into righteousness, wisdom, understanding, "evangelism", etc., often discounted by others as "spiritual kicks" and "jailhouse religion". Interestingly, no one ever doubts the sincerity of my pursuit. I have to tell them how incredibly different I am now, how lost I have been. Few see both sides. Is this dishonest? I think NOT. The problem is not the completeness of the shift or validity of either state. The only "problem" is impedance by perception, identification and limitations imposed by our own limited understanding. I've learned to ALLOW the cycle. Allow souls to both climb and fall quickly; whether we accept it or not, our souls do go through such cycles, even if we only observe one tendency in a given lifetime.

We, I do this that I might assist others to rise from the depths themselves. Each "dark period" in my life has had an immeasurable positive effect on others. I believe my soul chose this life of repeated success/failure. Not that the cycle must continue, but that it's only important I do my best. Practice due diligence. Attract not the "end of addiction" but "sobriety". Not the "end of forgetting God's power" but the memory of it. I can't help but think these notes, the physical manifestations of the crystallization of understanding will have lasting effect.

93

THE VALUE OF FAMILY: So much of teaching speaks to non-favoritism of persons when it comes to living spiritually. Whether by death or otherwise, all acquaintances come to pass. I feel bad for not being around this past year, but I also know it was/is necessary. What's more, I may leave the U.S. I guess it's impossible to say what will happen, but I'm seeing how important it is to enjoy each other NOW. Who knows what tomorrow will hold.

Anyways, I'm very tired,
I love y'all, sorry I've failed again,
Cory

P.S. Please give me an update and send *The Count of Monte Cristo*[25] as well as Oprah's book list and some well-reviewed book on Einstein, his quotes, his spiritual beliefs. Also, *BHAGAVAD GITA*[26], and *Inside-Out*[27] by Bo Lozoff.

August 27, 2012
Mom and Dad,

Greetings and all hopes of wellbeing. It's too late for me to write much, but as I reflect on the frivolity and general empty ramblings of my last couple of letters, perhaps brevity should be preferential. Happy Labor Day! It has been a good one here. I have been thinking of both of you very much, sending loving intentions and patiently waiting to hear from you. (I say this as though there were any other way, given my current situation.) Lately I've spent considerable contemplation on the inevitability of death and the unexpected nature of its incursions into the human experience. In doing so, a newfound appreciation for the very patient, tolerant love that the both of you have shown me has been conjured up. So, suffice it to say, I love both of you dearly and pray I can live in such a way that remains mindful of these consecutive moments we share, ready at any time for any of our departures from this realm.

My perspective on my conduct, disciplinary segregation too has changed since my 8-24ish letter. I see that this experience is the manifestation of long since elapsed karma and is best though I am very sorry it will adversely affect my availability- phone, email, visits. Though I am in no position to request any more favors, please stay in more frequent contact, even if there seems nothing to update.

I have a new celli here in the SHU (aka "Hole"). I was amused to hear he's here for almost an identical situation with the same guard in the kitchen I stood up to back in June. So, though I could have handled it with far more compassion and personal neutrality, at least I can be sure this small portion of my learning process was just that...a lesson. He's a high level Mexican businessman and multi-ton importer of _____. Yes, ton. That's multimillions. He owns and operates a myriad of legitimate businesses in and throughout Mexico as well, a trucking company, one of Mexico's largest among others. He's an interesting guy, very humble despite his infamy. In Mexico, people like this have a number of aliases. Not sure why, but all the major kingpins go by "Veinte-cuatro" and the like. Some kind of running list of all the biggest movers and shakers in the "game". It turns out on the same floor is one of Mexico's biggest top 5 cartel bosses. These guys are such a big deal, they literally stop everything for them. Just interesting to watch and hear about while doing time. Anyhow, I'll leave it at that and hope to hear from y'all soon.

With love and respect,
Your Son,
Cory

P.S. I have settled in and am in a much better place emotionally now that I've made some sense of the circumstance.

August 29, 2012
Greetings Mom,

It's too late to write a full letter, but it occurred to me to write until the lights do go off. Book-lights, my treasured token to midnight solitude, are no longer allowed in the hole. So at 9:30 pm, every night, I now have two options, sleep or sit in the dark.

I've spent most of the day in still quiet reflection and meditation. Since so many of my resources have been taken, rather, as days go on, I am less concerned with all I can DO and more and more concerned with who I can BE. I've always been intrigued with the concept of BRAINWASHING- that is the superimposition of a belief or idea onto a mind regardless of its beginning state through various techniques. What intrigues me is the idea, if we could tap directly into a mind and rewrite its beliefs and ideas as definitively and as

95

absolutely as, say the constitution. We would wield an incredible tool to reshape reality, destiny and human potential. If we genuinely believe "faith the grain of a mustard seed is sufficient to move mountains", then perhaps this power could be "BRAINWASHED" in. Some very promising progress is being made in this area- see Bruce Lipton and *Psych-K*[28] for what I'm talking about. Science is finally catching up with faith, and not a second too soon. The more I see, the more I'm convinced our consciousness, as a world, is very sick and indeed on the brink of demise. This is not paranoid. Virtually every quantifiable measure of harmony and sustainability is rapidly deteriorating. Navigating realms of understanding that lie beyond the immediate collective is a delicate issue. It's only natural for one grounded in compassionate concern to say, "Ok, you're flying a bit too high. That looks dangerous." But this is my life and a common theme to my story- people telling me I'm wrong, and I can't do whatever it is I'm doing. Meanwhile I just sigh at how lonely it can be climbing supposedly unscalable mountains alone or with small groups. I am frequently wrong. I do fall. I do get hurt. But I'm not shooting in the dark. In time you'll see, of this I'm sure. All the stuff about the government, all the stuff about new consciousness, telepathy, telekinesis, "novel" forms of interaction, emptiness and corruption of religion…In due time…

I'm having perhaps the roughest time since March- if you can even really call it "rough". I'm at peace but still a little disappointed about losing my friends on the 9th floor. They were so glad to see me back, and I'm fairly certain I will not get to see them until 2013, if ever. The counselor on our floor, Mrs. Martin, made it clear she does not like me and will make sure I don't get to go back to 9, which I know means probably DORM living, 7th or 8th or the hole for the rest of my sentence. I'm okay with that. I had thought to myself, "The most productive way I can do this time is alone with books," last month while I was here. So now, albeit somewhat contrary to my attachments, it seems it will be so. I'm just disappointed at the way it came about. I don't understand why I did what I did. It was one thing to go to the hole for helping a guy call his mom, another to go over something so trivial. It also brings up guilt for not being able to let y'all or Meimie [maternal grandmother] visit and anger, hatred really for the injustice of our government. [Both Meimie and I, his mother, were able to visit, contrary to what Cory believed was permissible.] How is it right to disallow a grandmother to see her grandson over letting someone use my phone? Or to take halfway house time for taking a bag of laundry that I could have had FREE. [His halfway house time was not affected in the end.] I don't spend much time thinking about it, but it's still there. I am sorry. You probably will not be able to visit me. I did not want you to anyways. See me free. I hate being expected to be compliant with this system. It makes it seem as though you are one of THEM and trust me, you don't want me to think of you as one of them. So be mad at them for punishing me incredibly unreasonably, not me for causing minor mischief. Anyways, I don't give it thought. Neither should you. At worst, this will be over March 25, 2013. Anything other than mail between now and then is lagniappe. And do NOT EVER SIDE WITH THEM if you ever want to speak to me. This government and all its workers, though good people, deserve the ultimate penalty. And I'm quite sure all karmic debts will be paid. Anyways, I miss y'all and hope to hear from you soon. It's been a while.

Love, Cory

P.S. Sorry if I floated off there for a bit. I'm here alone in the hole-no friends to pass notes to or collection of books this time. So, I'm kind of spaced out. I'll get over it. I'm glad I'm here, excellent opportunity.

September 12, 2012

Book Requests:

1. A good Emerson book
2. A good Thoreau book
3. A good Balzak book
4. A good book about Jefferson
5. A good book about Tesla
6. An almanac
7. A dictionary
8. *Be Here Now*[29] by Ram Dass

September 2012
Mom and Dad,

Greetings, How are you? I'm technically not in "solitary"- I just call it that sometimes because the majority of time down here I'm in a single-man cell. They randomly move and combine people. I'm always reluctant to move when they tell me "pack up" because of apprehension about who they might put me with. It's very hard doing time with someone like Boston Bob or worse. But I oblige in the name of grace and just hope for the best. (If I really wanted, I could refuse without consequence.) I was amused when I had spent most of the week with Veinte-Cuatro, trying my best to stay devoted. Yet, inevitably proximity of any kind to another transfers bad and good energy (undesirable and desirable), habits, tendencies alike- a simple fact of life more and less pronounced in certain personalities. Others' "energies" tend to rub off on me in some regards pretty easily. So while our exchange was mostly positive- He to me with knowledge of entrepreneurism and elitism in Mexico and I to him with meditation, principles, certain culture of Austin and Louisiana- we both got into a bad habit of making fun of "Southsiders", heavily tattooed Mexican Americans who associate themselves with petty street gangs. They make a ritual of yelling out to each other constantly between cells and conducting a very loud cadenced workout routine early in the morning while everyone else is sleeping. We began to rather hate them honestly, as it's our only real acute annoyance. I knew I shouldn't and was disappointed even with my annoyance with the incessant yelling. (Most of them went to prison at 18 or 19, so they're almost all stuck in that mentality, with only perhaps a cumulative year or two each of freedom during their adult

98

life.) Anyhow, I knew I shouldn't make fun, but it's hard not to get into such small bad habits with a celli, especially one who's not especially subscribed to ideals like tolerance and impartiality between self and others. So, he left and I started to pray to somehow overcome my animosity. An hour later, the guards came and told me I was being moved. I went upstairs, and the first thing I saw was this guy's tattooed wrist come out. I was thinking, "You've got to be kidding me! They're putting me with a Southsider?" (Normally not even allowed by policy to mix Whites with Southsiders.) To backtrack, Veinte-Cuatro had joked, "What if after I leave, they put you in the cell with one of the monkeys (Southsiders)? While they're working, you'll have to hear it even louder." We both laughed at the absurd notion (and even unlikelihood). "I bet they don't even workout. They just make all the noise and yell to look cool." (The Southsiders in general love to seem "hard" and cool.) We both laughed. Well, come to find out, out of 48 cells, I end up in a cell with a tatted-up Southsider, next to the cell of the main yeller who facilitates, so to speak, the workouts. And, as if that weren't a funny enough joke for God to play on me, the guy, "Cosmo", admitted, "I don't actually do the routine. I just yell out with the cadence to make the other homies happy. Hahaha...Wow! But, it turns out this particular homie is actually a very good-hearted guy, intent on breaking out of his tough guy identity and embracing the pursuit of the Divine, as manifest for him in nature and sacred symbology. It's amusing how happy some of these guys get to have a celli. Many people it seems really need other people's company and deal with isolation really hard. For a while I thought Boston Bob was going to cry when they took me out of his cell. Hah! Anyways, "Cosmo" is really a good guy; 30 years old, but a 100% teenage mentality. He's been in and out of prison since 21 in 6-month intervals. But he was also convinced of Divine serendipity when I came into the cell, for not only had he been asking for a celli for some time, he really wanted something to read. I just so happened to have two books perfect for him. One was even in Spanish and specifically about some stuff he had been studying. The main "yeller" introduced himself and welcomed me (through the air vent, adjacent cell's primary means of communication), thus vaporizing any contempt so easily grown at a distance, yet so quickly dispelled by a small gesture of courtesy. Today during the nerve-rattling "routina" (yelled cadence exercises), I made it my meditation to dive into the sounds, try to feel the intensity, which the futile attempt to ignore had previously rendered annoyance. I sat through the entire routine paying deep attention and focus. It seemed to work. The mind normally seems to experience annoyance as a result of sensations penetrating consciousness and interrupting thoughts, something virtually impossible to prevent, for our thoughts- the action of neural firing, has some "automatic" segments. That is we can't expect to stop thoughts and reactions so much as to redirect them. I first started using this technique when I had cellis who wouldn't stop talking. I find if I just give 100% attention, eye contact and preoccupation without even so much as judgement (analysis) of what they're saying, it becomes sort of a guided meditation. Even the vilest subjects of their monologues dissociate into a benign string of sounds- the judgement (and comprehension) still takes place by the "automatic" nature of thoughts and perception, but it's let to be in favor of the stream of sound. It becomes apparent the real source of displeasure in listening to such outpourings is not the vulgarity, nor is it even the "automatic" neurological response, but the additional and voluntary energy we put into it (judgement). So this demonstrates that it's not really possible to be entirely "nonjudgemental", only to redirect focus and spend attention wisely and skillfully. One thing that strikes me as novel about this practice/technique (absorptive listening, we'll call it) is it calls for/results in essentially stoicism perhaps undesirable or less preferable than expressive "facial sympathy" or expressing agreement, but it seems to satisfy the elocutioners; and it leaves me feeling even more peaceable than not having tried to listen. So, it's not just a diminishment of displeasure, but a transmutation (even if slight). It's also practical, for I find even if I focus so intently on the sounds themselves, they begin to digest and separate into a string of words or syllables. The overall memory and comprehension seems to establish itself even if unaided. As a bonus, insights into the stated seem to become even more profound than if "trying" to listen the conversational way. All this is the fruit of necessity, for it's a tall order to be asked to spend hundreds of hours straight in close proximity with the varied personalities presented. Still it seems perhaps useful in a world that normally can't seem to spend 5 minutes in conversation with people we deem of something as obscure as a different background or culture. So that's my lesson for the day. Hahaha...More another day.

September 12, 2012
Dad,

To continue where I left off, I do plan to stay in touch with many who I have met, and in that group I would expect a subset will remain "on the good side of the recidivism line." There's also an organization run by spirituality guru Bo Lozoff, which spearheads the "prison as an extraordinary spiritual opportunity" movement- largely in the way I have envisioned even before I was sent a copy of his book *We're All Doing Time*[21], an awesome read. Anyways, he has a conscious living community- sort of like a retreat center- in Durham, North Carolina that I would like to spend time at. There I am sure to find inmates who have resolved to stay on the "good side".

Don't be misled. I by no means want you to think my relaying of the profiles of these "successful" criminal masterminds reflects an inclination to follow their examples. On the contrary, the vicarious experience they've afforded me serves as a preemptive. I could not have designed better examples for myself of why NOT to lead a life of materialistic pursuit, let alone one which risks many more years of incarceration. In this regard, their acquaintances have proven invaluable. They're both attractive and interesting idealized examples, yet represent an ultimately undesirable end: excommunication from the realm of the spirit- both of these men, while generous, knowledgeable, talented, amiable, tasteful, etc. were almost devoid of the sort of transcendent wisdom and communion whose life purpose is explicitly mine and implicitly all of OURS to seek. Just as vegetables cannot grow in saline soil, so transcendent knowledge/wisdom quickly withers in the presence of carnal pursuits.

In an excellently timed confirmation of concept, later the same day my celli left, I received a number of books, one of which *Ideas and Opinions*[30] by Einstein confirmed eloquently the inherency of selflessness in our pursuit of life's purpose. I ate the first 50 pages with considerable relish as his expressions on "spirituality"- really the nature of consciousness and space-time continuum- paralleled so perfectly all else I've been reviewing:

- The Limits of a Personal Conceptualization of "God"
- Insufficiency of Dogma/Religion/Belief Systems to Approach an Accurate Understanding of Unity ("God")

- Inseparability of Entities from God or Each other (selflessness), aka Infinite Entanglement of All Consciousness and Existence
- Cultivation of the Dissociative Feeling which is Re-assimilation with God.

Einstein was a great guy. Before reading this book, I had no idea how multifaceted he was, very virtuous and wise in seemingly every field.

Well, the lights will soon cut off, so I'll leave it at that.

With love,
Cory

September 13, 2012
Dad,

Greetings! I hope this letter finds you well and in good spirits. I write from my little floor cushion, a folded over mat wrapped in a sheet, where I spend 98% of my waking hours. The past few days have been the longest of my sentence, thus far. I can't help but be disappointed that I affected the end of my friendship with Mark, the nuclear market analyst and Dimitrov, the Bulgarian crime boss. We all sort of helped each other so well. Dimitrov helped me learn culture, refinement, prudence, wisdom, sophistication, good taste. Mark, achievement of the American dream. Mark and I helped Dimitrov transcend cynicism and pessimism, and they both helped me learn maturity. (Apparently too little too late.) To watch Dimitrov's demeanor change so drastically was such a joy. While he'd never admit it, Mark and I could see it. He lived such an insular life, though very social, very detached. Everyone was either: a whore, a card to be played or a greedy acquaintance who was around only for his fine food and liquor, money, women, etc. He had clearly lost hope in human goodness, but couldn't see it was his own actions that "polarized out" the greediness in others. His wealth was his ruin. Really Mark too, but to less an extent. While they both see prison as terrible, it was clear as day how the removal of their constructed worlds of luxury was a huge part in a radical transformation. Will it last? Who knows? It's likely their return to that world will challenge the newfound joy it's clear they're both experiencing. But at least for now, I watched major change in these old guys. I feel so guilty for stifling that by leaving. Well, God has a plan. I'm well aware of how powerful this stint of hard time can be for growth and purification.

What would you say was your most powerful period of growth?

Gretchen Rubin of *The Happiness Project*[31] asserts that psychologists seem to agree happiness, satisfaction, lies in "positive growth", the notion of the "thrill of the chase", except large scale. That contentment and disillusionment can both be used as indicators of growth, personal progress, if you will. It makes sense then why things like winning the lottery and becoming paraplegic tend to have counterintuitive effects on happiness.

I must say, I'm a bit concerned because I haven't heard from y'all in almost 2 weeks. I hope all is well. It's a bit unnerving to be this isolated. I wouldn't even know if WWIII broke out, let alone something happening to a family member. So please keep me in the loop.

Anyhow, Much love,
Cory

P.S. Contemplating Death- "Of all mindfulness meditations, death is most powerful." – Buddha

"One day this body will become a corpse. Death comes without notice." – Buddha

September 26, 2012
Mom and Dad,

I just wanted to drop a line and tell y'all I pulled some strings and got approval to have a visit anytime from y'all or Meimie. We'll probably be allowed more time if it's after October 26th, but if y'all feel so inclined, come anytime. Just let me know and send me a copy of your tickets to submit to administration to get approval for a "special" visit of increased duration, and two or three days in a row. Days are passing well watching the sunset over the Coronado Island and listening to my cellis talk about growing vegetables.

I would like to ask if y'all would be willing to extend me some credit to keep a supply of books constant. So far so good. I've been finishing just about the same rate they come in. However, to pass days and weeks simply idly writing seems to me a waste of a precious opportunity to contrive the mind-expanding education I consider on par in value with a college education. In fact, in the ways that count- culture, vocabulary, history, anthropology, psychology, etc. - I think self-directed education is even more of a benefit. Sentiments expressed by Einstein support this notion. My highest priority is making the most of my time. And in this regard, the mental agility, culture, refinement and even tangible payoffs this pursuit promises would justify the investment made thus far many times over. I know lately my pursuit has been rather exclusively spirituality, but I seek to expand into the study of virtuous and accomplished people who brought the wisdom of the heavens to earth and applied it in excellent ways. Also, I seek to study the example of the various cultures, past and present, as it is clear each has its own valuable offerings. As a bonus, these books have begun to enrich the progressive atmosphere of this place slowly but steadily, an offering I can claim no pure selfless motive, since it is secondary to my own intentions.

September 27, 2012
Mom and Dad,

Hello, While I am awaiting "lights out", I thought I'd write a little and say Hello. I've got just shy of two weeks left in the hole. I was doing some metrics earlier and realized a few things about my time:

   a. I'm just over halfway through with custody (officially).
   b. I'm just over halfway through with my stay at MCC San Diego (4 more months)
   c. I'll have done >1/6 days of confinement in segregation.
   d. I have done > 1/6 of my time fasting.
   e. I'm averaging 2 books a week.
   f. I'm glad to say I'm more or less still persisting daily towards the same goals and mindset of when I came in.

With that said, I am displeased with one important aspect: I still find myself susceptible to negative spiritual influence when forced to be around people of a different mindset. Even though I find I maintain an awareness and consistent daily devotion, it seems like having my spiritual life suffer is an inevitable consequence of being around people. For example, my last celli who just left, I was so glad to see him go. When we first became cellis, the first three days seemed like they were excellent for the both of us. He was very eager to learn whatever it was I knew and would tell me he'd never been so at peace. He let go of a lot of baggage in a short period of time and was intrigued by some of the spiritual books and knowledge I brought. He even asked me if I was Jesus a bunch of times. He has a tattooed third eye of a Native American Indian on his leg and told me it was me. I did in fact watch him go from hyperactive, super-distracted, anxious 24-7 and negative to relatively calm, clear-headed and attentive in a few days' time, which I attribute to the latent awareness of "a better way" needing only an opportunity of an environment with someone likeminded and resolute about the pursuit. (His identity/appearance, as well as his allegiances did not lend themselves to such "soft", "weak" pursuits being acceptable.) Anyways, he also helped me a lot as I sat and listened and watched and observed. I was blessed with an endless stream of traits, patterns and tendencies that disgusted me, alerting me to just how perfectly they each reflected my own shortcomings. I made it a point to just listen and observe my inner reaction to these deficiencies I recognized. A strong feeling of repulsion was my mind's unsolicited reaction. I had long suspected a difference between "primary" and "secondary" thoughts. A book written by neurologists who are also practicing Buddhists confirmed this suspicion: a certain amount of chain reaction thoughts are simply inevitable and are more or less involuntary. The path to self-improvement is not to fret that often very developed, negative primary thoughts occur but to strive to institute corrective or "absorptive" "secondary" thoughts, as well as foster an inner environment that reduces "primary" thoughts altogether. So, in a sense, I suppose I can't blame myself for some measure of failure at transcending judgementalism. What troubles me is the degree to which it accumulates despite conscious efforts at releasing it. After a few days, I couldn't stand him. I was as careful as possible not to let it show, especially because he was still using me as some kind of example (desperate, I know). One of my favorite authors, Balthazar Gracian, has an aphorism that summarizes it in secular terms: #269 from *The Art of Worldly Wisdom*[7] circa 1650:

"Take advantage of novelty. You will be esteemed as long as you are new. Novelty pleases everybody because of its variety. Our taste feels refreshed. And remember the glory of novelty lasts little. In four days, people lose their respect for you. Take advantage of the fruits of first esteem. Once the warmth of novelty has worn away, passion grows cold, and pleasure turns to irritation."

So, at last it seems I'm not the only one who experiences these "shifts". But I still feel let down with myself for not being able to offer more compassionate support and not just some knowledge and an example of living. I feel like I failed at a perfect opportunity to demonstrate the same unconditional love I have been shown. It was a big learning experience. I felt I could relate to how Dad must feel when he observes my glaring character deficiencies, and I can tell he's bothered yet unsure or unwilling to validate any "secondary" thought critiques. I had in the past allowed myself to be offended by unspoken critiques, never taking the time or patience to recognize: Our brains cannot prevent themselves from thinking any more than our heart can stop from pumping blood. If someone is irritated by my actions, it's unfair for me to get mad (exacerbating the problem). It's just chemical reactions in the brain. I must try to limit my response to voluntary action. Even then, the line is thin or even nonexistent. These truths, coupled with a feedback loop model of interaction, make a strong case for tolerance/patience and the idea of keeping passions out of our interactions. I guess I'm trying to explain/understand I'm seeing the answer to the problem (contagious spiritual regression) is simply to try to maximize beneficial exchange, minimize negative and accept the rest. "You become like those you hand around," for better or for worse, voluntary or otherwise. I guess it's just God's way of showing me where weaknesses remain, since most undesirable "trait rub-off" requires some remnant of that trait in both parties.

Anyway, I'm so glad to be alone again. I think it will be different when I have other positive people to be around (in Austin). So far here they've been few and far between. I apologize if this seemed like a rant. I just needed to try and mentally sort things out and explaining seemed to help a lot.

I highly recommend *The Intention Experiment*[6]. The world its experiments and studies suggest is nothing short of WONDEROUS. You both would be amazed at what science has now proven, a magical world of telepathy, telekinesis, sentient plants (who can read our minds) that doesn't just exist, but PERMEATES and COMPRISES our world. Really, it's worth a read. You don't have to read it all at once. It's a good book for piecemeal reading. Or check out the website. In ten or twenty years, this book will be considered a major landmark in the beginnings of the new consciousness, for it undeniable affirms the previously esoteric notion of infinite interconnectedness- that we are literally all ONE consciousness.

Also, the images of Korotkov's biofields in and of themselves is probably a fascinating spectacle. It turns out all living cells use (emit/receive) light to form a sort of internet, capable of communicating even complex, coherent messages to each other and the world.

With Love, Cory

September 2012
Dad,

Good afternoon! How is everything? I participated in the "routina" today. It felt good to exercise, but it quickly became apparent six months of being sedentary has taken effect on my stamina. It has motivated me to pursue and be open to exercise opportunities in the future. I was particularly pleased with how much easier and more gratifying working out is when practiced with the principle of mindfulness "in the fore". I always have seen mundane activities- working out, driving, repetitive tasks at work, etc. - as opportunities to "mentally multi-task", daydreaming or obsessively measuring, calculating, analyzing the task, deemed in its own to be of insufficient cognitively stimulating value, necessary of amending with "something for my mind to do." As so many spiritual gurus and neurology experts have pointed out- I was DEAD WRONG. Spiritually speaking: our only access to the Divine is through each moment, that is to say, to deny the complete and satisfactory nature of any moment is to deny Providence. Complete focus is the least we can offer every task. Neurologically speaking, simultaneously entertaining multiple unrelated processes, inevitably leads to a web of unwanted connections, an inaccurate and ineffective "algorithmic reflection" of reality- and ultimately the degradation of both processes. I liken it to the pruning of a garden. The Eastern Way is to devote 100% of attention to each second's task. That has some very liberating implications for our culture, conditioned more and more to multi-task. Talking while having a meal. Listening to music while walking. Texting during conversations. We're tangling our neurons. I can't tell you how good it feels to be untangled, at least untangling!

With Love,
Cory

October 2012
Mom,

Hello. How are you? I've been doing a ton of reading and writing. The writing has been a joy. I've written a few short essays on various subjects that represent a summary of the understanding of ideas upon which I've focused my time and energy reading/studying. What is Karma? What is God, Spirituality, Feeble Fiction or Fantastic Fact, Wrong and Right. I can't say they're anything special. They'd win no awards for composition. They'd make no one laugh or cry (except maybe at their sheer inadequacy). They're no revolutionary concepts. They're intended as a feeble, simple, comprehensible primers to "spirituality", especially for the disillusioned and agnostic. They're first draft, unedited, inadequately annotated and cited writings whose only saving grace is that I am certain they would have been valuable to me not too long ago, so I'm certain they will prove useful to some others. Reading Bo Lozoff's books, especially *We're All Doing Time*[21] really inspired me: Simple, easily understood summaries of powerful concepts with direction as to where to dig deeper, written from the heart to the people who need it in a way that's so righteously candid; we know it's the truth as soon as we read it. It's worthwhile reading for simpleton and scholar alike. He, Grethcen Rubin of *Happiness Project*[31] and even *Eat Pray Love*[35]

were all written rather amateurishly, yet they still pass along even more appreciably and personally, a potent dynamic worthy of reading. Plus, one must start somewhere. I guess until now I haven't felt versed enough in the "primary documents", these dense, profound, enigmatic texts that next to first-hand experience of God are unequaled in wisdom. Now that I've spent some time daily studying them, I am sure I have at least some potential as a "secondary writer", one who digests, summarizes, reframes, connects these dense works to "real life" or at least, common man's understanding. When it will really become worthy is once it's edited, rewritten 100x and cited (for those who already know but could use the

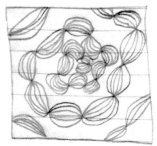

opportunity to know where to dig deeper). I'm almost powerless in these regards without a computer. OK well that's all for now. Have a nice day.

With Love,
Cory

October 3, 2012
My Intention

I used to think, "What could I possibly write that would help others?" Every idea is already explained in far greater detail by a more qualified person than I could ever surpass. Then I read Bo Lozoff's *We're All Doing Time*[21], Gretchen Rubin's *Happiness Project*[31] and other EXTREMELY helpful books written in simple ways by more or less amateur authors. It's not that their ideas were better, in fact, I often disagreed with them, but what made their books so life-changing was the way they didn't really write so much as read, digested, tried, summarized and relayed information. Even though they hardly presented me with one new idea of their own, they pointed me to and introduced me to a whole world of people, books, movements that could. They wrote in everyday language for everyday people about things they tried and lived first-hand, and that was even more valuable than all the scholarly original works I could ever read. I saw that anyone willing to seek out information and practice it then relay the info for the rest of us, has something to offer. So I decided to write. I'm going to keep this writing very simple and present mainly others' ideas. I want to write for the people who aren't experts, who haven't studied all the world's religions and read all the classics and philosophy, yet at the same time, I hope to write in a way that opens new doors for even the highly educated among us. Most of all, I hope to serve "living knowledge", writing in a way that expresses experience and understanding, not just dead intellectual knowledge. I seek to remind people of the truth lying fallen in a clouded spirit. I seek to awaken ways of looking at things, not convince people of beliefs. I will use generalizations and strategies, pointing people towards purer, more precise truths rather than trying to perfect it myself. I trust and believe my experience will help others – even if few, that's enough.

What is Karma?

Have you ever looked back at something you did, said, wrote just months prior and shuddered at the sheer idiocy that must have been behind that act? Personally, I find myself reading notes on my journals I wrote mere weeks prior (and especially entries from YEARS prior) and think, "What ignorance!" and then I'm happy. Why? Because I've proved myself an ignorant shmuck for the 100,001st time? No, because I know even though it means if I wrote something today, later it will become the 100,002nd proof I'm incredibly ignorant, and it means PROGRESS. Progress is all about those times in your life that make all the struggle worthwhile. As humans, we will struggle. We will also triumph. If we're lucky, we'll experience more triumph than struggle. Quantum physics has proven electrons somehow "know" which route to take to navigate a simple "maze". Energy it seems "knows" how to take the shortest possible route. Even such a simple thing "knows" how to avoid dead ends and make its way to "triumphs". How much moreso does a living organism? This is conscience- our internal navigation system guiding us to more triumphs. Conscience is not some old man God watching your every move, waiting for you to make a wrong move, so he can chew you out or tell you you're wrong. No, I see it more as an older, wiser version of ourselves guiding us to a happy, joyous and free future. It's a version of ourselves from the future sitting in a mansion in "heaven" trying constantly to help us get there quicker, live healthier, happier. Karma is the "maze". Karma is the word that means, "You reap what you sow." Karma is every turn we make in the maze. Karma is the boomerang effect of actions we take, every single "good" action coming back to benefit us and every single "bad" coming back to hurt us. Are there really good and bad, wrong and right? No. There are only types of actions and lessons to be learned. Karma is also like the way we train our dogs not to pee in the house or drink from the toilet. Since we're not so intelligent as to learn everything from thinking, sometimes we need to be taught by feeling. Our old, wise self may smack us on the nose for peeing in the house sometimes. If we still do not get the lesson, our old, wise self in a frustrated, last-ditch effort may even lock us in a room so we don't ruin our own house. Our "conscience", really our own "Overself", our own "success navigation system", does only what's best for our long-term happiness. If we understood this completely, we would become saints very quickly, and our lives would become unfathomably good. We are so ignorant of how good life can and would become if we followed our conscience through all the difficult lessons, that even if we could see our perfected lives, we wouldn't understand- much the way a young man cannot comprehend the joys of parenthood or a rich, but miserable banker cannot comprehend a poor man's smile. The pursuit of happiness and freedom from suffering is a path that will constantly deceive us. The only way to avoid all the dead ends is to practice nonjudgementalism and do our best to "tune" our inner guidance to match our outer actions. An interesting thing about conscience: if we repeatedly disregard it, it shuts off communication and resorts to using pain, suffering and prevention (feeling locked up/ being locked up) to teach us/ guide us to its lessons. We cannot avoid it because it is our own selves! We can reject it completely, and very quickly our lives will become painful and constricted. We're preventing ourselves from causing even more damage. Only by tuning in our minds, hearts, speech, actions can we stop working against ourselves. It's a battle we cannot win, like arm wrestling yourself. Even if you kill yourself, you still must answer to yourself. What's notable about this model of thinking of ourselves and karma is: it means there is really no "right" or "wrong" per se- only actions and the perfectly reflected consequences for those actions. Does this mean if a billionaire steals a dollar from a homeless man he'll only repay $1? That's an eye for an eye, right? Wrong! Karma looks to motivations. Karma takes into account thoughts, motivations, context, actions. The billionaire's dollar of repayment would never be enough to repay the act of selfishness stealing from a person in poverty. No, often karma reshapes lessons to affect a better more effective lesson. The other thing it means is this: even ignorance of the path to our triumph- land (heaven, success, etc.) is "punishable". That is, when the dog pees on the rug before you've taught it not to, you still have to spank the dog. Just because he didn't know, doesn't mean he wouldn't get pain in return for wrong actions. So it is in life. Just because we don't "know" smoking kills, does not mean we won't die from lung cancer, hacking and heaving our way to a premature grave. All this requires an open heart and open mind. Karma won't even allow you to understand what you're not ready for. In some instances, if we're too emotional about an issue or we would respond in such a way that would hurt us, karma keeps us from even being exposed to such information. That's why we learn so much once we become broken, humble, imprisoned, hurt, after a period of indulgence. We can make life easier on ourselves if we simplify, become open to "karmic lessons", meditate, reflect, study. The same way we learned to avoid time-out or getting a spanking by showing our parents or teachers we already learned our lesson,

111

we can reduce the more painful-type lessons by opening up to mental lessons. Remember the important part is motivation. If we purify our motivation and "feed the wolf of love", we will begin to get pure, loving karma back from the world. We truly get what we give? Does that mean giving a vagrant a $20 bill every day is a sound investment strategy- out of selfishness? You're likely to receive very little in return. If you volunteer in big public volunteering operations, you may receive some payback, but nothing compared to giving in secret. If this all seems very complex, that's because it is. What's simple is how we should act and what we should expect in return:

"Do what is right."

"Work makes worth."

"There are no shortcuts in life. You can't trick God (future self)."
"What's worthwhile is never easy. What's easy is never worthwhile."

"If you want to be miserable, live for yourself. If you want to be happy, live for others."

"Do unto others as you would have them do unto you." (Golden rule)

"Do unto others as you suspect they would like to be done to." (Platinum rule)

"Love hurts."

"You reap what you sow."

"Give and it shall be given unto you."

"You get out what you put in."

"When the student is ready, the teacher will appear."

"We create all our own problems, and so our solutions."

"Life isn't fair. [Existence is.]"

"You can't always get what you want, but if you try sometimes, you get what you need."

An excellent book, *What is Karma?*[32] available for FREE to any prisoners, can be requested from:

Brunton Philosophic Foundation
4936 Rte. 414
Burdette, NY 14818

It's a bit "academic" with some rather complicated language and ideas, but it's an excellent source for understanding karma. Most of the ideas I just presented "come from" or at least are echoed in that book. It's set up as a compilation of short concepts, a sentence to a paragraph each, 140 pages in all. Talks about "What is Karma?", "How Karma Works", "Grace", "Working With Karma", "Karma and the Great Liberation", etc. Takes philosophical Christian and Eastern concepts and really explains/presents some profound insights.

One thing to keep in mind: while karma, with all its pitfalls and responsibility, can feel burdensome- hence the real reason we rebel, not because of our families or religion- we rebel against our own conscience. If it were anything less profound, we'd easily free ourselves from the grip of its deception. The flip side of this is true: it also means we have a POWERFUL, WISE, EXPERT personal advisor/ personal trainer. Yes, your workouts get more intense, but you see the results. After all, it's yourself from the future, who is constantly sharing notes with other souls, ancestors, nature, etc. So don't get discouraged. You're here. You're in it. There's no escaping it. May as well go big- apply yourself.

What is "God"?

I am not a fan of the word "God". It's a word whose meaning is constantly abused and perverted by those Pharisees who pretend to "know" the Source better than anyone else. So, please excuse me if I use a variety of words with the first letter capitalized to mean "God": Source, One, Unity, Wisdom, Love, etc. As humans, it's impossible to accurately name or describe "God", and the closest we can get is bits and pieces. In simplest terms, Unity is the force that brings parts together, parts that, on their own, tend towards chaos. Science tells us, as does personal experience, without a destination, we choose everything- without a leader, society crumbles- without a purpose, we please ourselves and fall apart.

113

Any structure, without constant purpose to keep it restored, will degrade into nothing. Unity is such a force. At different times, we see different aspects of Unity- sometimes Romance, Sex, Collectives, Nature, even Altered Consciousness or our Bodies may seem like "God". The truth is, these all contain concentrations of "God", so it's only natural for us to mistake a part for the whole. The truth is, "God" is in EVERYTHING, so it's easy to get confused about what "God" is like. It's our nature as human beings to constantly pursue Unity (unification). Every act that brings us pleasure, peace, joy, satisfaction, is in some way a connection with "God". Even "terrible sins" are acts we commit to feel a little Source in our lives. The only difference is "bad things" ("sins") produce pleasure, a tiny glimpse of the One, often a tiny glimpse that costs us a much bigger slice later on. That's the purpose of conscience! Not to stand over you, like a critical grandparent constantly badgering you. No- our conscience is our Greater Self- the "God" within saying, "Don't do that because in the long run, you'll be happier you didn't." It's not some angry "God" getting angry with us for spending our last $5 on cigarettes. It's really just the part of us that can see the future (we all can) that's warning us- "Hey, save that dollar. You're going to need it."

I don't believe true atheists exist. I do believe there are plenty of people so fragmented they cannot perceive any "God" greater than Sex or Drugs or Pleasure. It's very easy, even natural for our awareness to break down this way. Deep down we all know that Science is pointing 100% to INTELLIGENT DESIGN. That Einstein, Newton, DaVinci, all the world's greatest and most inspired thinkers believe in some sort of constructive unifying force that keeps earth inhabitable and builds all creation. The mathematician can show us "his" fingerprint in numbers. The great cultures of the world can show us their shrines. The universe shows us its expansion from a tiny speck. It's no wonder tribesmen, islands unto themselves, without culture, all find Divinity. It's 100% necessary for long term survival. See *Spirituality- Feeble Fiction or Fantastic Fact*[34] for more examples of how our understanding of God is constantly morphing. The thing of it is, experiencing the One is such a powerful experience, even the most impure dilutions can satisfy us. We stick a needle in our arm and say, "Oh, God...yes" in ecstasy. Yes, indeed, this is God. It's just a tiny sliver, killing 99% of us and exciting 1% to feel "God". We have a one-night stand and say, "Oh, God...yes". Yes, that too- the connection of souls- even if a tiny fragment is "God". It's like picking a broccoli sprout to eat it. Sprouts

114

are 100% delicious, 100% super- nutritious and generally desirable things. But every sprout is a future plant. Eating it as a sprout means you'll miss out on 100 times the mass of a full grown vegetable. If you go around eating sprouts all day, ignorantly, and not allowing your garden to GROW, which takes time and care, you'll eat only 1/100th of the meals your garden could produce and still not have anything to trade. We begin to starve and start eating every seed we get our hands on. Eventually we start to steal to get our nourishment. The only way out becomes jail, institutions, death or learning a better way.

Now for a few quotes on "God":

"There are not atheists in foxholes."

"Seek and you shall find."

"I am that I am."

One more thing: beliefs are not "God". Religions are not "God". They are approximations of God. You may say, "How could there be a God if"

- So many belief systems contradict. (They're all wrong to some extent.)
- God allows evil/ bad things. (YOU say they're bad.)
- People kill each other for "God". (They're not killing for God. They're killing because they are misled.)
- What's the point? (Beauty, Truth, Love, Happiness. Pick one. I choose all.)
- Evolution… (Yeah, so? You thought creation was a true story?)
- I tried it. It didn't work. (You cannot "try" it. You ARE it already.)
- Sounds like bullshit. (It is. The truth is inexpressible. Feel free to "steal" some spiritual practices for purely selfish reasons. They work even without believing, science confirms.)
- I believe only in science. (Great, let's talk about science, shall we? See *Spirituality- Feeble Fiction of Fantastic Fact*[34].)
- I hate God. (How can you hate what you don't know? Emotions like hate are toxic and useless for survival. Embrace hate and die or let go and live.)

October 2012
Mom,

Good afternoon. I hope this letter finds you well. It's my 29th day on the 5th floor. My current celli leaves in 2 days to go home to a halfway house. His paperwork isn't clear. He's been going out and coming back within 6 months or so for 7 years. He hopes this is his last time. I won't make any judgements (though years of using drugs is excessive) about that likelihood. It does remind me how terribly broken not just our government is but also our "network" of peers. I read a study where three groups of alcoholics were used to test the efficacy of prayer on alcoholism. One, a control (no prayer), two family and friends, three strangers. One stayed the same, two got worse and three got better. To me this demonstrated a familiar effect the "family" of alcoholics "fit" into or their respective "local system" as a particular role, and despite fragmentary efforts at using the same network to raise them out, the overall system of energetic exchange had worked them into a particular role – any energy spent treating the "alcoholic" was transmuted into negative. In short we collectively contribute to our alcoholics and addicts. Our "sins" form together seeking an outlet, a human sacrifice. It's something we become. We can no longer seek "normalcy". Thrive, that is – become a living sacrifice – or die, go kicking and screaming. So it's not all delusion on the part of a "self-pitying"/ego-centric addict. The only real distinction between the two mindsets is RESOLVE – will I die as a screeching pig or a docile lamb? It seems the more freedom I see – the more I'm aware of what's determined.

Anyways, I've been doing the designs. [I asked Cory to make lines on small squares of paper for a project I was doing to help people access their creativity.] It will take me 1-2 more probably to finish. I enjoy them at times. My celli showed me how to soak pencils, split them and dislodge the lead. That way the lead can be advanced without sharpening, at least without sharpening the wood. It helps a lot. I can simply remove the whole lead and sharpen a 1cm. long tip, refastening with a rubber band. No more endless scraping to keep a tip. The "flower" exercise really wears pencils down.

I hope you find time to order those books. I'm done with what I have. I seek to broaden my horizons to include all sorts for a well-rounded education suited for nobility – a study of historical "role models", philosophy, naturalist's writings, classical literature, (certain)

116

esteemable works of fiction, the lives of great spiritual examples, ancient astronomic/geometric/astrologic wisdom, etc. Also I seek to keep up with contemporary popular nonfiction, increasingly difficult as the rate of advance skyrockets. I need books only 1 and 2 years apart – say 2006-2010 that make it very quickly apparent modern science struggles to keep up with itself. (Hence the emphasis I put on the ancient wisdom which skips science and draws conclusions based on esoteric formulations combined with existential ones.)

Have you considered going on any spiritual retreats lately?

Well just checking in,
Love, Cory

October 3, 2012
Mom,

Hello! I'm responding to your Sept 29th letter. Thanks for writing. I too am baffled by 80-hour work weeks. Honestly – I wouldn't get near a traditional teaching job in this day and age with a 10-foot stick, let alone sacrifice myself to 80-hour weeks. I have had a couple of brief periods of 70-hour weeks. I must say there is a certain satisfaction to be had with such complete absorption with a task. It's easy to feel like life's pulling me in 1,000 directions even from here. I try to spend almost the entire day in mindful absorption, but I also see great value in planning ahead. "Plans are nothing, planning is everything" – Winston Churchill. "The mark of an educated man is the ability to simultaneously entertain two conflicting ideas" – Socrates. . . So plan I will, trying to distinguish between unconscious, passion-driven future-tripping and concerted, due-diligence foresight (and presenting possibilities to others).

I am convinced we all have different 'energetic profiles' – sensitive to irritations and even toxicities others are oblivious to while each thriving on other types. What's food for the goose is not necessarily tolerable for the gander. You both like Baton Rouge very much. I find it deplorable, regressive, stagnant, and generally uninhabitable. Truth be told, I consider 98% of the U.S. toxic wasteland from an energetic point of view. Yet for y'all's interests and purposes, it's a great place to live.

117

Well, I'm just rambling. Perhaps I'll write some later.

Love, Cory

Please send Corey: *Art of Worldly Wisdom*[7] – Gracian, *It's a Meaningful Life*[34] – Lozoff, *4 Hour Work Week*[10] – Ferris

October 4, 2012
Mom,

"Never put off till tomorrow, what can be done today (especially when that something is for others)" – Personal Mantra

Even though I have already written you 2 other letters, I am making an effort to be more complete and expedient in service to others/fostering connection so I'm responding now to the letter I just received (9-30) from you.

What book on meditation are you listening to? What is its background/author? One thing I found helpful was the Dalai Lama's suggestions about meditation. It's really easy to over-complicate and/or get discouraged by our own expectations. If you will allow, I'd like to offer you a very brief summary of meditation practices as the crucial factors common to a wide variety of schools and lineages.

1. All meditation is – as summarized excellently by a semi-famous bit of graffiti in Austin- "Focus on one point and breathe."
2. "Posture points" are often observed for two reasons:
   a. To facilitate neurocerebral fluid flow
   b. To minimize distracting sensations

These are all optional – keeping the spinal column perfectly straight is the most important (but still optional/unnecessary).

3. Your mind will wander. This is normal. Teach it to come back. Don't react to thoughts. Absorb. Neutralize. Release.

4. #1 most important thing – practice. 2-4x daily 10-30 mins. Frequency over duration at first will help build concentration.
5. Many types exist – pick one main one and stick to it, daily 10 min. at the same time is better than 1 hour 3x/week. It can be rewarding to mix in different types (Bhastrika Mahadevananda, Sun Yantra), but keep the rhythm of daily practice consistent.

Just my 2 cents, for what it's worth. OK well I'll talk to you next week.

With Love,
Cory

October 2012
Mom,

Hello, You probably already have sent a letter since your return so I'm waiting on that, but meanwhile – I will write a little. I finished the little art assignment you gave me. I ran into a "creative block" halfway through but picked up the project today and just started drawing, overcoming it quickly. The hardest part is/was the ever-dulling pencil tips. The pens I have access to are terrible, so I just had to keep inserting new lead and filing new tips. I enjoyed it and was surprised at the results of the exercise. An excellent demonstration of how simple concentration and repetition mixed with even a drop of creativity can become beautiful. It reminds me of construction work I've done or gardening, starting in one place with a simple task – seemingly monumental, say, spreading 2 tons of mulch over a half acre. You get into a pattern and lose yourself in it. Next thing you know, it's reached spectacular fruition.

Hopefully the pattern of daily regular practice at mindfulness and structured introspection will reflect the same effect onto my life. I've been "outside my comfort zone" lately as I study the writings of Gracian, Lozoff and Paul Brunton and constantly consider life from the perspectives they present. Gracian presents a sort of noble virtuosity, drawing from both his background as a Jesuit priest and a well-studied political advisor – an excellent blend of where divine meets secular. Ninety percent of his wisdom concerns being prudent/reserved, managing not only to contrast oneself well but to interface with others in a way that reflects the wisdom and experience of history's greats. Brunton – whose book *What is Karma?*[32] is all I know of him – seemingly a compilation of short passages compiled by one of his followers after his death in 1981. He's a philosopher and theologian of sorts who explains very lucidly how he suspects karma works. Most people mistake the notion of karma as some kind of hopeful system of divine vengeance and in a way it is – but it's more like "a curriculum" or a system of tutoring if you will, a way for "God" to condition us to become One with all. It, in Brunton's opinion, is nothing more than divine cause and effect. The book – while a bit wordy – has really reminded me of some profound concepts concerning personal conduct, fate, how to maneuver in a world of constant temptation, etc. Lastly, Bo Lozoff, the founder and president of the Human Kindness Foundation and the Prison Ashram Project, has written *We're All Doing Time*[21] and *It's a Meaningful Life*[34], writes very simply, very compassionately and most importantly very practically about living a good and meaningful life. He's a man who practices what he preaches 100% and fearlessly dives into the wisdom and practices of just about every spirit path imaginable – reporting back a confirmation that they all lead to the same place. Lozoff presents the most comprehensive collection of spiritual techniques of anyone I've ever heard of. He's 100% at home with everyone and every situation, from the Dalai Lama to Death Row to the Synagogue, to family life. Reading from him is like discovering Solomon's temple with all its treasures. A person could live an excellent life in every regard just by reading one of his books. These three authors – plus sometimes Mother Teresa or Buddhist author Thich Nhat Hanh- I read and study every day. Not that studying can solve all my problems, but it's a good start. In psychology, there's a concept of 'conscious competence' which has 4 stages:

1. We react (or fail to act), and do not realize it (unconscious incompetence).
2. We do wrong and realize it, but cannot stop it (conscious incompetence).
3. We start to do wrong, but stop ourselves (conscious competence).
4. We vaguely remember or forget altogether we used to do wrong (unconscious competence).

So studying, coupled with frequent introspection brings us quickly from 1 to 2. Then with help and a vigilant emotional barometer watching, hopefully to 3 (the hardest transition). Then 4 comes naturally over time. My last letter spoke mainly of a stage 2 -> 3 hang-up with my celli – I know I should have been more tolerant, but felt powerless to change. Can you relate?

Did you subscribe me to *Shambhala Sun* magazine? I received a copy – wasn't sure if it was you. I enjoyed it a lot. It's very inspiring to become aware of like-minded people living the way I aspire to. Also, it opened my eyes to a whole sea of possibilities – conventions, temples to visit, authors to read, retreats to attend, etc. So – if it was you – thanks! Great choice.

It contained an article about Chögyam Rinpoche – founder of the Shambhala movement that really inspired me to embody not just peace and detachment but laugh more – smile more – be more personal. It makes sense – nobody wants to follow our example no matter how composed we are if we don't appear to be able to joke around. It's just difficult in an environment where most humor is both vain and vulgar.

Well, I look forward to hearing about your trip. I hope you had a great time.

Well, talk to you soon.
Love,
Cory

October 4, 2012
Dad,

Hello, I hope this letter finds you well, thought I would say "hello" here before the weekend. I'm over here reading and writing my days away. Picking through the 5th floor (the "hole") book shelf, which is actually the first stop for books donated in bulk from outside, so I end up with some good ones. *All I Really Need to Know I Learned in Kindergarten*[36] by Fulghum was hilarious. I've got a book on the identification of plants in Yellowstone. I asked Landon for some selections – thinking he should know some good ones – so far he's sent 4. One was a large book called *Seven Tips to Make the Most* of the *Camino de Santiago*[38] written by a very American lady who packs "neck coolers" on month-long backpacking trips. My first reaction was – ha! This middle-aged housewife tourist is going to teach ME about hiking and survival? But as I read, even though it was comically basic, it brought up all the pleasant thoughts of backpacking and travel that make it all worthwhile. Do you think you'd ever join Landon on a pilgrimage to Santiago? I had no idea one can BIKE the trail, in fact – on bike the whole trail is do-able in <10 days. (500mi). Well anyways – we'll see.

The other 3 books are all very deep and cryptic books on Catholicism theology, etc. It's clear Landon's reading level compared to mine is like comparing caviar to Cheerios – much more sophisticated but not quite as easy to digest. But he holds these texts in high regard, so, I'll do my very best to chip away at them. Work makes worth. No challenge, no improvement. Six more days till I'm out of "the hole", always bittersweet as I'm sure even my release will be both, representing shifts in occupation from highly focused progress towards a goal, simplicity, peace, to pastimes, socialization, increase in "creature comforts", which unavoidably weaken one's ambition. Such is the great paradox of human nature – enjoyment and comfort versus progress and deprivation. The basis for the saying, "It is harder for a rich man to enter 'the kingdom' than for a camel to pass through the eye of a needle," and, "Blessed are the poor in spirit, for theirs is the kingdom [of heaven]." I am getting much closer to an intellectual understanding that can break the intellectual paradox which has been near the core of my struggles (breakdown/narrowing of the scope of reward-seeking circuitry). The basic answer seems to be to detach from the satisfaction we/I seek in things. Not so much to avoid pleasures, though that is one necessary strategy, but to perceive their emptiness through mindfulness and meditation and to try and redirect it towards Unity (God). Where the trouble comes in is the innate "rewardingness" of choices not particularly troublesome – even GOOD ACTIVITIES but still simply diminishing of time, motivation, etc. to apply to BEST ACTIVITIES. Choosing to go play guitar with someone and jam over studying Landon's books, per se. The immediate quality of life goes UP, but the lasting effect goes down. The rate increases, but the derivative steps down. It's a complex economy of dopamine reward circuitry in our brains – arguably no simpler to maintain than one based on little pieces of paper and expansive countries. But fortunately, I've got some of the world's foremost "spiritual economic advisors" hanging out in a pile

122

stacked neatly under my bed. So with luck, prayer and time – we'll end the recession. . .

Well, talk to you soon. With love,
Cory

When I was a baby, I sought only love with every little cry.
When I was a child, I sought wonder within my parents' bounds.
When I was an adolescent, I sought curiosity within society's bounds.
When I was a teen, I sought fun within all that was forbidden.
When I was a young adult, I sought pleasure within all that was forsaken.
When I was a little older, I sought comfort within the last few options left.
When I was a little older, I sought survival, with the threads that hung.
When I became a young man, I sought hope, with nothing left at all.
When I became a little stronger, I sought the senses, within all creation.
When I became a little wiser, I pursued till- I tripped.

And saw I wasn't wise at all.
With all this seeking (and finding) the world became so small.

And no, I'm not done seeking.
Not until I find it all.

- Cory Roussel

October 7, 2012
Mom,

Hello! How are you? Thanks so much for the recent books! I get the feeling it's taken me all six months to really identify which books I really want to read. I spent a whole day just flipping through the almanac, getting a bird's eye view of so much about our world, how the money moves, how many people live in it, how much money each industry makes, how much beef, chicken, fish we eat on average per capita, comparing it all to the world. Learning everything from a "bird's eye view". Really cool. As I write I can hear the Southsider next door explaining some of the peace-abiding practices and compassionate ideals presented in *We're All Doing Time*[21] – Bo Lozoff's book on enlightened living behind bars. Considering these guys are two of the more violent, hardened people I've met doing time (for point of reference – most of my cellis have killed or brought people to death's precipice) it brings great joy. The possibility, however remote, of playing a role, however minor, in decreasing the chance, however, marginal, of a person killing again is very encouraging. Truly Lozoff and his writings are one of the greatest American contributions to the pursuit of sanctity of yet I am aware.

I got in touch with Bryan who is doing well and has generously offered to help me populate my bookshelf. In true Bryan-style, he's kept up his education by resolving to read at least two books/month – the result – a book list perfect for me to follow along with. I will likely end up bringing some to Austin to read at the Halfway House, but better too many than too few. Perhaps another ambitious reader with a taste for learning (versus escape, the prevalent purpose of reading here) will show up to benefit from this growing collection in tandem.

Anyways, I've got many more letters to write, so I'll let you go.

With love,
Cory

October 2012
Bethany,

Thanks again for the books! I've read most all of them, taking my time to digest *The Heart of Buddha's Teaching*[38] and taking my time on *The Language of God*[39]. *Tuesdays with Morrie*[40] was deeply inspiring, fit perfectly into recent renewal of contemplations or temporality (of life, etc.) in my spiritual practice. Morrie was a really great guy we can all learn from. I think he "got it right". It's very nice to see secular thinkers, the world's GREATEST secular thinkers reach the same universal conclusions as the most devout "spiritual" ones, just to know "proof" (living proof) exists of the universality of Truth is comforting. It's a very easy read when you do get the chance. *Buddha's Brain*[41] was very insightful, rich with practical insight on the lifestyle that is Buddhism. While both books on Buddhism are helping "flesh out" my practice, I strongly encourage you to start elsewhere if you're interested in experimenting with the meditative arts. Had I started in these books, I probably would have over intellectualized and "dogmatized" such simple, still, poetic acts. I would be glad to direct you towards a workable beginning if you are interested. As far as *The Language of God*[89] – I'm still working on it. He seems to be striving to answer many questions which – quite frankly – have already been expertly handled by men more qualified than he. Furthermore – his models for understanding intelligent design, science of biology for that matter, are outdated – the zany "quack scientist" Bruce Lipton PhD all but singlehandedly destroys notions of a mechanistic DNA-based ecosystem in *Biology of Belief*[16] – a VERY good read. Alas, science is progressing SO rapidly that progress has become fragmentary – and even a year can drastically change the state of our collective understanding. All in all, you are an excellent book selector. I would have had to order twice as many books to find the number of good ones you found (ordering "duds" is inevitable to an extent). Anyways, just wanted to say hi!

With Love, Cory

October 7, 2012
Dad,

Hello I am very well, very pleased to have received so many letters and 3 excellent (or at least very promising) books. Yes 16 hours of waking freedom lends itself to finishing a book every day or two. Do I reread them? Depends on the book. Fiction – never – but I've only read maybe <15 fiction books here. The nonfiction I keep and reference frequently all the good ones; plus I have about 4-5 I read and study, memorize and copy quotes from daily. There simply is too much on my "waiting list" to read to have time to reread entire books. But I find the really good ideas tend to "stick". I often find I can remember all the most pertinent info, 80/20 principle applies here – as does, "do it once, do it right". I read the 80% to find the 20% best, put 80% of my attention on it, study it, memorize it.

[Referring to his father's comments on a band reunion.] I often wonder if my high school will ever do a 10-year reunion. Regularly I dream of being back in high school. How it was. How seemingly minor choices had such profound effects. Notably – almost all my

125

close friends are now very materially successful, have kids, wives, homes, good jobs. At times I have regretted choices – specifically morally deficient choices, others that came very close to costing my or other's lives or freedom (often involving alcohol, not drugs) and of course a couple of seemingly perfect women I LET GO. As I reflect, two huge tendencies become apparent – 3 in truth: 1. Sheer unpredictability shrouds any valid judgement of "what if". The woman could have turned out later to be painful divorces. The "straight and narrow" could have led me into a mediocre commitment and missing out on two amazing years, etc. (Wistful reflection is to me, that is to say – inherently inaccurate, an illusion of fantastic perception.) 2. Certain times and places tend to bring out the wistfulness – seeing all the college kids at LSU enjoying carefree lives of parties and ignorant bliss - Graduation times, weddings. Weddings can be particularly hard with all the introductions and focus on "eligibility", etc. 3. More often than not, my own wistfulness is a glaring reminder of a more pressing failure – failure to lead my PRESENT life in a fulfilling way. The poor man's smile – the noose around the child actor's neck who had it all. The great paradox of fleeting Satisfaction. How is it I sit, in a prison cell, twenty-five with almost nothing but faith, hope and love yet the wistfulness of a time abundant evades me? Truly we live in a world of paradox and illusion: how can we explain the blind man's simple smile or the jackpot winner's assertion, "I wish I'd never won". Yeah, I have some experience of wistful retrospect. I prefer the pain of realistic introspect – it stands up better against the test of time.

Well, as usual, been learning a lot lately, notably: Learning about Thoreau and Emerson, two REALLY exceptional American authors/virtuosos, supreme examples in the Art of Living. Emerson's eulogy to Thoreau (they were friends and at times lived together) was particularly captivating. I found I could relate to Thoreau's example as though he were a perfected version of myself. We share MANY eccentricities, aversions, tendencies and philosophies. He is me, perfected, in a great many ways, more than I've ever seen (read) another human being. It's VERY refreshing to have identified this, like having discovered the cure to a rare disease or a perfect tool for a tough job. The promise of his example stands to revolutionize my life.

I have also been studying a book on Financial Analysis (donated college textbook) as well as the Almanac – man, the Almanac is SUCH a priceless book. Never before have I been able to take a

126

bird's eye view of the economic, cultural, historic, statistical metrics of our world. Studying the Almanac should be required for all middle high schoolers. It could single-handedly do more good than all the superfluous humanities studying we begrudgingly digested. Sure I'd studied all sorts of Wikipedia articles, but one, simplified summarized, comprehensive collection has done in a day what hundreds of piecemeal articles haven't- painted a CLEAR picture of our human existence.

Particularly interesting:
- Rice's tuition - $40k/year
- AVERAGE New Yorker's income - $5,800/month
- Crime, diet, health, economics, trade statistics, profiles and comparisons, living expenses, religion for various countries and states, gives FASCINATING perspective on what's wrong with us vs. world and where we all sit in relation to other countries, individuals.
- Risk Statistics – fascinating to calculate things like:
  - Guns cost each American 3 days of life
    (risk of death, population, years alive)
  - I have an estimated 51.6 years of life left
  - Chances of suffering X, Y, Z

Really cool. I spend whole afternoons just calculating odds. If you get a chance, I highly recommend taking some time to flip through one.

Anyways, until later. Love, Cory

October 11, 2012
Mom and Dad,

Greetings! How is everything? What's new? I moved to the 4th floor today – the "new admit" floor where everyone is still coming to grips with their predicament, either just sentenced or just arrested. Some are learning for the first time they may not see freedom for the next 20 years. Some are crying and biting their nails wondering how violent prison will be, while others still simply laugh and joke about it all. As a "veteran" of M.C.C and the Federal System, there are plenty of questions to answer and concerns to dismiss. Indeed the density of emotions here surpasses almost any other place but court. Even in court, the sheer volume and speed of stimulation somewhat dampen the depth of emotions felt, whereas here, it's very empty and restricted. Virtually all there is to do (for the new admit, 90% of the floor) is come to grips and tickle each other's' speculations in ignorant (but endless none-the-less) conjecture. Were I free to come back at my leisure for a few days to visit the 4th floor and remember the struggle and watch the drawn, personal, human unfold, I probably would. I apologize for the poor handwriting. I had to "rent" a contraband pen to write this letter, as pencils and paper aren't even provided here. Yes, they must specifically design this experience for intense reflection.

The stack of books I have almost is as high as my hip. Bryan has been generously sending me his "best of" selections. He's proven exemplary in his diligent perseverance in the quest for personal improvement through education and is one of VERY FEW who I know who make themselves keep reading regularly despite the technological richness that tends to deflate our motivation to do so. We share many interests and outlooks, so the 25-item list he's promised to send is – well – promising. The first 3 seem great – including one by the author of *Outliers*[42] – remember that book you were listening to Dad?

Well, I'll leave it at that.
With Love,
Cory

P.S. I will get visit info ASAP. I am learning SO much, but don't want to bore without dissertations. Existence framed correctly fascinates.

Quotes:
"Do not flatter your benefactors. Their reward is unavoidable on its own." – Unknown Buddhist

"Buddhism is a practice, not a belief/dogma; otherwise it's nothing."

"Understanding is the basis of love. When you truly understand someone, you can't help but love." – Thich Nhat Hanh

"Good thoughts are no better than good dreams unless they be exercised." – Emerson

"Eat not to satisfy, but to work." – Variant of Emerson

"If I speak, I define, I confine and am less."

"Readiness is the Mother of Luck." – Gracian

"When we become completely satisfied with God, God becomes completely satisfied with us."

"The honorable man does not forget who he is because of who others are." – Gracian

"If you want to be miserable, think of yourself. If you want to be happy, think of others." – Sakyong Rinpoche

"Once declared, resolutions are never esteemed." – Gracian

"World – you are beautifully clothed."

"We each possess every trait, virtue, defect, possibility. Which we choose to water is the essence of mindfulness."

"Love is giving attention. Giving attention is love."

"Great worth requires great work." – Gracian

October 15, 2012
Mom and Dad,

Greetings. I hope this letter finds you well. I'm currently on the 4th (reception) floor awaiting transfer to 8th (dorm living like the 7th floor) then to 9th floor. I like it here very much, very quiet, very close to street to see people, people constantly coming in and out from the street or the facilities. When I got here, a group of 6 guys who were friends from a local church (involved in some stupid tax thing) were here getting acclimated to prison life. It was a joy to ease their concerns and help set a jovial, playful, optimistic tone to their experience. Also very glad to lend some books to the (rare) appreciative reader. Two cellis have passed through, both white, college educated, exceptionally successful guys who began hard drugs and eventually became rich drug dealers with unsurpassed crazy stories. One, a Bay Area guy who was all into Hollywood etc., the other a sort of mechanic/hot-rod fabrication virtuoso with many appearances in top magazines, etc. It's quite refreshing to have met not one but two cell mates who are around my age that are at least near my level in education and have a ton of worthwhile knowledge (experience to learn from and share with). Both really respectable solid guys I hope to keep up with. I've finally started working out, taking advantage of having athletic cellis (one was ex-marine, the other a track and field record holder). Having a good source of ideas for a routine makes a HUGE difference in the reward of working out — Most do the same few workouts over and over — no diversity or consideration for maximizing time and effectiveness. Learning more and more about entrepreneurism and lifestyle — the Bay Area guy was a loan officer and real estate agent and the hot-rod mechanic made > $2500/wk. just trading on eBay (not including his regular jobs and freelance fabrications). Meanwhile Emerson, Tesla, and Thich Nhat Hahn are still amazing me with graceful understanding that are more effective than 8 years+ of my own personal philosophical pursuits...yet remarkably similar conclusions! If only the nation's greatest thinkers were required reading in school! Really — these people's contributions are unbelievably under-rated in all but the most learned circles.

Well, it's late, must go for now.
With Love,
Cory

October 18, 2012
Mom and Dad,

Hello! I hope this letter finds you well. I'm sitting here on the roof, enjoying the cool fragrant fall air for the first time in almost two months. Yesterday I made my way up to the 8th floor (much like the 7th, dorm style) where I am assigned to a nice, cozy secluded cul-de-sac bunk next to the home for the guitar. Within a week I will be back to the 9th. Really none of it matters much. I'm content anywhere they put me. It's a matter of mere specifics — the types of comforts and advantages each affords, the people whose paths I cross. In this regard — going to the hole has been immeasurably rewarding, despite even IN SPITE OF my original concerns about failing my opportunity to participate in certain other circles (personalities, pursuits) on the 9th I was growing to appreciate. Reading *Siddhartha*[43], Emerson's essays (highly recommend), a book on Tesla who is perhaps the single most brilliant inventor American ever to have lived, virtually every electronic instrument we use he pioneered, but failed to monetize, and had stolen and commercialized by others. The success of Edison, the father of modern electronics and Marconi, the father of modern telecommunication, all of modern chemistry and medicine, as well as the advent of X-Ray imaging AND the electron microscope were more than anything else his ideas. The modern conception of history, particularly as it relates to scientific development/modern technology is hideously mistaken in its placement of credit in that regard. All but the most educated (along with those credited erroneously with the various inventions he demonstrated, often some 40+ years before the one credited with it did) are completely ignorant of him. It makes me sick – if we can overlook, marginalize, rob, such a revolutionary, what hope is there for anyone intending to offer the world innovation? Well, it's loud and distracting. I'll write more later.

Love,
Cory

October 26, 2012
Dad,

Hello, I hope this letter finds you well. It's 8 PM here, just received a substantial stack of pictures, letters, books. Sometimes provision even skirts excess – the "tides" of volition alternating between days of sending letters and later receiving big stacks of the same often having all but forgotten I sent some. It's the sensation of "plenty" exemplified, even if almost overwhelming at times.

Interrupted to go watch a gang-related fight in the "common area". The one guard nonchalantly lets each group back into their ranges, stepping around the 220 lb. gang member A pounding on 140 lb. gang member B, essentially saying, "Do as you will. In a few minutes, a team will handle this. It is of no concern to me." Eventually a very bloody B scampers his way back to his "pod", leaving A pacing and catching his breath unscathed but covered in blood, retrieving the glass of water his friend offered through the grate. More than likely the two don't even know each other. "Prison politics."

The perspective I'm getting while in here is priceless, both from studying books like the Almanac, so-called Pop-psychology books,

131

spiritual books etc. Yesterday a program came on the history channel called "What's the World Worth?" or something to that effect – looking at the overall metrics of the world and its nations, giving an idea of our overall resource condition as humans, materially and economically. This I think is POWERFUL information. Also it seems we produce about $1,000/person/month on average worldwide, and some multiple of necessary provision to sustain life acceptably, yet, we still see over half the world living on <$1000/YEAR. The ready availability of this information framed in various interesting (that is – engaging to the common man) forms gives us some reason to be optimistic about curing our macro technological cancer (extreme disproportional supply and endless pursuits of misperceived advantage).

Restructuring policies of who I associate with has been VERY beneficial. Not that I was associating with undesirables, but even people who have some qualities but look down or around instead of UP toward principles and ideals and IN to eyes and versatility of each moment, really seems to render days of joy. This policy has actually resulted in strained relations with fellow "woods" – other white guys – mostly rebellious guys who spend the days wasting time playing cards. As I socialize with select "Paisas" (Mexicans) and blacks they look on suspiciously, not seeming to see the vulgar, immature mush of a mindset that's ailing them. For better or worse, I'm sensitive to such stagnation.

I am eager to get back to the 9th floor to get back "jamming" with the guys. This professional mariachi in here has singlehandedly improved my technical skill significantly by showing me a few things.

- continued on October 28, 2012

"Wealth is the accomplished technological ability to protect, support, nurture and accommodate all the growthful needs of life. Money [by contrast] is only an expediency adopted means of exchange, disparately sized, inequitable items of real wealth" – Buckminster Fuller

"All fiat currencies are designed to fail." - Maloney

When I'm released? My feelings? Challenged. Overstimulated. Bittersweet. I've got my work cut out for me at least the first 4

132

months. There is very much to be done to repay karmic debts and return seeds to the soil of provision.

Previous release? Completely different. Then, staying was DYING, wasting away from the inside out. Now, this is an ideal life. The next chapter holds great challenges, necessary progress. All is and will be. I try not to speculate too much, plan a lot, approach it as any other great challenge. Well, three more letters to write. Thanks for writing! Talk to you soon.

Love, Cory

Quotes and Points of Research:

"Nothing bewitches like service to others. The best way to win friends is to act like one." – Gracian

"Liability is invisible loss, readiness, inevitable gain." – Unknown

"Anxious people make good consumers and good workers. Government and big business therefore love terrorism." – Tom Hodkins

"Nature never abhors seemingly idle trees, snails, grass, coral reefs and clouds." - Buckminster Fuller

"If to sweet freedom you would cling, submit unto righteous king." – Claudian ~ 300AD

"No one truly lacks time. We all have exactly the same amount each day. What we lack is priorities." - Unknown

"Be known for your courtesy, it alone can make one worthy of praise." – Gracian

"One cannot escape the effect of giving. Good karma will catch up." – Deepak Chopra (paraphrased)

Smoke and Mirror Free Economics Reports:
Shadowstats.com - Independent, bullshit adjusted economic analysis
David Walker: Former G.A.O Head
Hodges Grandfather Report

October 25, 2012
Mom,

Hello from the 8th floor of the Mexican Country Club, where I sit in my bunk, in a sort of Cul-de-Sac of bunks, a very tight yet cozy partition where I, "Zapata", "Bon Ice", Salvador and our little crowd of aspiring Mariachis spend days dying of laughter and singing "corridos" to Zapata's expert "tocando" [playing] (professional Mariachi and-at least now-guitar teacher). It's like living in a cantina, except with mugs of freeze-dried instant coffee instead of glasses of Corona, and it's considered acceptable passing out [sleeping] amidst festivities (if you can sleep). Better still, one of the best-read and smartest people I've ever had the pleasure of meeting – Nikko Briteramos (wiki "AIDs Huron State") is here and has become a friend and chess opponent. Our conversation often last 5-6 hours straight on everything from the role of cellular nuclei to the embarrassment of government intrusion. Nikko towers at 7', spearheads the ESL and the GED program here, as well as acts as a walking repository of historical, scientific, medical, cultural scholarly perspective. He's the subject of a great expanse of (political, ethical, social) debate and general exposé around his being the first person in South Dakota to be charged for "non-disclosure". He's appeared in various movies and his ordeal has been all over world news. I have no idea what it all says, but he's a great guy, very much like Landon – obsessed with BIOETHICS, reads 100x the normal amount. It's very refreshing to be able to share some books with him. There are other very likeable characters I won't spend time profiling. While the constant interpersonability refreshes, and latent wit and personability (which I'd begun to suspect I'd lost) has been re-emerging, days are "busy", whimsical, playful. The carefully constructed routine of intentional effort towards a Greater Good gives way to making the most of limited opportunities to engage fellow man. I guess it's like a vacation to some cultural immersion – nice, stimulating, hilarious, colorful – but – I'm ready to go "home" – 9th floor. I've also come to the conclusion (as has Shakti Gawain) caffeine IS a drug, indifferentiable (fundamentally) from other sorts of recreational "drugs". The jury is still out on the ultimate answer to the question, "Are drugs* (broadest sense) an acceptable part of a truly progressive life?" Simplified: "Are drugs bad?" and its corollary – "What role/ context/ rhythm should drugs be introduced to the human experience?" Simplified: "When is it OK to use drugs?" I am speaking philosophically, and I encourage you to try not to let the imagination run on this

134

consideration. Light penetrates all darkness, and reason penetrates all truth. If a large part of my purpose is NOT to courageously and equanimously penetrate the confusion around drugs and humans, then I am the victim of a great tragedy, and I do not believe this so. I'll write more on a separate page.

* *In this designation I include any substance that has even imperceptible effects on consciousness: caffeine, SSRIs, sleep aids, antihistamines, etc.*

To your letter (Oct 21):

You speak of the process of expanding into new beliefs and the tact of not exciting others' suspicions. I listen (read) and feel a mixture of remembering the alienation, the guilt for breaking others' belief systems carelessly, without sufficient solution, the pain of being dismembered, spiritually, before I knew what to replace the pieces with, the longing to invite others in, etc. Just as death is an inevitable part of any revolution, losing common understanding and even whole relationships is a part of growth. It has often been a lonely process for me, which is why I love Austin so. I've been blessed with some revelations lately, which have "bridged the gap" to connect with Christians – ideas that tap into ideas Jesus presented which open minds to new perspectives. So called "Eastern" ideas do much to UNLOCK otherwise cryptic "Jesus concepts":

"Be still and know that I am."

How will we know false teachers? "You will know them by their fruit." "Fruit of the spirit: love, patience, kindness, tolerance, generosity, wisdom, hope."

Can Good exist out of God? No. So look at the good of all "practices".

The historic perspective of modern Protestantism, as an only 300-year-old concept, built off, but not at all independent from Catholicism.

Historical perspective of the Bible accepted/rejected books arbitrarily chosen by politicians of questionable virtue. The tone of Paul in the New Testament, one of uncertainty and addressing conflicts within churches imperfectly. How could we possibly treat the text as infallible? There is power in the Bible, but it's nothing more than a questionable collection of writings from a handful of imperfect, uncertain, inspired but human writers.

"God does not [give] us a spirit of fear but of POWER of LOVE and of a SOUND MIND." How can the shunning of pure and wholesome pursuits possibly match this idea?

"You will know a tree by its fruits." Just look at the lifestyles and cultural effects of the various belief systems and one can see modern "Christianity" has no monopoly on fruits.

Jesus came specifically to destroy dogmas and judgementalism.

As far as RELIGIONS – 1) Service and worship of God. 2) Practices which reflect a set of metaphysical beliefs. 3) A set or system of beliefs in the metaphysical.

So let's be honest – we're quite religious. We just need no labels, no stamp of dogmatic adherence.

Lastly, I tell doubting Christians: I regularly and have for some time, pray to God to show me if I am deceived, how I am. I offer wholeheartedly to become an "exclusivity doctrine"-evangelizing Christian if it's my calling. So far I remain unanswered.

I'm very glad you are enjoying Lozoff's *We're All Doing Time*[21]. Once one sees the practical way his spritualty translates into dialogue and advice, one can't help but see the light. The world's very diversity of needs point to many expressions of the ONE SOLUTION, as opposed to a few expressions of one idea of a solution. It takes all the world's religions to treat all the world's ills. If it didn't, God would not be being fair to the indigenous people, the people with no virtuous exemplification of Christianity and the culturally predisposed to other religions.

Lately I've been seeing powerfully Godly beings in many who know/ practice no religions. The notion of swimming back and forth through "Samskara" [a mental conformation or latent karmic tendency shaping one's present life] in various lifetimes has opened this beautiful POSSIBILITY (not even important whether accurate or not, still bears some fruit) that even enemies are spiritual masters in

136

disguise teaching tough lessons. Thus the jokester, the Mariachi, the machismo, the DECEIVED, all are exposed as carefully chosen "costumes" "God" wears to teach the lessons suited for each stage of spiritual growth. In this model, even the "tragically lost" intravenous drug user "could-be", IS Jesus if you will, coming to show us something. What a precious sacrifice these "junkies" have made for the rest of us to learn from. They willingly take on great pain and consequence even loss of life to bring us these lessons. The rapist even teaches forgiveness. Or perhaps the raped chooses to teach others how deep-seated resentment can kill us and rob us of joy. Either way, what a sacrifice the afflicted made in choosing their life of covert sacrifice. We really need not even KNOW or TRY to be Godly to be God. Our only option is WHICH PART TO PLAY? Willing recipient of Providence? Or martyrdom in sin and pain? Truly righteousness is for our own OPTION to exercise good and experience blessing. We cannot cheat God or deviate from HIS plan. His kingdom on earth IS here, and we visit it regularly. Just a thought I had as I noticed some telltale rays of light seeping through these cheap and imperfect* costumes God wears (we call them strangers, friends, enemies).

*There is no such thing as imperfect, only incomprehensible.

[The following is in response to a situation I, Denise, shared with him from my own life.]

Being here in prison has showed me politics are a very real, daily, unavoidable part of life. The best way is NOT ALWAYS to fight it and definitely is NOT to ignore it (as I had up until this term). It takes techniques and skills (often uncommon to the pure-hearted) to groom our inner politicians and stop haphazardly bumbling through life playing the too-honest-to-be-savvy/ victim/ "people-are-idiots" card. We must play or lose by default. . . Fortunately certain Godly, virtuous people have invited us to be their students (Gracian, Saints, godly Politicians) and learn the basics of managing our interactions with others. It's powerful stuff. If one believes all people are unique manifestations of God, it can be said political savvy is about learning to honour God (in "imperfect"* ways reflecting imperfect perceptions of imperfect people). Really it's a matter of being courageous and discerning enough to choose the lesser of evils. To acknowledge imperfections and learn where to place them so truth, goodness and beauty can be their best. Anyways, it's late, I'll write soon, Cory

137

November 2, 2012
Mom and Dad,

Hello! How is everything? Seasons changing yet? Over here things are well. I'm still here on the 8ᵗʰ floor living in a jovial Spanish-speaking dead-end hallway, the tiny 10'x10' space doubling as a gathering grounds for singing and joking. The consequence – my Spanish, which is still very rudimentary, has improved tremendously, as has guitar skill. So in no rush to move. The Mexicans have been very amiable and generous with me. I've made a few good friends. One who we call "Bon Ice" (a popular popsicle/frozen fruit brand in Mexico) has over 20 deportations, most of which SWIMMING the (4.5 hrs) span from Tijuana to San Diego in the 50-degree water under cover of night. WOW! Lots of noteworthy characters.

Getting deeper into books others have sent and lent has resulted in exposure to many seemingly conflicting sentiments. It seems like every persuasive argument has its paradoxical contradiction in a later text: leisurely living vs. productive living, awareness of merits vs. humility, idealism vs. materialism (realism), frugality vs. abundance mentality. Obviously these aren't contradictions, only calls to define the razor's edge of discernment. This, for me, is a great joy. Going through the day observing and later analyzing the applicability of the widely varying ideas in personal interactions and vicarious phenomena. Recording it all, journaling its identifying subjects, experts, places, literature, movements to look up when I leave here. This process has exponentially expanded my perception of possibility. There are so many things to get involved with, and I know it's impossible to get involved with all. Spiritual movement, cultural movements, business movements, technological, artistic, etc.

Well, it's late I've got to send this before count. So will talk soon.

With love,
Cory

P.S. Been having much more luck lately providing others with books, now that I've got more selection. Very refreshing to see people getting some good stuff out of them – making a difference. I am ready for some more, especially to diversify studies. It helps to be able to cover more ground (can only digest so much of a given type of book):

Another Almanac – *Farmer's Almanac*[44] – more technological, less cultural

Something called: *Mathmatx*[45], I THINK this is it. I'm looking for a book on learning to perform math more rapidly, techniques for doing math in your head. "Speed math". . . there should be some good book designed/used by middle and high school math competition students to compete in speed events – long multiplication, mental exponents, etc.

FENG SHUI – some well rated book on Feng Shui fundamentals

The Life of Samuel Johnson[46] by Boswell

Boy Scouts Handbook[47] – some very extensive book of techniques that include: survival, knot tying, other general skills a handy naturalist should have.

Acclaimed Book on/by:
- Ghandi
- Muir
- Thoreau
(preferably published BEFORE 1970)

November 2, 2012
Mom and Dad,

Hello. I am sorry I have not written more. Much like "free life" the 8th floor is full of distraction, both willingly engaged and not so willingly exposed: hollering, horse-playing, people coming by to arrange the sale of their food tray or borrow a book. I frequently find myself discarding letters I write to y'all and others in environments like this, either most often because they come out as empty intellectualizations, wanting of personability/ intimate* revelation OR I feel a gut feeling not to send it after review: an inclination I do my best to obey/ trust. The result if you can imagine is sometimes a 3-page letter simply being archived, hours work not reaching fruition. Maybe 1/3 of my letters meet this end.

Meimie came yesterday. I was very glad to see her, and look forward to seeing her today as well. We had a very good visit. She talked about life in Jordan, told stories, etc., laughed, smiled. Yes, half of the visit was devoted to militant defenses and attacks on spiritual pitfalls and looming dangers, none of them directed specifically at me. She seems to grant me on almost complete amnesty from critical attack: a fact I find interesting considering I've probably got far more "ammunition" and even Christianity-specific arguments than any other she encounters simply because I've gone the deepest into her fortress of dogmatic self-righteousness than any other. I try my best to simply, strategically redirect the conversation towards more "human" subjects, to some success, but I do find myself succumbing to the urge to contradict certain more troublingly self-defeating arguments. Meanwhile, inside my own entertainment of the DUALISTIC ideals, looms like a dark and suspicious cloud above the now flourishing monistic landscape below. My mind has been thoroughly ravaged by dualism, and now that the destructive blazes have subsided, I'm left to wonder the significance of such "looming danger, dualism". Einstein put it perfectly when he said, "The most important questions any human being can ask himself: is this a friendly Universe?" While everything good and beautiful in me screams YES, God is All, is in All, sanctifies all, and in doing so secures our fate perfectly and permanently as saints to be saints in-fact, still I can feel a certain plausibility coming from the old world of my upbringing in zealous dualism. I see arguments throughout our world for this sort of looming danger we're constantly at the risk of tragically overlooking- mistaking the good for the best – complacently trudging onward towards terrible damnation, lulled away from the supposedly finite path so oft contested by every rite since Jesus as their own. Could Jesus, when he said, "I come not to bring peace but a SWORD" have been a mere anarchist seeking to seal his place in history as he introduces fatal, materialistic dualism to a monistic world? If Jesus really came to bring an expression of God's wrath, a final ultimatum on salvation or damnation, his teachings failed to find a home in the heart of the world's spiritual leaders, who all implicitly argue for monism or suffer a life of marginalization, fighting an endless battle against an invisible enemy (think Inquisition, Jihadists, cults, etc.). "Is this Universe a friendly place?" Mother Teresa, Buddha, the Catholic Church, Dalai Lama, Einstein, Emerson, Chopra, Lozoff suggest it IS. A look at nature, psychology seems to suggest it COULD BE. But our whole American society is built around the notion IT ISN'T. Where does the motivation to act decisively come from if we're

140

always satisfied God is in All, and we simply choose which reality to live in even though they all exist equally righteously. Indeed this seems like the only possible way for "omnipresence" to manifest itself. The scriptures do say: "There is a way that seems right to man, but in the end, it leads to death." This could mean anything. Somewhere else it says, "The heart will lead you astray." But it too says: "You will know a tree by its fruits". And "You will know the truth, and the truth will set you free," and "I come not to bring the spirit of fear, but of power of love, of a sound mind." Additionally we look and see the notion of a kingdom on EARTH not some dualistic eventual achievement of the strongest fighters- the 0.1% who "got it right" (actually more like <0.01%). So Meimie's claims and points are not so easily dismissed. Like any other decision − I must weigh the arguments and come to a conclusion, day by day. For now, MONISM which is PANTHEISM is the prevailing force, and it serves me well − even MAKES MY SURVIVAL POSSIBLE. I do not think I could survive dualism again. But I still must pray to be shown if I'm committing some great blasphemy thinking the Jesus I've been served a god, LITTLE G, just like you and ME. "God" couldn't ignore a willingness to embrace fatal dualism were it truth and allow this so completely convincing, empowering, endearing, peace-giving notion of unity amongst all to persist, could He?

Back to my * on "intimacy", I've been very empowered by Monistic thinking (techniques, practical implications) and philosophies (higher ideals). Watching others makes it clear the ability to connect with others manifests itself in widely varied forms and degrees from person to person. When I meet highly "magnetic" persuasive, charismatic people (Corey is one), I can't help but wish I were that way. I often feel like I'm missing some sort of mental agility key to personability. At various times I've felt downright like a different SPECIES. I engage others in an original way, and it's a major pursuit to determine what to make of this. It's not that it's bad or needs fixing, it's just UNCOMMON and as such I've got no example to follow to show me how to direct it. It's clear it has its place, as I've repeatedly observed people unlocking long closed or repressed parts of their personalities to me after short acquaintance. I suspect as a result of perceiving my stoicism as a safe receptacle for sensitive subjects, a more responsive person may betray dissonance with inadvertently opening. I don't know, I do know it's important for me to respond to this "uncharted territory" where I exist with vigilant introspection and effort to cultivate empathy.

November 4, 2012
Mom and Dad,

"It takes luck to think well, as it does to write a good letter." – Gracian

Hello, I just thought I'd say hello again. I missed the mail on Thursday (actually, the C.O. ignored my letter), so I'm sending this Sunday night (no mail goes out Fri, Sat). Meimie visited again yesterday (Sat). It went well. She still preached, but I just listen and pray to best understand. I wrote down her more important points so as to review them later. A big one she mentioned was "honor your parents." I asked her what exactly this means, but didn't really get a clear answer. Perhaps the two of you can shine some light on what this has meant for y'all with your parents or in general. She mentioned respect and contribution – time, attention, money, etc. She talked about how this is the only commandment with a promise (longevity). She talked about how we as a society do not respect our elders. I wondered how many years dishonor cost me. I saw how the thickening of technological illusion/ confusion/ progress contributes to an independent thinking youth. I thought about trying my best to keep experienced people around, even at preference over others my age. I thought about how I've used differences in beliefs, values and strengths to justify parting with my own parents' guidance. I thought about expectations, misunderstandings, cultures.

Well, I'm fighting a throat sickness, so I am going to go for now. Thinking of y'all.

Love, Cory

"On the heels of humility and fear of the Lord are riches, honour, and life." – Proverbs 22:4

November 2012
Mom and Dad,

Hello! It's Thursday so I thought I'd check in. I've been fighting a cold (or something similar) for a week now, but it seems to be subsiding. It's Thursday so we had our weekly chicken-on-the-bone today after our weekly exposure to fresh air. I'm still on the 8th floor, (dorm environment). It's all good, just not exactly ideal for writing &

142

reading. None the less, I've been reading a book Bryan sent on neurology – specifically plasticity – the ability of the brain to adapt and morph. To me this is very good info since karma, spiritual cause and effect, acts as divinely designed "lesson-plans" to condition us to act "Godly" (which is to say for the Greater Good). Since optimal education caters to the brain, neurology can actually help us understand our personal experience as humans. I've come to conclude (or employ) the notion that INDEED, THE UNIVERSE IS A FRIENDLY place. This premise unlocks a world of significance in every perception. It says, simply, God is in every sound, smell, texture telling us all the answers to every question ever posed. Thinking an "evil", a "0", a darkness looms to deceive, instantly evaporates this sort of unified transparency. We cannot trust our senses if a "devil" who seeks to tempt us away from God's will exists. In a way – of course evil exists, but we're exempted from its influence when "tuned-in". As y'all can tell, unified theory of practical living, truth, science consumes my thoughts. Not that I'm serious all day. In fact I've learned to be "common" and irreverent with the "commoners". This just comprises my private thoughts, studies, writings most of the rest of the time. It's not easy to write about how, for whatever reason, the Paisanos (Mexicans) never tire of laughing at me calling them delinquincias (trouble makers) and other perpetual inside jokes, pranks, etc. I cannot write of happenings, since they mostly don't exist, aside from the occasional fight. I cannot write of personal growth, since that would be to define, confine, reduce. I prefer not to divulge resolutions and intentions (for the future) for various reasons. So I write about my studies, various reinterpretations of ideas my "professors" Einstein, Gracian, Emerson, Lozoff, Chopra, etc., present. Feedback would help, but is unnecessary. I study all this, everything from the most transcendent to the most practical only as expression of "due diligence". Contributing the best I can to our reality, given what I've got. If my ideas seem abstract, I assure you, they find DAILY TANGIBLE practical expressions. They're really no more profound than the nonexistent ideology of an impoverished, uneducated peasant who finds reasons to laugh and give in his completely, not-religious, obviously inherent nature. One idea taking root: there is no attainment, no past or future act that can exempt us from DAILY effort, even daily mindfulness (remembering). There's a great temptation to "rest" from devotion, a persistent urge that follows all who "seek" perhaps their entire lives. Much like a race, we crave a "break". If we do stop, we very soon "cool down" and starting again hurts worse. The trouble is – we normally lack a practical collection

143

of personal maxims for living. Without DAILY reconsideration of ideals and their practical implications, we're deciding to "devolve" into a more obscure, meaningless existence, one we'll inevitably tell ourselves works more "naturally" and feels more "human" (as sin does). All the best invitations to return to mindful living, even our own previous statements attesting to the pleasantness and peace of this state seem foreign, impossible, deluded. We decide it was a "bubble" and go on looking elsewhere for comfort. In certain schools of Buddhism, such regressions (although only referred to as a multi-lifetime cycle) describe the path of the Bodhisattva, one who travels to nirvana only to look back to the suffering and return, descending into deception and illusion, voluntarily relinquishing enlightenment to guide others back. Who are we to prescribe a particular "state" of "acceptable attainment" for "salvation": in doing so damning (implicitly) all those below our mark? Isn't it inevitable our impractical idealism diverge from our reality, giving us plenty of reasons to doubt ourselves. Due diligence, practical, proportionate/ devotion. Just REMEMBERING. We know the truth. We experience profound demonstrations of truth in our lives. Indeed, given an opportunity to encourage OURSELVES IN THE FUTURE from this place of inspired clarity, we'd present a most compelling argument for "right perspective". (The popular example of this is the regretful old man on his death bed wishing he'd remembered *insert simple yet sublime notion here*.) So, bridging the "gap" between natural forgetfulness and "right perspective" (remembering, mindfulness) holds great promise as a DAILY TECHNIQUE. Favorite examples as of late (for daily reflection):

"Death will come suddenly and without notice. One day this body will turn to stardust."

"All those I love will die, and I will lose everything in life."

"All self-seeking is sin."

"All unity seeking is salvation"

"Put weight in gut instincts."

"Never complain or offer excuses if AT ALL possible."

"When emotionally charged (angry, excited, etc.) STOP. WAIT. Do not act."

144

"Focus deeply on every moment (never multitask)."

"Listen to each as though from their lips God speaks."

"There is no 'attainment'. We strive daily." (Can't simply eat enough today for the next month.)

"Please others."

"Readiness in all things – readiness is the mother of fortune."

"All sufferings are 'God's' priceless lessons. All difficult people are great masters in disguise 'testing' us."

"Self-satisfaction, pride always results in humiliation."

"Hide benevolence, devotion, resolution's explicit expressions of good except to a SELECT few (lest seem self-righteous)."

"We're all only temple façades."

"Nothing means anything, yet everything has infinite significance."

"Use techniques to bring the temporal into eternal and the eternal into temporal."

"We can't CHEAT "karma" (God). Benevolence begets good. Self-gratification begets bad."

The more people purposefully put 5 minutes - 2 hours/day rekindling whatever perspective-giving remembrances they so choose, the happier, freer, and less regretful they'll be. Y'all already know all this. I know y'all tried to teach me the value of this practice, but honestly, "Christian" devotions never quite cut the mustard. I need practical, applicable practices. Well, it's late. With Love, Cory
November 21. 2012
Mom and Dad,

Greetings, I hope all is as well there as it is here. Thank you kindly Mom for coming to visit on your birthday. It was a very special time, really helped me to gain some perspective on things, reminded me much of the world outside.

I received your letters dated 13ᵗʰ and 14ᵗʰ of Nov. Is it just me, or was in person cooperation more common before the advent of digital communication? Perhaps when y'all were in high school. It seems like I recall much greater interactivity in the 90s than now. I was particularly touched by Mom's transparent empathy with all the people you described intimately interacting with. As our days are fragmented, this sort of disarming openness we'll find more and more desired. For better, or worse, we've got 24 hours per day. As we commit to engage an increasing amount of technologically disseminated activities, our opportunities to connect are slowly divided and conquered.

Theoretically Average American Day:

24 hours
- 7 sleep
17 waking hours
- 10 work (+/- commute/preparing for work)
7 hours personal time
-3 hours meals + hygiene + cleaning
4 hours "free time"
- 1 hour phone/email/mindless technology
3 hours /day REAL FREE TIME

Y'all have done very well to position yourselves near human interactivity. Truly community is becoming rarer and rarer.

A time will come when I will be out of contact for a period as well, not to mention the fact in time we WILL lose every single person (and thing) we love. How is it, we can say all at once with our death is the best way? We can only value our time and connections all the more when we do have them.

Things are good here, but very screwy sleep schedule: 2 AM (work) – 6:30 AM (breakfast) then meals, so I basically only get to nap, stay rather tired. I'm still getting along very well with my Mexican friends, practicing Spanish, guitar, chess. (I won a tournament last week; another I have a 90% chance at this week.) The prize is 6 candy bars – the cost – decrease in my skill level by playing people less experienced. I am ready to go up to floor 9. I like my friends, but being social with so many people has its cost in my progress, studying, etc. Been studying the work of Buckminster Fuller, one of America's greatest innovators. He's got an annoying, clarifying

146

perspective on human civilization and the role of technology in our affairs. WHY was THIS (instead of lifeless junk) not required reading in school? It's taken a lot of work to UNLEARN the propaganda of traditional education and IDENTIFY the REAL history of the Universe as we know it. I can hardly believe how dry, empty and outright misleading traditional educations curriculum on history is/was. It's no wonder only NOW has history become relevant and interesting for me. (Not just Fuller, but recent literature in general). More and more traditional education begins to look CRIMINAL in its danger and harm to our culture and through our minds, our realities. Since, most of our society's great shortcomings from seemingly practical ideals have solutions in simply improving understanding, we can do much to help change the world by simply committing to practice even a portion of our education time being communally directed (suggestions from people we know). "Know OR have someone who does" – Gracian. None of us know! We delegate it all to experts. I can now greatly appreciate the desire to homeschool. I also feel like 95% of the population or more are unacceptably ignorant to where we are as the human race (our situation), in space and time. In only one 3-hour class, one could completely change their outlook on existence.

Dad, you ask if I've thought about going to college for philosophy. I have, and it's a very enticing prospect, but when I look deeper into my motivation, I realize college, as I'm thus aware, is not capable of providing the quality or quantity of valuable knowledge per unit of time and energy spent. My interest more lies in the ENVIRONMENT of thought and personal improvement/human evolution. Ironically, the instruction itself designed to be "digestible" by all, represents a deterrent. It's hard to "unlearn" wrong and irrelevant material, so I don't know that I can justify it (even if it were free). INSTEAD I can seek to create my OWN and FIND MY OWN stimulating environments, engage MIT Open Course Work and other online top-of-the-line free course, etc. I don't know if you realized it, but many of my Austin friends are PhD holding people who devote their lives to the pursuit of human evolution. How much better than to just learn communally? Perhaps I'll consider it again when my finances are "right".

Just received a stack of books including the 3 you sent, Mom. The two autobiographies look great. I think I'll be able to learn a few techniques from the "Speed Math" book even though it turns out I already know most of them. Thank you very much for sending them.

I've been longing for some personal examples of the embodiments of principles these two seem to "fit the bill" well. It seems Samuel Johnson's biography, who I chose on suggestion of a variety of awards (Best Biography, etc.) and reference in other books, was a bit of a scoundrel, so we'll see if his biography's 1000+ pages are all worth reading. Genius perhaps, but who cares to be a genius if you're miserable and vulgar.

Anyways, I'm out for the night.
With love,
Cory

November 30, 2012
Mom and Dad,

Greetings! How is everything? I'm enjoying hearing of the outpouring of inspiration and innovation, Mom. Speaking of accomplishment, I won my second chess tournament a few days ago. The final games took less than 5 minutes; my killer instincts have developed significantly. One of my opponents even forfeited when he saw he was pitted against me. But all that said, I'm a 1250/2400. A full 200 points below any serious players online. So by that standard, I'm terrible. Truly, we only race against ourselves. As far as workout regimens – I suppose I'll get in on one of my friend's routines at your repeated suggestion. I'm so used to heavy stimulation and interactivity any time I exercise, it's a big shift for me to participate in a "regimen" or routine. Well what's outside our comfort zone is exactly what we need so...good enough...Between all the work, (including some 10 PM – 4 AM and 10 PM-8 AM shifts), talking to my friends, practicing guitar, chess, lots of journaling – my reading has dropped to 30-50 pp/day. Meanwhile I've got some 3,000-4,000 to read. But it's all good, I've been able to lend out 4-5 books at a time, plus, I've decided to take many of them with me, so I'll get to them later. I just finished *Why We Get Fat*[48], a good book on the state of superior understanding on diet and obesity. (Speaking of, the Officer's Gym's scale says I'm 170 lbs., then heaviest I've ever been!) The answer to the question *Why We Get Fat* is basically because we're defying millions of years of evolution in favor of a 2,000 - 3,000 year old practice of eating high percentages of carbohydrates (insulin regulation not designed for this) – a practice we adopt partly out of addictiveness and partly out of economics (priorities: money > health). The book bases its
148

argument on a 2,000 year anthropological study of diets of ancient man. They found the vast majority of our ancestors ate 70%-99% meat, specifically, the fattiest animals they could find. The science flies in the face of research aimed to prove obesity is a result of overeating and under-exercise. Much of the research they tout evidence failure of this stubbornly imposed theory comes from the notorious leading obesity research center –Pennington Medical Center. So, this doesn't suggest the readily available meat (treated and also itself unnaturally carb fed) is superior, just that meat in general is the solution. Specifically meat FAT. Perhaps I will sometime try some heavy fish and fowl dieting, see what happens...The deeper question becomes this: Even if recent discoveries of our inherently carnivorous diets prove we're almost surely better off eating meat, is the pursuit of the vegetarian ideal a worthy or practical "next step" in evolution? Even if it is, it becomes "it" being eating > 30% of calorie intake as plants becomes a voluntary choice. To try and defy our nature and eat grains/veggies becomes an extremist form of activism. In Gandhi's book, he talks about how the common belief at the time of his childhood was that the British were so superior in strength and resilience to rule as a direct result of their meat eating and the Hindu's vegetarianism. Also I think of Jesus and the Jews. Both eat generous amounts of meat and fish.

The notion/verse "There is a way that seems right unto man, but in the end it leads to death," has always laid heavily on me, never sure what exactly it means, practically speaking. I end up with no real interpretation, so it just sort of hangs as an ambiguous threat/warning. It's this sort of unworkability/ambivalence that keeps me praying God keep me from falling prey to whatever exactly it is this refers to, and as of yet, unanswered (at least explicitly), keeps me at arms-length from the writings called "Scriptures" (Bible). Surely if God wants me to see my folly in this He'll tell me, right? "God, if I'm wrong, tell me!" Perhaps we should all pray this, if nothing else, as homage to Meimie.

Well, with that, I part. I look forward to hearing again from y'all.

With Love,
Cory

Books Wishlist: even though I've got a lot to read, I try to keep it diversified, and right now I lack spirituality books for daily devotion. Plus I lend them out.

A Taoism book or (*Tao-Te-Ching*[52])
The I-Ching[49]
Book on Confucius' teachings
Book about "God being in Numbers" – been experimenting with symbolic geometry (aka Sacred Geometry)

December 3, 2012
Mom and Dad,

Greetings! It's 9 PM Sunday night, and I'm sitting here listening to half the range sing along with the Mexican songs they play. ("I think I'm Going to Cry"). I've been enjoying practicing guitar very much, and feel like I've passed into another threshold of competency with it. Still, my finger-plucking style isn't quite conducive to many songs, so I've got my work cut out for me to reach the "next level". I've taken "the belt" on the floor in chess, which I guess isn't saying much other than that it's hard to find opponents and less pleasure to win, knowing winning is only necessary to maintain position. I suppose it's time to start making secret "mistakes." This and other experiences regarding the never-ending ebb and flow of competency, comfort zone, and challenge brings to mind a quote from Michael E. Gerber, small business/entrepreneurship: "The ordinary man sees only blessings and curses, while the warrior sees everything as a challenge." I can see powerful arguments for the superiority of each role: warrior and easy going "ordinary man". It's the question of, "To what standard of achievement do we hold ourselves?" In Landon & Amanda's case: a very high one. In most people we interact with, simply meeting life's demands, at whatever standard that arises, is sufficient. On the one hand, we are inclined to see the great difference in achievement between applications and laxity. It would seem a tragedy to live anything less than a rigorous, god-driven life of quantifiable impact. On the other, even the greatest works seem utterly futile in consideration of eternity, expansivity and temporality of human existence. We see noble examples coming from BOTH extremes, people who did almost nothing and simply WERE, and people whose intensive action left permanent legacy. It's interesting to me how God seems to allow opposed ideals to all work together for the good. It would seem God

150

is even indifferent to our explicit acknowledgement of his singularity: the man who says, "There is no God," often makes a very strong argument for God's omnipresence; we discover he's really only opposed to conventions and mysticism. Anyways, a more regimented lifestyle than I've ever lived has been developing step by step. I see now that many seeds lay dormant and many flowers never blossom without many consecutive, uninterrupted days of watering, weeding and fertilization. I remember now a decision I made in 1995 to willingly take my time developing certain habits and stages of development, the same concept as arbitrarily employing lesser methods so as to exercise the rest more strenuously. Well, it's time to return to greater methods. (I've done the same with cycling, chess and guitar.) With cycling, switching to a road bike resulted in a level of speed otherwise unattainable by a consistently consciously imposed challenge. I guess it can be summed up as adopting a material/inherent challenge instead of relying on consistently deciding to challenge oneself consciously.

Anyways, it's time for work.
Talk soon!
Cory

P.S. Will you please send me a book on "Feng Shui" as well as one of these: *The Jataka Tales*[50], *Ramayana*[51] William Buck translation or *Tao Te Ching*[52]?

December 2012
Mom,
Hello! Thank you for your last letter. Nice artwork. I imagine it took quite a while to complete all those little lines. I like the simplicity and clarity of that piece. There's something nice about B&W drawn pieces that speak directly to a concept. It's Thursday, roof day and soon I'll break from writing this to go upstairs to the roof and get some fresh air, maybe play some volleyball. Today I woke up at about 3 AM, full of energy for no apparent reason. I opted to simply take it as an opportunity to write, reflect, etc. I've been in the habit of recording and analyzing dreams, at least the tail end of them that I can recall when I wake. I do believe dreams are good indicators of the reality which we've been creating during our waking hours – not

literally, but symbolically and not irreversibly, but tentatively – a sort of imagery inertia, a chance to work with possibilities before they enter, manifest reality. It's a good chance to prove beyond the shallow façade of conscious attention to see where our subconscious is at and how we feel about things. What we'd do, given the opportunity. Lately I've seen a few favorable trends: certain agreeable landscapes I'll travel to, time spent with you, Bethany. Bike riding, living in some plush, agreeable space, etc. Another recurring theme is school, not college but high school. At

first I had been attributing this to a sort of return to a vibrant youthful social situation in many ways manifest here in prison. (Return to high school dreams have been going on for a long while before this time.) Last night I recalled some young women about my age speaking favorably about the possibility of attending a high school science fair. I responded, "Then we'll go." When I awoke and recorded this dream I became aware of an additional possible meaning: the call to participate at some level with the development of education. I'm not sure how. I feel like being a teacher in the most conventional sense is more or less out of the question. It doesn't not want me, and I do not want it. I have some ideas. The biggest question is under what context can the greatest willingness/desire for learning be engaged? It's the same question that's emerged about the attempt to bring learning into prison – I've found its best to seek and respond to receptive minds personally, case by case, rather than some contrived mass provision attempt (aimlessly donating my book to a book shelf vs. keeping them and loaning out 1 by 1). I see some ideas forming (about how I could find a way to serve in education.) This is so independent from my ideas of how to earn money.

Well I look forward to hearing how things are going.

Sincerely,
Cory

December 2012
Dad,

Hey how are things going? It's ~ 7:30 AM, sitting here waiting to hear the call that means our weekly hour of volleyball, fresh air and the fulfillment of our orders from the available commissary (mostly junk food). This week I'm supposed to get my 3 candy bar reward for winning the chess tournament. I've got one more opponent to beat conclusively to be floor champion, but we've been going back and forth (I think its 6-5, him). It's been a bit of a strain lately being expected to work a 10 PM – 2 AM janitorial shift. My sleep schedule gets all sort of mixed up. I am making it a point to get up and stay up 6:30 AM – 12 PM in appreciation of the supremacy of early rising/mornings and have been fairly consistent about this. I've found a clear intention combined with a couple brief meditative sessions is sufficient to get my body to allow this. Without either I've found trying to stay awake on such little sleep like trying to stop the rain: only possible by moving around. I've watched this ~50-man range almost completely turn over, all my old friends are gone, slowly but surely replaced by new ones. Lately it's been a couple of guys from Riverside. One called "Show" who was flown down in the middle of serving his 7-year "Rico Act" (one phone call to the effect of "Hey, Can you find some kilos of ____ for me? Maybe, hold on.") term, it seems to be asked to witness against some friend of his that knew some pilots who got caught smuggling – it turns out this friend is the same guy who I mentioned I need to beat to win 8th floor title. Anyways, "Show" is a good guy, owns a couple successful auto shops, likes building hot rods and driving nice cars, many of which are featured in hot-rod magazines worldwide. It turns out he's from some town my next best friend (here), Dave, is from: Dave ALSO is an accomplished custom car fabricator who was an instructor at the local tech school in hot-rods. Needless to say, they hit it off and turn out to know many of the same people. Show is a spare-no-expense kind of guy who likes to eat the best possible in here, so the past couple of weeks we've been making all kinds of crazy dishes from black-market food and commissary. Last night we made shredded beef tacos with habanero cheese and refried beans, with honey banana nut skewers. The other day we made "mackerel ceviche soup" with black-market lemon pepper, fresh onions, soup packet, rice, and mackerel (with honey-drizzled bananas, peanut butter, honey-bun, warmed). In all honesty it's on par with "outs food".

I have been practicing speed math (stuff like mentally doing 1.24 X .097 (.12024) in a few seconds. In this case ~ 15 sec (but I was off by .00001, still working out some kinks). I am also studying geometry, not so much to learn it, as to develop a fundamental familiarity with it as a meditative practice the way the ancients of all history did; they saw the deeper symbolism in fundamental formations, the signature of God that pervades all nature and reality. Our civilization's great minds paid this understanding homage in their architecture and development planning. Even D.C's streets are designed around sacred symbology and numerology. The dollar, the statue of liberty, pyramids, cathedrals of Europe. All conceal hidden relevance in their subtle shapes and dimensions. This has to do with the fact our perception, human consciousness operates on hallucination, which is the arbitrary extension of possibilities into the data received by our senses. When we work with fundamental designs, we improve our ability to "hallucinate more productively," extending more and more likely shapes out to be "tried on for fit" with our senses. The improvement in mental clarity has been perceptible as a result of this practice. It's a wonder to me we neglect this pursuit, which would have been considered central to a good education in ancient schools, today.

Well I hope to hear from you soon.
With Love,
Cory

December 2012
Mom and Dad,

Greetings, I hope this letter finds y'all well. It' a cold rainy day here, also "roof day", so it was somewhat nostalgic experiencing the first cold rainy day since last year. It brought back many memories of long, trying days out in the cold, wet. Days spent laboring in a muddy pit in near freezing weather in Boone, others of commuting through winter downpours in Austin, others still of the nights spent enduring wind and rain hiking many miles to stay warm, waiting for the laundromat to open to get dry. Putting on warm clothes after twelve hours of bone-piercing cold is an experience of unsurpassed relief. It's hard to imagine how our pre-civilization ancestors dealt with the elements when it's so hard for me to imagine enduring the elements without state of the art of synthetic clothing.

Have y'all tried the Google glasses yet? It's always amusing talking to some of these guys who have been down > 1 year who haven't

154

experienced certain technology – Facebook, Skype, iPhones, etc. It makes me think of the whole lifestyle of using technology I'm about to get reintroduced to: changes in fundamental nature of thought and perception are inevitable. The trick is isolating the most beneficial aspects and compounding on them, while maintaining the focus that's increasingly challenged by technological distraction. Everybody likes to watch the video of the kitten wearing a cantaloupe helmet, but no one wants to recognize it's exactly these small wastes of time that accumulate and multiply, consuming large chunks of our day and reprogramming our reward center notifications.

Then there's the question of which goals to focus on. The whole world seems to invite me to participate, yet I now know to choose everything is dangerously close to choosing nothing in practice. I've got some ideas of what to commit to.

Well, looking forward to talking next week.
With Love, Cory

December 13, 2012
Dad,

Thanks for your letter. The Ecclesiastes verse you mention seems almost to suggest a sort of sensual hedonism. – "All there is for man is to enjoy his food and drink." Perhaps there is room for people to exist in a variety of "karmic positions" in life – some just taking it easy, some striving, some striving to rise out of suffering, some seeking transcendence of all imbalance (detached enlightenment), some defying personal inclinations to serve others (Jesus, Mother Teresa), others seeking the place where personal satisfaction/ provision meets service to others – "win-win-seekers", (my personal subscription, by deed rather than intention). Perhaps there is a place for it all, and none is more right, per se. It's obvious to me striving towards experiences outside our "position's" comfort zone is of supreme importance. Last night I started to read a book that talks about human understanding from an evolutionary perspective. Really good book. One of the ideas it develops is the idea, "Knowing is doing and doing is knowing." Basically, that all intellect is only as relevant as its effect on action, since there are no factual designations to be found in reality or science. It's a difficult concept to fully understand without much meditation & reflection. I'm

155

eternally grateful I have found an (intellectual) community in Shambhala that seems to take the most reasonable intellectual yet practical approach to principal living.

I'm going to be interrupted to go to work, so sorry I end abruptly.
With Love, Cory

-CONTINUED-

They honor ancient teachings and eternal truth yet suppose no rigid modern interpretation. They embrace and incorporate the modern science of neurology and quantum physics. Indeed, science seems to both confirm their convictions, while also building on them. If Austin was for me arriving on campus, prison studies have been entering the library, and Shambhalism (which really is a mere secular tradition, not even a specified doctrine or true branch of Buddhism) is my major.

I will continue to consider the option of college. I DO desire to find a way to focus on the lifestyle most conducive to evolution for the next 2-3 years. We shall see what that turns out to be.

Well, Until later,
Cory

December 14, 2012
Mom,

Not twenty minutes ago I was writing out questions about the very things your letter answered, which I just received.

Dad's experience with "words with friends you want to lose" reminds me of mine with chess. I agree the goal is not to simply win. It's very limited as a game to build bonds with others, as it's like poker, best played in expressionless silence. The goal is to compete. Winning is just the evidence of successful competition and challenge. If the goal were to enjoy one's self alone, many of the most productive, competitive games would prove failures. It's a delicate balance. Glad to hear you're doing more art, it's clear to me it's a great way to serve others.

That's good Debra enjoyed *We're All Doing Time*[21]. As I read more, I'm being increasingly pointed back towards the primary documents all these books are based on: *Tao Te Ching*[52], *I-Ching*[26], *Bahgavad Gita*[49], *Upanisads*[53], etc. So many of the American books are essentially "Tao-lite" and Gita-simplified.

Lately I've been struggling to find real inspiration to write. I'm hoping that will change soon.

For now, I must go write others.
With Love,
Cory

December 17, 2012
Mom and Dad,

Greetings. Just wanted to say hello briefly here this Sunday night. Well, I'm still on the 8th floor, trying as best I can to focus and be progressive despite spending the whole day with 4-5 people who have a very "different" idea of personal standards of progress. We all get along, but that's exactly the problem. Inevitably a person becomes like those he spends time around. The person may maintain many qualities of his own but inevitably will adopt some and compromise others. In this case, its best summed up by vulgarity. Now vulgarity is a deceptively malicious fault. It seems benign and subject to contextual censorship, but it finds its expression in slowing the flow of inspiration, a necessary component of all communication, including better writing. The correlation between thoughts, actions and speech has been becoming clearer. Truly good thoughts require good actions. Good speech, good habits. Words are the shadows of actions.

Well, I'm about to have to go back to work, so goodbye for now.
I love y'all very much, Cory

December 20, 2012
Mom and Dad,

It's Thursday, crystal clear, and the sun is shining with a penetrating silver clarity. While Christmas no longer holds the sentiment that it did when we used to drive around looking at Christmas lights in

Victoria, this time of year holds a certain charge that with increasing attention proves unique. A sort of shining snow day feel. With our recently explicit awareness of a sort of "soul-internet", and its relations to solar circumstance, what I once devolved as meaningless sentimentality, now appears to be profound shifts in the very state of our collective consciousness and demands closer attention. I am sorry I could not spend this time with y'all, and hope y'all will find time to meet me in Houston/Austin on the 25th of January during my trip to the "Halfway House" and associated 2-day gap in custody. I suggest Houston because I doubt Landon and Amanda will go to Austin to show me the baby, so San Diego →Houston→ Austin will have to do. I will be very glad to finally see you all again. Perhaps we can run, play some tennis, sun bathe (I want to correct this paleness ASAP), etc. I feel good, but not actually excited per-se about the Halfway House. Only diligent execution of my plans can resolve this time. I'm hoping they will allow me to serve, not at a residence or home-confinement, so I can wrap up the mass of the "to be researched" objectives all this studying has accumulated.

Days have been going well, lots of reading and talking to "Show", who's been able to tell me more still about the life of a very successful entrepreneur. I'm flattered he devotes me so much attention, as his time here seems to be in great demand from just about everyone. Truly God has put some great people of action and principle in my path this year. I'm never quite sure what it is that sparks their interest in building a relationship with me, but I wouldn't doubt if it it's sheer novelty, nothing meritorious per-se. My words exceed my deeds pitiably, and my aspirations stands like the Himalayas next to the hills of accomplishment. One can say all they want about "it's what's inside that counts" and what not, but what happens outside is an indication of what has been going on inside. Even the tiniest external failures indicate internal ones, even the most seemingly uninitiated experiences of seeming injustice found their root in previous karma. (Perhaps from previous lifetimes, but more likely this one.) So, as I look around at disorder in my life I feel a call to improve.

Well, I will be calling y'all tomorrow first thing in the morning, so I can going to go to bed for now.

With Love, Cory

December 29, 2012
Mom and Dad,

Greetings from Sunny San Diego. Things here are going alright, ready to get back into an orderly rhythm after holiday laxity. Major changes in sensory and literal "diet"/exposure: listening to music, eating less meal food, more nuts, fruit, cheaper and more regular phone calls. From outside, I'm sure it's hard to imagine such "small things making appreciable difference, but since days are made up of small things, it has made a difference, a big difference.

Landon mentioned his graduation in April. I guess that's another trip I'll be taking next year. It's a bit overwhelming, all the plans and obligations waiting for me. Well, I'm sure it will all work itself out. Honestly, I feel at a loss for what to say. I'm just sort of observing right now. I've spent a lot of time theorizing, envisioning, etc. It's getting to be time to just observe and act. Best I can tell, I've got less than four weeks left. This year has passed too quickly. Even with effort at maximizing it, I still feel I could have done better: learned more, wasted less time on redundancies. Also, there's the issue of work. I do not want to do that which I should do, neglected in favor of self-directed study. Blah Blah….

We just ate some shredded turkey burritos that we made with leftover turkey carvings, jalapeno cheddar cheese and refried beans, cooked till crispy/flaky, very tasty. "Show" has really got me spoiled eating all this good food. Everyone else in our range is constantly coming by hoping to get some of our leftovers. Normally, there is. To me, "Show" exemplifies the law of "Giving and Receiving". He's 33 and many times a millionaire with many cars, properties, businesses, employees. What strikes me most about his resilient abundance is his resilient giving, supporting not only his employees and immediate family but extended family, associates, girlfriends, and even the local "prison economy." All without pretense or expectations and not in a compromising way. So far, this is the best example of giving I've seen so far; many also give but also expect and/or do so only strategically. As best I can tell, giving is an art. A fine line exists between giving well and either wasting or being partial.

I am considering going to school to conduct LEED or Energy Star rating on residences while I'm in the halfway house. This would enable me to pick up jobs writing reports on the energy efficiency of homes entering the market, as is now required by law in Austin. Honestly, I don't particularly want to make a career of home inspection, but it would make a good "backup plan" and supplemental income source. It promises to be a growing market, as efficiency ratings become the status-quo nationwide. It's also a segue-way into home improvement sales, bridging the growing gap between the state-of-the-art in living systems and popular implementations. I am still considering completing a 4-year degree, but will need more time to consider before I make this huge commitment again.

Well, That's all for now.
With Love,
Cory

January 1, 2013
Mom and Dad,

Greetings, How are things? I am sorry I haven't written lately. Honestly, I've been reluctant because I've been in a phase of perceiving the emptiness of communication. All the sallow judgements, monologuing on recent events. "When I speak, I define, I confine and am less." I've noticed these phases of periodic withdrawal, and they just are what they are. Things have been progressing "very well", a nice rhythm of life, lively rapport and steady flow of inspirations mark my final days as satisfying "all's well that ends well." We have spent the past week or two fasting, jamming local radio stations, feeling more or less perfectly provided for, treated with a respect that borders reverence, working towards goals daily. Today a brief riot broke out during my daily evening nap (~5 PM – 9 PM). Bunk beds were thrown, boxes flew, C.O.s were yelling. My friend Show was called out to discuss whether they would lock the whole prison down. They perceived it to be a possible start to a major power grab by the American gangster Sorrenos against the decided majority-rule Paisas, more or less average Mexican farmers who try their luck at drug smuggling periodically, and often unwillingly. (Using people who don't know they're trafficking drugs has become the modus operandi for these cartels.) Show assured them it was nothing of the sort. I did my best to ignore it and go back to sleep.

Y'all asked me to express my emotions here as I approach the end of my time: honestly there is less and less to express. There is this flowing sequence of manageable challenges, encapsulated in a very safe, provident, consistent environment. Things just are...

Well, That's all for now, more soon.
Love,
Cory
Happy New Year!!

January 2013
Mom and Dad,

Greetings! It's about 3 AM, and I just finished work. It's so pleasantly quiet that I thought I'd take the opportunity to write a bit. Lately 10 AM – 11 PM have proven very difficult times to write or read. (Hence the reduction in letters sent.) Fortunately it's mostly agreeable distractions; people come "visit" me often. We then have good conversations. But I'm left with the answerless question(s):

1) Am I getting enough accomplished?
2) How should I be spending my time?
3) What standard do I hold to?
4) Will I regret not reaching goals?

It seems like these two questions either directly or indirectly shape our entire lives...For some – their answers seem to tend towards "no" on 1), whereas on the other extreme are the majority of the inmate population who imply there is nothing worth accomplishing except the murder of time. Somewhere in the middle sits y'all's example, which seems more or less inherited/ taken from popular local standards of productivity. Correct me if I'm wrong. So far, my conscience seems more or less noncommittal. Who knows? We spend much time working towards perfection of these careful balances only to have them made irrelevant by major changes. I just feel like maybe I should be accomplishing more. But then when I examine life, I see socialization is about all I can cut out, and even that would be tough to cut gracefully.

Just a thought, not sure y'all have any,

More later, Cory

161

January 2013
Mom,

Greetings, Thank you for your thoughtful reply. You mention not neglecting the practice of handwriting letters. I too hope to continue handwritten letters even after emails and even exiting prison. It will be a challenge, because regular phone, skype, email access has a way of deflating motivation to write. Modern neurology explains this: different regions of our brain "compete" for control over particular tasks. Naturally, when we're reading emails and making phone calls our brains relocate resources away from writing − conducive sectors, and we end up choosing the more popular medium to express our vital ideas. So, this being said, for better or worse, a certain degree of "forced changes" are bound to occur as lifestyle changes demand neural accommodation. All I can do is my best. The idea occurred to me to type emails first to take advantage of neural advantages, then rewrite/rethink them by hand. We'll see. I do not get phone and email back till 12-20-12, the second to last day on the Mayan calendar.

Well, I must go to work.
With Love,
Cory

January 6, 2013
Mom,

I started reading *The Artist's Way*[54] today. Have you read it? I also did some contemplation of letter writing vs. email, one of the subjects we've spent considerable attention on over the past few months (as I likewise have for many years now). It came up in the context of *The Artist's Way*[54] suggesting hand writing 3 full pages of flowing free writing every day upon wakening to sort of get the creative juices flowing. She suggests everyone from lawyers to dancers to businessmen swear by it once they've practiced it for a few months. Have you used this exercise?

The only trouble with this otherwise sensible idea is this: Considering it takes me a full 19 minutes to cover even ONE SIDE of a page (in a hurried rush at that), that would put the practice at almost an hour and a half each day. This competes with a great number of other practices for limited daily devotion/ morning ritual

162

time. In order to be realistic and sustainable, it seems like there should be some time cap on daily rituals, otherwise one ends up having to cut them short. Then the continuity necessary for resolution is compromised.

What is the most time you've set aside for daily devotion on a regular basis? The idea of how to spend time in devotion/ reflection has risen to utmost importance. It's become clear that this time, more than any, has the power to direct the course of one's life (followed closely by what we read and who we spend time around).

Anyways, I got to thinking about the fundamental differences between reading and typing: I started to realize back some thousand years ago, there probably was a young man somewhere debating on the transition from pictograph symbols and the more or less bastardized symbols that make up an alphabet. Some many years before him, another young man debated the merits of moving from caricatures to symbols. Some many years before him, further predating man, debated on the transition from gestures to pictographs. Of course, each of these transitions were very different steps, unique costs/ benefits and ways for evaluating them.

What marks typing as inherently different than all of the aforementioned methods is this: Typing loses almost ALL the evidence of human movement, and visually conforms to a global standard, whereas writing only retains a few commonalities that characterize them (for people with terrible handwriting like mine, very few). This isn't necessarily a bad thing. I consider my own handwriting, which even at its best is not very good. What does the visually-rich expression really even say?

More than anything, handwriting a letter says this: I spent a little bit more time and effort writing this. It follows then we're that much more willing to put weight in what's said. This difference begins to look more and more romantic and less and less fundamental as I look into it. It IS tragic that when I get out, the rate at which I handwrite things will drop dramatically. But ALL progress contains certain tragedy: the tragedy of the more historically-rich experience typing replaces being lost.

Even when a tribe builds its village, it must destroy some trees, trample some grass, evict some insects and small animals. Fast forward a few thousand years, and we "pave paradise to put up a

163

parking lot." All progress is tragic until it itself becomes romantic. It doesn't even become romantic until it's threatened by a still more progressive movement, and we realize all the richness that will be supplanted. In time, this new practice grows in nuance, richness as it takes root in our collective conscience and cultural experience.

Writing has some 4,000+ years of cultural reinforcement and development. Typing has barely over 100. I look forward to searching other's thoughts on this matter. While it may sound trivial to spend so much contemplation on ONE decision, to write or to type, since writing and typing make up at LEAST one hour of my day every day, that represents as much as a cumulative 4 years of my remaining life, and of course the possibility of contributing to an understanding that will shape the course of many others' lives as well in this regard.

January 26, 2013
Mom and Dad,

How are things? We're behind a silvery veil of rainy winter fog here. I spent the night reading about monks in Dharmasala and the origins of philosophical thought, an excellent book, *A Brief History of Thought*[65]. I came across the philosopher you quoted, Dad, Rousseau. It turns out his major contribution to the world of thought is the idea of what it is that differentiates man from animal. Previously we had some vague idea of rationality/ sensibility being what separated us from the beasts. In the 18th century, Rousseau said it's none of that, but "perfectability". The way animals are born with their essence, instinct and can act more or less predictably according to it their entire lives, whereas humans are more capable of striving towards perfection, spending large portions at the beginning and end of life incapable of providing for themselves. It's on this foundation that the idea of all men are created equal is based. The idea is that all have the same opportunity to pursue perfection, and as such should be treated with equal respect.

It's an interesting idea because in truth we really don't know to what degree humans are "unique" in our "perfectability". Every day neurologists are finding out more and more of our behavior cued if not determined by instinctual traits, and animals demonstrating more and more human ones. Either way, the idea of humans being

164

equal is one that we "thought up" and widely accept as beneficial and good. It is not a-priori, which is to say fundamental.

Well, have a good day,
Cory

January 22, 2013
Mom,

Greetings! How are you? Since no news is good news, I'm going to presume – "well". I have little to update on as I equate consistent, equanimical progress with successful completion of my "retreat" be it three more weeks or nine more weeks. I just keep chipping away. Days pass like sand through my grasp. Soon all that will be left is an immense beach whose borders extend around the world.

I shaved my head. Protesting nothing in particular. Except maybe the haphazard haircut an inexperienced inmate barber gave me. It turns out I like it shaved.

I highly recommend: *Creative Habit*[66] by Twyla Tharp and the 30-minute daily free-writing touted by the *Artist's Way*[54] as more or less essential for freeing up "the flow", uncensored. Such exercises always seemed to me too simple or unstructured to be of appreciable benefit, but the last week's experiment with the practice assured me, writing daily doesn't mean uncensored, free writing. There is much that our souls are just waiting for an opportunity to express to us clearly, given the right opportunity. Even if we think meditation or other types of purposeful writing should meet that need.

Well that's all for now.
Love,
Cory

January 29, 2013
Mom,

Hello, How's it going? Thanks for the pictures. You asked me to write how I am feeling. I'm feeling balanced – challenged, yet provided for, in every area. Things cannot and should not run too

165

smoothly. Right? When ALL is well, things are optimal, we can expect a challenge. When all is challenging, we can expect progress that will later mean "provision" or "good fortune." The trick is to bring each into the other. Lately life's been doing this for me. Ever noticed people who intentionally bring challenge into their lives are more pleasant to be around and popular, while those always seeking an "easy way out" fade into distant oblivion? When we bring one into the other, we stop needing our challenge to come from anywhere and everywhere (others) and others begin to flock to the person who challenges themselves because to them everything else comes easy: money, knowledge, achievements, culture.

Examples: Today was my first day working at medical. I can tell it will be an easy job, but today was stressful because I had to get used to everything- procedures, people, etc. Then, when I left, well, rewind. I had wanted this job for a while. It's easy, only a few mid-day hours. I get to socialize with nurses and doctors all day, meet other inmates, etc. I was concerned I wouldn't get the job because of my record here "stealing" (even though it was all stuff FOR US anyways plus less than $1 in value). Well, I went to work and worked hard trying my best to set a good impression, etc., went back and in the elevator the C.O. was like, "What's this?" He reaches in my pocket and finds two keys used for opening and closing soap dispensers. DUH! I had forgotten to return them in my haste to thank & say goodbye to my supervisor. I tried to play it off. "I'm glad you found those. Can you bring them to my boss, please?" He wasn't convinced and proceeded to go show them to my counselor, the C.O. on duty, etc. I really wasn't trying to steal them. They're useless anyhow. I spent this afternoon scared they'd send me back to "the hole" over it. Who knows, I may not even have a job tomorrow. We'll see.

Anyways, I'll talk to you soon. It's getting late.
Love,
Cory

January 29, 2013
Dad,

Thanks for writing. Managing certainly is a big difference from creating isn't it? Your management technique sounds like 3M president William McKnight's* "Hire good people, and leave them alone." (* McKnight's employees created "Post-It" notes during free time- which 3M gives all employees 15% pick of any task they'd like to do.) It mirrors the growing body of research on motivation, performance. You may remember a video I posted on my Facebook called "Drive: What Motivates Us." It was about the growing body of evidence that traditionally fundamental tools of management-imposed schedules and performance incentives don't measure up to self-directed ones. It's BIG. This research will revolutionize the economy as well as the workplace. What they're finding is that so-called "intrinsic motivation," the playful, creative, doing it because it's in line with our skills and or the "big picture" is far more productive a motivator than "extrinsic motivation" – coercion or incentives. Bryan highly recommended and sent a book called *Drive: the Surprising Truth About What Motivates Us*[57], and it's basically talking all about these things. Essentially, when it comes to "heuristic" tasks – tasks in which we're free to decide how to approach a problem (most of all we do), incentives positive and negative stifle our creative abilities, narrow our focus and tend to lock us into "the box" (which ideal outcomes are often outside of). Incentives (and coercion, which is simply a negative incentive) work for mechanistic repetitive tasks. I've found often what one would think of as a "mechanistic" task often is really a heuristic task. For example: I've been working on the "Elevator Crew", basically traveling throughout the quiet, empty prison while everyone, guards and inmates alike are asleep. Wiping elevators and sweeping offices. I started off hating it, constantly considering going back into "retreat" (the hole, where we go if we choose not to work). After a while, I resolved to endure, and I began to play with various algorithms for completing the job in such a way as to reach a decent level of approval in the shortest time possible. I utilized every possible option I could think of- different orders of performing the task, circular vs. sweeping motion of stainless steel polishing, focusing on cleaning elevator tracks vs. polishing doors, rags vs ripped blankets. Eventually, best techniques were established, and the C.O. began to trust me to do the job. Everyone knew I was the "elevator expert". Now that the techniques were established, experimentation on what to focus on, how to breathe, walk, deal with the others (when I did work with another…once in a blue moon) became the game. Thus this much-hated seemingly monotonous task became a flowing, meditative "game".

Then one day a black guy named Lawrence came on the elevator and decided he wanted to tackle elevators. So I took him with me, tried to give him suggestions. At one point, he decided one particular way of getting dust out of the tracks of the elevator was best. He liked sweeping it right to left, something I'd found leaves dust under the skirt, unnoticeable until later when the Lieutenant did her very detail-oriented rounds. Sometimes, if she found dust, she'd actually come at 2 AM, wake inmates to go back to work and fix it, or keep us an extra 3 hours (10 PM to 1 AM vs. 10 PM to 4 AM) to punish us. So I told him, first gently, "Be careful, sometimes right to left leaves dust under the skirts." He was bent on doing it his way, and we ended up getting into an argument over it. My first thought was, "This is idiotic. Clearly, my way is better." Later I thought about it, thought about how even if my way was significantly better, it was more important that he have the same opportunity to create a game out of the job. I realized that if someone had taught me my EXACT METHOD, even if it was what I'd develop ANYWAYS, it would have been torturously constrictive. I enjoyed the work because I'd developed a system and in doing so "charged" every aspect with the memory of that "creative flow". We can also "charge" environments with dissonant repulsion. So I quit elevators, left it for him to play with. Now I work in the clinic where the name of the game is make stressed-out prison nurses, and doctors feel accommodated. A new, more sociable "game".

On a different note, the notion of "freedom" being superior to regimented scheduling is one that has consumed my contemplation at many points in my life. I have vacillated between both extremes, totally available for spontaneous human interaction and totally scheduled for progress towards a goal. To me our issues with business are a direct reflection of the spiritual flow between singular unity and pluralistic manifest reality. God is One. We are two. Yet we are all aspects of God too, so we are also One. Theraveda Buddhists and certain Hindu ideologies promote renouncing all attention/ attachments to pluralistic reality and simply meditating, merging with the One, all one's life. They sound a bit crazy, but there's a certain truth to it: if God is omnipotent, why bother? Just bask in Divine Bliss all day. We actually have strong evidence some of those Buddhists actually disintegrated, merging directly with the spirit realm. On the converse, we've got Mother Teresa, who found sainthood in busily serving others. My recent idea is that neither is better or worse. What's important is that we just "do what we should." This changes from person to person, season to season, as we desire, as we aspire, as we get "burnt out". We cannot discount business as inherently wrong, as long as we're in this reality, we will have different ways to serve, some demand insane commitment. Take doctors – 1 extra day with the family could mean another person will not get ANY days with their family. Or say – YOUR JOB, a few less days of productivity could ultimately reduce our GDP by a few thousand, which could have a new effect equivalent to three Cambodian who make only ~$1,000/year becoming homeless or starving to death. These are obviously imaginative exaggerations, but still. What's important to me these days is trying to consider "dharma" "mindfully." Dharma is a concept that relates to "the art of living in harmony with purpose and natural order" and mindfulness is "maintaining awareness of fundamental, pervasive "clarifiers." So I spend time each week (and consistently every day) considering living in a way that reflects: temporality – the economy of time, resources in general from a daily, weekly, lifetime perspective, Maslow's hierarchy of needs, various roles and how to best fulfill them, reflect on time spent and how it aligns with all that. The list goes on. Studying Dharma is a very important aspect of both Hindu and Buddhism, something the authoritarian religions seem to overlook almost entirely: "How to Play the Game of Life." Expect this subject you're raising to be a continuing theme of future writings personally and also of some imminent major changes in the world in general. Well, I am off to write more. Good to hear from you.

Love,
Cory

Chapter 4: The Way Out 7 page Project

Cory felt strongly about creating a document that outlined his process of growth and transformation as a way to help those who have experienced incarceration. Originally he wanted to fit it all on 7 pages so that practically speaking he could proliferate it by mail using only one stamp. He quickly realized that there was no way everything he had to share would fit on 7 pages. But he kept the name, noting that 7 is the number of perfection. After he produced this document, which he named "The Way Out", he created another document and encouraged others to do the same, which he named the 7 page project. He felt strongly that each of us have a responsibility, it is our "due diligence" to document our life's inspiration and truths by which we live. So, he created his personal 7 page project and named it *The Seed Collection: A Book of Proverbs*[1], which is primarily quotes and exposés and his take on Deepak Chopra's *Seven Spiritual Laws of Success*[2]. This prison 7 page project, "The Way Out", is partly his writing and partly verbatim writing from other sources that he felt did a more thorough job of explaining what he wanted to relay. In this work, he refers to himself as the "Editor". As you may have noted from his letters, this portion of the book is the culmination of his life experience and lessons learned from being a prisoner, first of his mind, then physically in federal prison. Both of which he found freedom from and longed to help others do the same. May you too find healing and transformation is these pages.

- Denise Roussel

Introduction

For most, prison means defeat. It means an end to a time of prosperity, greatness. It means being degraded, demeaned, blacklisted, exposed. It means being subjected to the constant threat of violence, disease and constant psychological attack. It's considered GAME OVER. But is it?

"The worst enemy of the best life you could live, is not the bad life you came from, nor is it the circumstance you are in now. But the good life you had been living, and fantasize in vain about getting back to. It's gone. Let it go. Time to move on to bigger and better things." Let's take a look at some men who came out of prison victorious:

Viktor Frankl
Viktor Frankl was a Jewish neurologist and psychologist who was sent to Auschwitz concentration camp during the Holocaust. He lost his wife and entire family, his job, his life's work, his dignity, and almost his life to starvation, frostbite and hypothermia. He survived it all by finding meaning in his suffering, just enough to pull him through the torture. He wrote a book (*Man's Search for Meaning*[3]) upon his release that has consistently rated in the top 10 most inspirational books of all time. He founded the field of "logotherapy", using meaning and purpose to bring people out of despair.

Quotes from Viktor Frankl:

"Everything can be taken from a man but one thing: the last of human freedoms - to choose one's attitude in any given set of circumstances, to choose one's own way."

"When we are no longer able to change a situation - we are challenged to change ourselves."

"Between stimulus and response there is a space*. In that space is our power to choose our response. In our response lies our growth and our freedom."

Editor's note: That space between stimulus and response is improved greatly by meditation.

171

"Each man is questioned by life; and he can only answer to life by answering for his own life; to life he can only respond by being responsible."

Major James Nesbeth

Major James Nesbeth spent seven years as a prisoner of war in North Vietnam. During those seven years, he was imprisoned in a cage that was approximately four and one-half feet high and five long. During almost the entire time he was imprisoned, he saw no one, talked to no one and experienced no physical activity. In order to keep his sanity and his mind active, he used the art of visualization.

Every day in his mind, he would play a game of golf. A full 18-hole game at his favorite green. In his mind, he would create the trees, the smell of the freshly trimmed grass, the wind, the songs of the birds. He created different weather conditions - windy spring days, overcast winter days and sunny summer mornings. He felt the grip of the club in his hands as he played his shots in his mind. The set-up, the down-swing and the follow-through on each shot. Watched the ball arc down the fairway and land at the exact spot he had selected. All in his mind.

He did this seven days a week. Four hours a day. Eighteen holes. Seven years. When Major Nesbeth was finally released, he found that he had cut 20 strokes off his golfing average without having touched a golf club in seven years.

Rubin Hurricane Carter

Rubin Carter was born on May 6, 1937, in Clifton, New Jersey. In 1966, at the height of his boxing career, Carter was twice wrongfully convicted of a triple murder and imprisoned for nearly two decades. During the mid-1970s, his case became a cause for a number of civil rights leaders, politicians and entertainers. He was ultimately exonerated in 1985. He spent the rest of his life fighting for the wrongly convicted as well as the mental liberation of all incarcerated.

While incarcerated at Trenton State and Rahway State prisons, Carter continued to maintain his innocence by defying the authority of the prison guards, refusing to wear an inmate's uniform, and becoming a recluse in his cell. He read and studied extensively, and in 1974 published his autobiography, *The 16th Round: From Number 1 Contender to Number 45472*[4], to widespread acclaim.

172

The story of his plight attracted the attention and support of many luminaries, including Bob Dylan, who visited Carter in prison, wrote the song "Hurricane" (included on his 1976 album, Desire), and played it at every stop of his Rolling Thunder Revue tour. Prizefighter Muhammad Ali also joined the fight to free Carter, along with leading figures in liberal politics, civil rights and entertainment.

Quotes from Rubin Hurricane Carter:

"Hatred and bitterness and anger only consume the vessel that contains them. It doesn't hurt another soul."

Editor's note: See "Taking Inventory" for the cure to toxic bitterness.

"He who bemoans the lack of opportunity, forgets that small doors many times open up into large rooms."

"It doesn't matter if you are guilty or innocent. The important thing is that you take the time to think about what choices you made, that got you where you are. And what choices you will make that will get you where you need to be."

"I understood that it was the law that put me in prison, not the individuals, not the jury, but the law which conditioned that jury to bring the decision that it did. When I understood that, I turned that prison into an unnatural laboratory of the human spirit to overcome the law, and in trying to escape the physical prison, I stumbled upon the universal prison, you know what I mean? And that gives me the ability to laugh."

Mumia Abu-Jamal:
Mumia Abu-Jamal is:
- An internationally celebrated black writer and radio journalist
- Author of six books and hundreds of columns and articles
- Organizer and inspiration for the Prison Lawyers' Movement
- Former member of the Black Panther Party and supporter of Philadelphia's radical MOVE organization
- Has spent the last 30 years in prison, almost all of it in solitary confinement on Pennsylvania's Death Row for supposedly killing a white cop, who shot him during a traffic stop.

His demand for a new trial and freedom is supported by:

- Heads of state and prominent politicians worldwide (France, Africa, the Caribbean, Latin America, and elsewhere)
- Nobel laureates Nelson Mandela, Toni Morrison, Desmond Tutu,
- the European and Japanese Parliaments
- City governments from San Francisco to Detroit to Paris and its suburbs
- Distinguished human rights organizations such as Amnesty International
- The Congressional Black Caucus and other members of the U.S. Congress
- Prominent civil rights groups such as the NAACP
- Numerous labor unions
- And by scholars, religious leaders, artists, scientists and countless others who cherish democracy, human rights and justice.

Quotes by Mumia:

"I spend my days preparing for life, not preparing for death... They haven't stopped me from doing what I want every day. I believe in life. I believe in freedom, so my mind is not consumed with death. It's with love, life and those things. In many ways, on many days, only my body is here because I am thinking about what's happening around the world."

"Politics is the art of making the people believe that they are in power, when in fact, they have none."

"Wiesel says that the greatest evil in the world is not anger or hatred, but indifference. If that is true, then the opposite is also true: that the greatest love we can show our children is the attention we pay them, the time we take for them. Maybe we serve children the best simply by noticing them."

"Prison is a second-by-second assault on the soul, a day-to-day degradation of the self, an oppressive steel and brick umbrella that transforms seconds into hours and hours into days."

Be Strong. Reject Oppression, Rule Yourself
"Nothing in this world can take the place of persistence. Talent will not; nothing is more common than unsuccessful men with talent.

Genius will not; unrewarded genius is almost a proverb. Education will not: the world is full of educated derelicts. Persistence and determination alone are omnipotent." -Calvin Coolidge

All overcame. How did they overcome? First they accepted their circumstance. They stopped looking for impossible outs, people to blame, stopped wishing. They started writing their own story.

"Here I am. Yes, what happened happened. That's out of my control. Yes, I'm stashed away from my people, my life outside. Yes, I'm confined, reduced, threatened, oppressed. What now?"

WHAT NOW?
I'll tell you what. Since you're stuck here anyways, make the most of it. If you can overcome this test, become it. Give in to it. You can overcome like the great men who've done so before you. Most of them suffered circumstance far worse than you'll ever know, and still they overcame.

The only difference: they made a decision. They mated imagination with truth and created a new reality for themselves. They adorned the drab walls of their oppressed existence with sacred beauty. They dove into their reality, and in doing so penetrated it, breaking free from their immediate surroundings and into the Universe at Large.

What's that mean in practical terms?

They lived with purpose, no matter their circumstance.

They started the day thinking these two questions:
1. How did I get here?
2. What can I do today?

And ended it likewise:
1. What have I done today?
2. What can I do better tomorrow?

They repeated this thousands of times, until their sentence ended and they had eaten an elephant, one bite at a time.

I'll tell you a few things **THINGS THEY DIDN'T DO**:

175

Self-pity
Sit and think self-defeating thoughts. Why me? I don't deserve this. I'm the victim. It's because I'm Black/ Mexican/ Asian/ White/ Native. It's because I'm a loser, etc.

Resentment
They want to get at you. They want you to be filled with hatred. They want that rage. Why? Because it will kill you faster than they ever could.

"Resentment is like taking poison and waiting for your enemies to die."

You want that? If so, give these papers away. You're already dead.

Wasting time
They did not say, "Oh well, here I am. I guess that's it."

Playing cards
Do you have any idea how many hours you have wasted playing games that benefit you nothing? Sure, a little fun has its place. But do you really need 5,000 hours of pinochle to have fun? Do you really need to spend multiple hours a day playing games? As you begin to find productive outlets for your time, you'll realize you need less and less "recreation".

Frivolous talk
It's easy to sit around and gossip, run it, bullshit. How much of that will matter even in one day? How many of your family members could you have written in the hours on end you waste talking to people who don't even care about you? So your friends and family are out there, wondering about you, and you spend hours a day giving the time you could have spent writing them running it with some low-lifes? Come on.

Negative talk
All those people who make mountains out of mole hills. So the Paisas let one of theirs shower without shower shoes. So you can't believe the new C.O.s really raided your cell for the 3rd time this month. So you hate "the man" and are sick of him always beating you down. WHO CARES? Shut up and do something 'bout it. You're in prison. You've got enough negativity for your lifetime. You cannot afford to dwell on it anymore. Move on. "If you have nothing nice to

say, say nothing at all." Remove yourself promptly from others who want you to share in their bitch-fest. It's diarrhea of the mouth, guaranteed to bring you down.

Drama
There's plenty of drama in your life already. You do not need a bunch of fools to add to it. Don't involve yourself in drama.

Prison politics
You may or may not need to involve yourself with prison politics, depending on where you are. But understand this: In history, many times the oppressed have tried to govern themselves and have ended up more terrible than their oppressors. Ever read *Animal Farm*[16]? Most of the time, prison politics is just a way for ego-maniacs to get some recognition and feel important. It's a chance for people who on the outside had influence over junkies and poor people to keep their power-trip going. You want a sure fire way to waste your energy and get used? Get involved with prison politics.

Living in fantasy of the outside
The outside is outside. You're inside. It's very important to stay as connected as possible with the outside. But staying connected is not the same as fantasizing about the outside. It's a fine line. Plan- but know that your plans are subject to revision and even abandonment. Keep in touch with people outside, but don't let it consume you. You've got your own challenge to deal with.

Giving up
"Well, I'm in prison. I may as well just give up. I can't do anything anyways." Focusing on limitations, not seeing the truth:

"Your limitations are exactly your strengths."

Even if you've given up, today is a new day. As long as you're vertical, there's still time.

Ok, so what DID they do?
Each of these successes stories are a little bit different. Mandela persevered in the name of righteousness. Frankl, to liberate minds from desperate situations. Former Black Panther Mumia, to achieve international acclaim despite incarceration. Vietnam POWs to live just one more day in hopes of reuniting with their family. Some, some do it for revenge. **Living well is the best revenge.**

Meditation
Meditation unlocks many doors for the prospective inductee. As you sink down into yourself, you may find the opening. It is the way people held in the most brutal of solitary confinement and have made it through stronger than ever. The universal Suit of Iron. If you intend to follow us, you'll need to regain control of your senses. If you cannot control your senses, how then will you control your thoughts? Didn't you once learn even how to use the restroom? There is a reason why a majority of this text is devoted to meditation.

Lived on Principle
Collect quotes you live by. Treat them as more important than anything in your life. These principles are like gods. Exalt them and they will reward you. Disobey them and they will punish you. Here are a few suggestions, but make your own lists. Get in the habit of collecting this kind of truth.

"What's easy is never worthwhile. What's worthwhile is never easy."

"We only have three responsibilities in life: give. receive. forgive."

"Proper Prior Planning Prevents Piss Poor Performance."

"Practice makes perfect."

"Give first. You want a friend? Be one first."

"Humility is the soil on which greatness grows."

"Greatest of all is servant of all."

"Do what you can and forget the rest."

"All things come to pass."

"Fish. Cast not, catch not, eat not."

Retreated
They didn't let the profanity, idleness, drama, politics, haters, cops, noise stop them. If the champions spent their time playing poker or dominoes, do you think they'd be champions? That's not to say

there's anything wrong with relaxation or recreation, but it has its time and place. If you are relaxing, it should be because you've been working towards your goals, and need to refresh so you can continue. If you're recreating, it should be because you spent time creating in the first place. Your safeguard against this will be your daily review, the time you take to ask yourself "What did I do with my day today? Was it all towards my goal?"

Read
If you don't read, you're captive to your own thoughts. Words are solidified thoughts. When we read, we bring someone else's thoughts back to life. We invite Socrates, Gandhi, Benjamin Franklin to come sit with us, right there in our cell. Even if we have good positive people to talk to on our block, it's still only our block. The highest you can rise surrounded by fools is Chief Fool. Want more? You'll need to stand on the shoulders of giants. "Creativity is the ability to hide your sources." – Einstein. Does that mean you turn into some kind of nerd? No. Keep playing the fools game. Conceal your new-found wisdom. "The mark of an educated man, is the ability to simultaneously entertain two conflicting ideas." -Socrates. Read. And DON'T just read fantasy and fun stuff. Read broadly. Try and find things to read that stretch you. On one side, you have things you read completely for fun. On the other, things that you barely understand, not fun to read at all. Try and push yourself towards the "not fun" end. Don't read stuff just because you think it's good to read. You have to enjoy it to some extent.

Write
"Journal writing is a voyage to the interior."

"Writing is the only way I have to explain my own life to myself."

"Only through writing can we pin our thoughts down long enough to evaluate them. Only then can we end their lives, or to nurture them."

"If you never write, you're doomed to repeat your mistakes for life."

All influential people write. Why? Writing is how we get things out of our brain, so we can work on and with them, and then put them back, organized. It's soul surgery. Writing is the way we plant seeds in others' minds. Writing is the way we super-charge our memories. Writing is the way we solidify the mush we call our thoughts. Writing gives ideas life. If our thoughts lead to actions, and actions lead to

179

results, writing is a way to design our results. Writing is a way of making sense of problems. Writing gives life to fleeting thoughts. Writing is also the way we continue to interact with the outside world. One day we'll die, our bodies will turn to dust and bones, but our writings will live on. The writer is IMMORTAL. Only through writing can a man make himself a force to be reckoned with, a true man. It doesn't matter if you are a skilled writer or not. Practice makes perfect. What's important is that your thoughts be given the chance to be seen. Not just bounce around aimlessly in some gray goop between your ears, but to be given a home. I can't tell you how many times just putting something down on paper made it crystal clear. Proper prior planning prevents piss poor performance. Proper reading/writing prevents piss poor thinking/actions.

Grew
"If you're not growing, you're going."

They all looked at what they'd come from and decided who they wanted to become. It's true our essential nature never changes. What changes is how we present that to the world. We may be the same person we always were, but we can choose to nurture different aspects of ourselves. We may always be the same old song, but we can be the remix of that song, dubstep, featuring guest artists, chopped and screwed, you name it. We can choose to turn the volume down on the noisy tracks, clean up the vocals, turn up the bass.

Escaped
They didn't let the drab gray walls and clanging metal doors keep them trapped. They escaped by diving inside. Prison doesn't end your life. It ends your life outside the walls of prison. Let prison be your crucible. Let it burn off the chaff and leave behind the precious jewels buried in your soul. Let prison be your classroom, your gym, your hiding place, your prayer room. Let the bastards be right- prison would be good for you- but not for the reason they thought it would be. Let it kill you- that's what they want- but like the Phoenix, be reborn. Let prison cut you off from the life you once knew. Give it to them. You won't need it now that you'll have a new one.

A CO is at the highest point in his life, you are at the lowest, and you are at the same facility.

So you want to know the WAY OUT, how to ESCAPE?
180

Wait. Occupy yourself. Eventually the doors will simply open, and you will be free to go.

Life sentence? Become immortal.

Food for thought:
The "world" we supposedly live in, is made up of molecules, which are made up of atoms, which are made up of protons, neutrons and electrons, which are made up of quarks. So basically, everything you "see" is actually just a cloud of quarks swirling around each other. But wait- there's more. These quarks are tiny. I mean TINY. In fact, they're so small, if you could take every particle in your body and put it in a container, it would be less than the size of a speck of dust. What's that mean?

Everything you see, is empty space, with a few tiny particles and waves mixed in. All those colors you see? You made those up. They're hallucinations. You're on a life-long hallucinogenic trip. One your brain made up just so you could wrap your head around living in this empty cloud (like outer space). There's no proof the world even really exists. We aren't even sure the particles are actually there, or if they're just balls of empty energy. Everything you see is a reflection of a reflection.

So does anything exist? Yes. We have reason to believe an entire world exists outside of this cloud world. It's the world of concepts. You see, the concept of a triangle exists regardless of whether we know what it is or not. The concept of life exists whether or not there is anything living. The concept of there being more than one thing exists even if there is only one thing. It's THIS WORLD of concepts we should strive to inhabit. Your mind is your space-ship. It's time to leave this planet of pointless clouds of dust and explore the world unseen. That's where the real power is.

Plato calls it "The World of the Forms". Some go on to believe there are additional levels of reality, spiritual realms. If you believe this, use your own spiritual practice to access these realms. If not, the conceptual world will suffice (aka the world of the forms, causal reality, the world of thoughts, ideas). Make yourself capable of traveling back and forth between these worlds with ease, and you'll never be able to be oppressed again.

181

The rest of this portion of text will be devoted to exposing mysteries hidden throughout the ages in sacred texts, secret groups and behind closed doors of the elite. *The Book of the Phoenix*[5] has been summarized and approximated with articles plagiarized from the internet, since the actual text is too cryptic for the uninitiated. These techniques were never intended for the masses, so we've done our best to find their closest approximations written in plain talk, without the Illuminati jargon and hidden symbology. We don't care if you "get it". The purpose is to return the favor done to us. We expect most not to understand this cryptic language. The following text is for those who do, that their minds might be expanded, and the Doors to the Kingdom opened unto them. We invite you to our ranks, you who do get it. For the rest, we hope what we've given you thus far will be some small consolation for your suffering.

We need to learn to speak the tongue of the subconscious, which speaks in symbols, sounds, imagery. And even higher still, the pineal, so called "god-within". We need to find a way to awaken these higher levels of self that the psychologists spent so much time identifying and differentiating if we are to take true command of our reality. We need to listen to them deeply. We need to learn to speak their language, if we are to activate their power. We each possess unlimited potential to influence the world around us. Everything from our physical reality, our relationships, even our own habits and actions depend on consensus between our cerebral conscious, our intuitive preconscious and our visceral meta-conscious. These terms are not concrete, as we are not really three entities. We are very much One, but it can be very helpful to recognize these parts as though they were separate, so we can identify techniques and tendencies. Simply reading and writing will not accomplish the goal of talking to the subconscious, or will do so in very limited fashion. Our subconscious needs pictures, needs to feel it. There are many ways to make this happen. Historically, symbols and ritual have accomplished this end. What do you think all the Freemason, Illuminati symbology is all about? Ritual has the ability to cement thoughts into our minds, in a more complete way that causes us to be more likely to change our actions. We are not robots, no matter how good an idea or how wonderful any words sound, they will be utterly inconsequential if we can't get our subconscious and our divine self on board. It's not a one way street either- while the world seeks to let the conscious mind dominate the subconscious/intuitive and the divine/visceral, we would be much better off allowing our divine nature to direct us. The problem? This requires faith. It's

182

impossible to understand our own divine nature in words, even abstract concepts are approximations. So to allow the divine nature to control us, requires a leap of faith. We DO have tools to listen to it (meditation, listening to your gut instinct). We do not really need tools to communicate with IT, because it's omniscient. It sees everything we do, impeccably. We can assist it by increasing our focus, decreasing spiritual and subconscious distractions. As far as our subconscious, we have tools there too. Creative visualization seeks to integrate our feelings, sensations with our conscious resolutions. Compassionate meditation helps strengthen emotionally charged sympathy, which gives us perspective that charges each thought: "How does this thought affect those I love?" or "How would those I love, the ones who understand, feel about this particular thought or action I'm having?" Contemplation seeks to spend time with a thought, nurtures it and allows it to send out roots, connecting with other dormant thoughts like compost and proliferating. For the divine part of ourselves, we need to meditate. Our divine nature is the most constant part of ourselves, and needs stillness to be activated. This one is the most difficult to understand, and it takes practice and experience. Faith is like that mustard seed, once planted, watered, we will begin to see a sprout. Eventually a seedling, then a small plant will one day evolve to become a tree. Faith is when it's impossible to prove there's something more, but you act as though there is. Not necessarily in absolute certainty, but enough sureness to take action. Action that cannot be justified by reason, cannot be proven to be of benefit by the body of solidified knowledge. This is what faith is. Neither can intuition be justified by reason. Thus, it is exceedingly important for the intuitive to become both persuasive and capable with the justification of reason through science. This has been the challenge presented to women in our day and age. Not only must they continue to be effeminate and intuitive, but they must become capable of competing in a decidedly rational, physical playing field. Women have recently been expected to learn science and math, in addition to the immeasurable expanse of intuitive knowledge they possess.

In the quest to awaken one's self, we must access the controls to these various aspects of our awareness. Having access to those deeper levels of your consciousness is of paramount importance to affecting them. They're affecting you profoundly. Why should you not be able to see them for what they are, and speak their language? Only then can a person, mind, body and spirit become whole. Of course, there exists no true delineation. These are simply

183

fragments of understandings we use to imply the full picture. (Any effort to pretend words are the complete picture naturally strikes us as silly or down right egregious). Think how you only need to see 2 or 3 surfaces to have a good idea of where you probably are. You only need to receive a couple impressions (sight or otherwise) to deduce where you are. Often two or three words can conjure up the exact image you're looking for on Google Images. Think how many things you can express in 3 words. (It may be an interesting exercise writing as much as possible in 3 words). So words are mere fragments. Occasionally, the word fragments match actual things that can be proven to exist. These are a-priori concepts of mathematics and geometry, certain philosophical ideas. These are called a-priori which means "relating to or denoting reasoning or knowledge that proceeds from theoretical deduction rather than from observation or experience." In other words, reasoning that just exists. It's infinite, and undisprovable. Everything else is finite. (Anything derived from applied sciences can be discredited or misperceived.) Words are this way to thoughts, and thoughts are this way to true understanding, as true understanding is to being. Words are mere fragments of the full understanding. They're often sufficient to recreate the "seed" of an understanding in another. That seed may fall on fertile soil, and grow to become a tree, or that seed may sit, waiting for conditions to be right to germinate. Or, it may simply be eaten by a bird. **It's our job, as people who've collected seeds, to play those odds. It's our job to distribute, trade, share and collect these seeds.** It's our job to penetrate the depths of secrecy to steal the power gems of knowledge. It's our duty to benefit mankind through the distribution of these seeds. Be they seeds of truth, beauty or goodness. A "seed" is my reinterpretation of Chopra's spiritual law #2. This law is of particular interest to anyone who has ambitious self-interests. If we really internalize this law, through constant contemplation, we will see that capitalism is very much based on this principle. I scratch your back, you scratch mine. I give you this, I receive this in return. In business, one thing that's been proven to work is helping others. How do you think Open Source software works? Some really smart guys give away their powerful creations to the world, and in turn become immensely famous and sought after, donated to, are raised to celebrity status.

Mate Chopra's 2nd law and this age old axiom and the result, is the concept of "seed":

184

#2 The Law of Giving: Today, bring whoever you encounter a gift: a compliment or flower. Gratefully receive gifts. Keep wealth circulating by giving and receiving care, affection, appreciation and love, for they are different sides of the same coin. - Deepak Chopra, *7 Spiritual Laws of Success*[2].

"Give a man a fish, he eats for a day. Teach a man to fish, he never goes hungry." - Unknown

Seeds are concepts you believe, if nurtured, will result in fruitful trees. They're things that cost a penny and result in thousands. They're autonomous. They can be coaxed into growing with intentional effort, but do not need this in the right soil. Seeds are collected in mass, easy to reproduce, and abundant- where they abound. Where they do not abound, they are rare, priceless beginnings. They're shade in a desert. They're fruit for a village. They're medicine to cure what ills. They're the materials to build a structure. It's pretty magical if you really think about it. These "seeds" exist in the conceptual realm too. Have you ever, just by short conversation, benefitted someone greatly? Maybe suggested they apply for a certain job or invited them to a meeting of your favorite organization. Maybe you suggested a restaurant that became someone's favorite? Maybe you taught, and in doing so sowed many seeds in the ripe soil of developing youth. That's seeding. Seeds can expound truth, goodness and beauty, often some combination of the three. Suggesting a particular song to someone that then falls in love with that group would be an example of seeding beauty. Graffiti is another. Seeding truth would be evidenced by quotes, short phrases of truth. Also, documentaries that expose new ways of thinking. Anything that inspires continued growth or change is a seed. Seeding goodness would be something like starting a movement. Volunteering, resulting in others being inspired to volunteer, etc. Giving gifts to the underprivileged. Funding a youth's education (also, some truth in there too). Having someone accept a book suggestion is a great honor of a seed as well, springing truth and if internalized, goodness. If a fiction, beauty. People have suggested books to me to read that completely revolutionized my life. Eckhart Tolle's *A New Earth*[6] is one book that grew into a phenomenal tree for me. Yes, for the one who seeks, it is his duty to distribute what he finds. In THIS distribution, the propagation of long lasting changes and ideas, does one become immortal.

185

MEDITATION

This is where things get real. Using modern technology like MRI scans, scientists have developed a more thorough understanding of what's taking place in our brains when we meditate. The overall difference is that our brains stop processing information as actively as they normally would. Even after one SINGLE 20-minute session, scientists have shown a decrease in "beta" waves, the waves that indicate we're trying to process information. Below are a series of articles stolen from the inter-web to help you get a better picture of what meditation is, how it benefits you and how to practice it.

Taken from lifehacks.com:
I've seen you guys post a few things about the benefits of meditation, and I only have one question: Really? I'm pretty skeptical. Is there some actual science behind meditation benefits, or is this just one of those trends?

Sincerely, Meditation Myths

Dear MM,

The meditation you've been hearing about isn't quite as stereotypical as you're probably thinking. And indeed, there is some science behind it: meditation has been a hot topic for all sorts of studies recently, and the supposed benefits range from jump-starting your productivity to improving your memory. Let's start by defining what meditation actually is, what the benefits are, and how you can implement it into your daily schedule.

Is Meditation Really Beneficial, or Is It Just Ridiculous?

If you see the word meditation and immediately conjure up religious images or deadbeats wasting time at work, you're not alone—but that's not exactly what we're talking about here. Mindful meditation, despite its awkward name, is really just about training your brain to concentrate and focus better. As Professor David Levy describes it to *USA Today*, meditation is just another exercise:

"Meditation is a lot like doing reps at a gym. It strengthens your attention muscle."

That's it. You don't need to buy yoga pants, burn incense, or even sit a particular way. The purpose of meditation is to train your brain just like you do the rest of your muscles. In this case, that means concentrating and focusing on one thing in your brain for a little while. As The New York Times points out, it's about being mindful of what you're doing:

"Though the concept originates in ancient Buddhist, Hindu and Chinese traditions, when it comes to experimental psychology, mindfulness is less about spirituality and more about concentration: the ability to quiet your mind, focus your attention on the present, and dismiss any distractions that come your way."

So, if you're struggling with concentration and focus, it's thought that meditation is one simple way to train yourself to get better at it. All it really takes is the ability to intentionally not think about anything for a little while.

The Benefits of Meditation

It's long been thought that meditation plays some role in concentration and focus, but only recently have we started to see studies that actually reflect what many societies have known for ages. For example, one study from the University of Washington showed that meditation can increase productivity and help you focus. Another study published in "Brain Research Bulletin" suggests meditation can decrease stress, and another by the University of Massachusetts Medical School has shown meditation can boost your overall brain power in a number of ways. Simply put, while researchers are still gathering evidence about the effects of meditation, it looks like even short stints of meditation have a positive effect on the brain's ability to concentrate. That in turn makes it easier to focus, retain memories, and be more productive. Can you say, "superhuman"?

We've discussed some of the benefits of meditation, including how it can help you at work and relieve chronic pain and stress, but new research shows that the mental benefits are much broader and can be achieved in as little as eight weeks of even short (but regular) meditation.

In a study published in the journal Psychiatry Research: Neuroimaging, researchers both reinforced previous research that

187

indicated that regular meditation (or other "mindfulness exercises") can produce measurable changes in the areas of the brain associated with empathy, memory, and sense of self. In an interview with the Harvard Gazette, the study's lead author explained:
"Although the practice of meditation is associated with a sense of peacefulness and physical relaxation, practitioners have long claimed that meditation also provides cognitive and psychological benefits that persist throughout the day," says study senior author Sara Lazar of the MGH Psychiatric Neuroimaging Research Program and a Harvard Medical School instructor in psychology. "This study demonstrates that changes in brain structure may underlie some of these reported improvements and that people are not just feeling better because they are spending time relaxing."

Participants in the study spent close to a half-hour every day meditating or practicing some other mindfulness exercise (notable because most people associate meditation with sitting and thinking quietly, and that's not the only type of exercise done in the study) for about eight weeks. They got MRIs of their brains before and after the eight week exercise, and when the study was over, many of the study's 16 participants showed significant changes in the areas of the brain associated with behavior, memory, and stress:

"The analysis of MR images, which focused on areas where meditation-associated differences were seen in earlier studies, found increased gray-matter density in the hippocampus, known to be important for learning and memory, and in structures associated with self-awareness, compassion, and introspection.

Participant-reported reductions in stress also were correlated with decreased gray-matter density in the amygdala, which is known to play an important role in anxiety and stress. Although no change was seen in a self-awareness-associated structure called the insula, which had been identified in earlier studies, the authors suggest that longer-term meditation practice might be needed to produce changes in that area. None of these changes were seen in the control group, indicating that they had not resulted merely from the passage of time."

Researchers note that their analysis uncovered a relationship between meditation and neurological activity. The study participants also reported improvements in mood, stress, and memory. The results show an interesting look into how quickly regular meditation can yield tangible mental benefits in your life.

If a half-hour every day is too much for you, there are ways to fit meditation into a busy lifestyle. Research done by Lift, a service used to help build positive habits, points out that while eight weeks may sound like a long time, it only takes about 11 days to really get into the habit.

Taken from Article in Harvard Business Review:
People say the hardest part about meditating is finding the time to meditate. This makes sense: who these days has time to do nothing? It's hard to justify. Meditation brings many benefits: It refreshes us, helps us settle into what's happening now, makes us wiser and gentler, helps us cope in a world that overloads us with information and communication, and more. But if you're still looking for a business case to justify spending time meditating, try this one: Meditation makes you more productive.

Our ability to resist an impulse determines our success in learning a new behavior or changing an old habit. It's probably the single most important skill for our growth and development. As it turns out, that's one of the things meditation teaches us. It's also one of the hardest to learn. When I sat down to meditate this morning, relaxing a little more with each out-breath, I was successful in letting all my concerns drift away. My mind was truly empty of everything that had concerned it before I sat. Everything except the flow of my breath. My body felt blissful and I was at peace.

For about four seconds.

Within a breath or two of emptying my mind, thoughts came flooding in—nature abhors a vacuum. I felt an itch on my face and wanted to scratch it. A great title for my next book popped into my head, and I wanted to write it down before I forgot it. I thought of at least four phone calls I wanted to make and one difficult conversation I was going to have later that day. I became anxious, knowing I only had a few hours of writing time. What was I doing just sitting here? I wanted to open my eyes and look at how much time was left on my countdown timer. I heard my kids fighting in the other room and wanted to intervene.

Here's the key though: I wanted to do all those things, but I didn't do them. Instead, every time I had one of those thoughts, I brought my attention back to my breath.

Sometimes, not following through on something you want to do is a problem, like not writing that proposal you've been procrastinating on or not having that difficult conversation you've been avoiding. But other times, the problem is that you do follow through on something you don't want to do. Like speaking instead of listening or playing politics instead of rising above them. Meditation teaches us how to not react, so we have both options.

And while I've often noted that it's easier and more reliable to create an environment that supports your goals than it is to depend on willpower, sometimes, we do need to rely on plain, old-fashioned, self-control. We can't always stop the distractions. We must be ready for those times.

Meditating daily will strengthen your willpower muscle. Your urges won't disappear, but you will be better equipped to manage them. And you will have experience that proves to you that the urge is only a suggestion. You are in control.

Does that mean you never follow an urge? Of course not. Urges hold useful information. If you're hungry, it may be a good indication that you need to eat. But it also may be an indication that you're bored or struggling with a difficult piece of work. Meditation gives you practice having power over your urges so you can make intentional choices about which to follow and which to let pass. On a more circumstantial level, meditation can also help you avoid information overload to help reduce the amount of noisy news around you all the time. Meditation is also helpful when you want to improve your powers of observation, or change habits and craving.

How to Meditate

So how do you do it? If you're just starting, keep it very simple.

There really aren't any special tricks, magic incantations, or weird brain hacks. It's just about sitting quietly and concentrating for a while. The Harvard Business Review has a meditation system we can all use:

190

A Guide to Meditation for the Rest of Us

Sit with your back straight enough that your breathing is comfortable—on a chair or a cushion on the floor—and set a timer for however many minutes you want to meditate. Once you start the timer, close your eyes, relax, and don't move except to breathe, until the timer goes off. Focus on your breath going in and out. Every time you have a thought or an urge, notice it and bring yourself back to your breath.

That's it. Simple but challenging. Try it — today — for five minutes. And then try it again tomorrow.

While a lot of the studies above dig into longer meditation periods, you don't need to dedicate that large of a chunk of time. Two minutes a day is beneficial, and you can even use apps to help you calm down for those short periods of time no matter where you are.

Taken verbatim from http://lifehacker.com/what-happens-to-the-brain-when-you-meditate-and-how-it-1202533314:
Because meditation is a practice in focusing our attention and being aware of when it drifts, this actually improves our focus when we're not meditating, as well. It's a lasting effect that comes from regular bouts of meditation.

Less Anxiety

This point is pretty technical, but it's really interesting. The more we meditate, the less anxiety we have, and it turns out this is because we're actually loosening the connections of particular neural pathways. This sounds bad, but it's not. What happens without meditation is that there's a section of our brains that's sometimes called the Me Center (it's technically the medial prefrontal cortex). This is the part that processes information relating to ourselves and our experiences. Normally the neural pathways from the bodily sensation and fear centers of the brain to the Me Center are really strong. When you experience a scary or upsetting sensation, it triggers a strong reaction in your Me Center, making you feel scared and under attack. When we meditate, we weaken this neural connection. This means that we don't react as strongly to sensations that might have once lit up our Me Centers. As we weaken this connection, we simultaneously strengthen the connection between what's known as our Assessment Center (the part of our brains known for reasoning) and our bodily sensation and fear centers. So

191

when we experience scary or upsetting sensations, we can more easily look at them rationally. Here's a good example: when you experience pain, rather than becoming anxious and assuming it means something is wrong with you, you can watch the pain rise and fall without becoming ensnared in a story about what it might mean.

More Creativity
As a writer, this is one thing I'm always interested in. Unfortunately, it's not the easiest thing to study, but there is some research into how meditation can affect our creativity. Researchers at Leiden University in the Netherlands studied both focused-attention and open-monitoring mediation to see if there was any improvement in creativity afterwards. They found that people who practiced focused-attention meditation did not show any obvious signs of improvement in the creativity task following their meditation. For those who did open-monitoring meditation, however, they performed better on a task that asked them to come up with new ideas.

More Compassion
Research on meditation has shown that empathy and compassion are higher in those who practice meditation regularly. One experiment showed participants images of other people that were either good, bad or neutral in what they called "compassion meditation". The participants were able to focus their attention and reduce their emotional reactions to these images, even when they weren't in a meditative state. They also experienced more compassion for others when shown disturbing images. Part of this comes from activity in the amygdala—the part of the brain that processes emotional stimuli. During meditation, this part of the brain normally shows decreased activity, but in this experiment, it was exceptionally responsive when participants were shown images of people.

Another study in 2008 found that people who meditated regularly had stronger activation levels in their temporal parietal junctures (a part of the brain tied to empathy) when they heard the sounds of people suffering, than those who didn't meditate.

Better Memory
One of the things meditation has been linked to is improving rapid memory recall. Catherine Kerr, a researcher at the Martinos Center

for Biomedical Imaging and the Osher Research Center found that people who practiced mindful meditation were able to adjust the brain waves that screens out distractions and increase their productivity more quickly than those that did not meditate. She said that this ability to ignore distractions could explain "their superior ability to rapidly remember and incorporate new facts." This seems to be very similar to the power of being exposed to new situations that will also dramatically improve our memory of things. Mindful meditation has been shown to help people perform under pressure while feeling less stressed. A 2012 study split a group of human resources managers into three, which one third participating in mindful meditation training, another third taking body relaxation training and the last third given no training at all. A stressful multitasking test was given to all the managers before and after the eight-week experiment. In the final test, the group that had participated in the meditation training reported less stress during the test than both of the other groups. Meditation has been linked to larger amounts of gray matter in the hippocampus and frontal areas of the brain. I didn't know what this meant at first, but it turns out it's pretty great. More gray matter can lead to more positive emotions, longer-lasting emotional stability, and heightened focus during daily life. Meditation has also been shown to diminish age-related effects on gray matter and reduce the decline of our cognitive functioning.

Editor's Notes on Meditation:

Meditation will change you, if you continue to practice. Not everyone will experience the same benefits; for some it may simply be a slightly increased attention span. For others, like myself, you'll find it completely transforms you in every regard. You may find yourself being smoother, calmer. You'll find you have more control over your decisions. You may find your speech beginning to clarify. You may find you are more satisfied with life. If nothing else, you'll find the patience to sit still, relax. If you are like us, you'll also become a better celli- better person to be around. You'll become more peaceful, and if you **were** to throw a blow, it would land closer to its mark. During the journey you'll most likely experience ecstasy, despair, bliss, torture, emptiness and fullness. You'll experience difficulty and ease at various times in your practice. One day meditation may feel great. The next day it may feel like torture. If it feels like torture, that means you need it more than ever. There are many forms of meditation, many that have benefits for various aspects of life. They are all explorations of consciousness. It is important that we not compromise; we should still work on our razor sharp attention, even if we use some of the other techniques. For example: when scientists studied accomplished athletes, to determine what they all did in common- they found "rehearsal" to be one main thing. They all took time to visualize their shot, stroke, throw reaching its mark. They created, played and replayed the tape of them winning over and over again. They saw it, heard it, tasted it, felt it, became it. While that's not meditation in the strictest sense, it does fall somewhere on the "meditation spectrum". On the one end of the spectrum,

Sitting Meditation (Primary Focus) ---> Rehearsal / Repetition ---> Contemplation ---> Mindful Living

Stillness ---> Confining Your Thoughts to One Area ---> Confining Your Thoughts to the Now

We need to operate in the entire spectrum. We regularly sit in stillness as our backbone. At times, we sit and contemplate, rehearse, or chant mantras. Then, as we live our lives, we strive to maintain our control over attention, and hold ourselves accountable for when we do not. This is where the rubber meets the road, where your practice affects your life.

More complete descriptions:

Complete Focus/Oneness/Emptiness/Sitting Meditation, intense thoughtless focus on one point. This is standard meditation, a necessary component of any enlightened life. No lesser form of meditation should substitute for your sitting practice. Next is:

Rehearsal / Repetitive Thought, within narrow parameters. Say-repeating mantras, or visualizing the swing of the bat leading to a home run. Next comes:

Contemplation, confining your thoughts to one particular problem or area. Next comes:

Mindful Living, Focusing on what you are doing, whatever it is. Your attention moves fluidly, but according to purpose, not instinct. There is no right or wrong way to be mindful; it's a direction not an accomplishment. Constantly you must be bringing your attention in. What am I doing this very moment?

194

Meditation Instruction Taken from Mipham Rinpoche - **Leader of** **the Shambhala Movement which seeks to bring Eastern Truth to the West:** Mindfulness in life is keeping a thread of meditation going throughout your life, bringing yourself back when your mind wanders, like a shepherd watching over his sheep. The practice of mindfulness/awareness meditation is common to all Buddhist traditions. Beyond that, it is common to, inherent in, all human beings. In meditation we are continuously discovering who and what we are. That could be quite frightening or quite boring, but after a while, all that slips away. We get into some kind of natural rhythm and begin to discover our basic mind and heart. Often we think about meditation as some kind of unusual, holy spiritual activity. As we practice, that is one of the basic beliefs we try to overcome. The point is that meditation is completely normal; it is the mindful quality present in everything we do. That is a straightforward principle, but we are continuously distracted from coming to our natural state, our natural being. Throughout our day everything pulls us away from natural mindfulness, from being on the spot. Our natural tendency to rush means that we're rushing past opportunities. We're either too scared or too embarrassed or too proud or just too crazy, to be who we are. That is what we call the journey or the path: continuously trying to recognize that we can actually relax and be who we are. So practicing meditation begins by simplifying everything. We sit on the cushion, follow our breath and watch our thoughts. We simplify our whole situation. Mindfulness/awareness meditation, sitting meditation, is the foundation of this particular spiritual journey. Unless we are able to deal with our mind and body in a very simple way, it is impossible to think about doing high-level practices. How the Buddha himself, having done all kinds of practices, became the Buddha was simply to sit. He sat under a tree, and he did not move. He practiced exactly as we are practicing. What we're doing is taming our mind. We're trying to overcome all sorts of anxieties and agitation, all sorts of habitual thought patterns, so we are able to sit with ourselves. Life is difficult. We may have tremendous responsibilities, but the odd thing, the twisted logic, is that the way we relate to the basic flow of our life is to sit com-pletely still. It might seem more logical to speed up, but here we are reducing everything to a very basic level. How we tame the mind is by using the technique of mindfulness. Quite simply, mindfulness is complete attention to detail. We are completely absorbed in the fabric of life, the fabric of the moment. We realize that our life is made of these moments, and that we cannot deal with more than one moment at a time. Even though we have memories of the past and ideas about the future, it is the present situation that we are experiencing. Thus we are able to experience our life fully. We might feel that thinking about the past or the future makes our life richer, but by not paying attention to the immediate situation, we are actually missing our life. There's nothing we can do about the past, we can only go over it again and again, and the future is completely unknown. So the practice of mindfulness is the practice of being alive.

When we talk about the techniques of meditation, we're talking about the techniques of life. We're not talking about something that is separate from us. When we're talking about being mindful and living in a mindful way, we're talking about the practice of spontaneity. It's important to understand that we're not talking about trying to get into some kind of higher level or higher state of mind. We are not saying that our immediate situation is unworthy. What we're saying is that the present situation is completely available and unbiased, and that we can see it that way through the practice of mindfulness.

SITTING MEDITATION PRACTICE

At this point we can go through the actual form of the practice. First, it is important how we relate with the room and the cushion where we will practice. One would relate with where one is sitting as the center of the world, the center of the universe. It is where we are proclaiming our sanity, and when we sit down the cushion should be like a throne.

When we sit, we sit with some kind of pride and dignity. Our legs are crossed, shoulders relaxed. We have a sense of what is above, a sense that something is pulling us up at the same time that we have a sense of the ground. The arms should rest comfortably on the thighs. Those who cannot sit down on a cushion can sit in a chair. The main point is to be somewhat comfortable.

The chin is tucked slightly in, the gaze is softly focusing downward about four to six feet in front, and the mouth should be open a little. The basic feeling is one of comfort, dignity and confidence. If you feel you need to move you should just move, just change your posture a little bit. So that is how we relate with the body.

And then the next part-actually the simple part-is relating with the mind. The basic technique is that we begin to notice our breath, that we could have a sense of our breath. The breath is what we're using as the basis of our mindfulness technique; it brings us back to the moment, back to the present situation. The breath is something that is constant-otherwise it's too late.

We put the emphasis on the out-breath. We don't accentuate or alter the breath at all, just notice it. So we notice our breath going out, and when we breathe in, there is just a momentary gap, a space. There are all kinds of meditation techniques, and this is actually a more advanced one. We're learning how to focus on our breath while at the same time giving some kind of space to the technique.

Then we realize that, even though what we're doing is quite simple, we have a tremendous number of ideas, thoughts and concepts-about life and about the practice itself. And the way we deal with all these thoughts is simply by labeling them. We just note to ourselves that we're thinking, and return to following the breath.

So, if we wonder what we're going to do for the rest of our life, we simply label it thinking. If we wonder what we're going to have for lunch, simply label it thinking. Anything that comes up, we gently acknowledge it and let it go.

There are no exceptions to this technique: there are no good thoughts and no bad thoughts. If you're thinking how wonderful meditation is, then that is still thinking. How great the Buddha was, that's still thinking. If you feel like killing the person next to you, just label it thinking. No matter what extreme you go to, it's just thinking, and come back to the breath.

In the face of all these thoughts, it is difficult to be in the moment and not be swayed. Our life has created a barrage of different storms, elements and emotions that are trying to unseat us, trying to destabilize us. All sorts of things come up, but they are labeled thoughts, and we are not drawn away. That is known as holding our seat, just dealing with ourselves.

POSTMEDITATION PRACTICE

The idea of holding our seat continues when we leave the meditation room and go about our lives. We maintain our dignity and humor and the same lightness of touch we use dealing with our thoughts. Holding our seat doesn't mean we are stiff and trying to become like rocks; the whole idea is learning how to be flexible. The way that we deal with ourselves and our thoughts is the same way that we deal with the world.

When we begin to meditate, the first thing we realize is how wild things are-how wild our mind is, how wild our life is. But once we begin to have the quality of being tamed, when we can sit with ourselves. We realize there's a vast wealth of possibility that lies in front of us. Meditation is looking at our own backyard, you could say, looking at what we really have and discovering the richness that already exists. Discovering that richness is a moment-to-moment process, and as we continue to practice our awareness becomes sharper and sharper.

This mindfulness actually envelopes our whole life. It is the best way to appreciate our world, to appreciate the sacredness of everything. We add mindfulness and all of a sudden, the whole situation becomes alive. This practice soaks into everything that we do; there's nothing left out. Mindfulness pervades sound and space. It is a complete experience.

Seven Point Meditation Posture - How to Position the Body

Editor's Note: *While this position is not necessary, many believe that there are added physical and physiological benefits to maintaining this posture. It's also designed to minimize strain and maximize subtle energies over time.*

1. Legs
If possible, sit with your legs crossed in the vajra, or full lotus, position. In this position, each foot is placed, sole upward, on the thigh of the opposite leg. This position is difficult to achieve, but one can train the body to do so over time. This position gives the best support to the body and mind. However, it is not essential. An alternative position is the half-lotus position where one foot is on the floor under the opposite leg and the other foot is on top of the opposite thigh. A third alternative is simply sitting in a cross-legged position with both feet resting on the floor under the opposite thighs.

Sitting on a firm cushion the raises the buttocks higher than the knees can help you greatly to keep your spine straight. It can also help you to sit for longer periods of time without having your feet and legs fall asleep or get uncomfortable pins-and-needles. If sitting on a cushion on the floor is not possible, one can use a low meditation bench. It is also perfectly acceptable to meditate while sitting on a chair. The most important thing is to find a suitable position in which you are able to be comfortable.

Editor's note: Use a chair if you've got back or knee problems. Otherwise, don't get used to it. The goal is to eventually be able to meditate anywhere, anytime, chair or no chair. Getting used to a new chair every time will limit your attention.

2. Arms
Hold your hands loosely in your lap, right hand resting in the palm of your left, palms upward, thumbs lightly touching, forming the shape of a teardrop, or flame. Your hands should be resting about 2–3 inches below the navel. Shoulders and arms should be relaxed. Arms should be slightly akimbo, leaving a bit of space between your arms and your body to allow air to circulate. This helps to prevent sleepiness during meditation.

3. Back
Your back is **most important**. It should be straight, held relaxed and lightly upright, as if the vertebrae were a stack of blocks effortlessly resting in a pile. This helps your energy to flow freely and contributes greatly to the clarity and alertness of your mind in meditation. The position of your legs can contribute greatly to how easy it is to maintain a straight back; often the higher the cushion under your buttocks and the lower your knees, the easier it is to keep a straight back. You should experiment to see what works for you.

4. Eyes
In the beginning, it is often easier to concentrate with your eyes fully closed. This is totally fine. As you gain some experience with meditation, it is recommended that you learn to leave your eyes slightly open to admit a little light and that you direct your gaze downwards, not really focusing on anything in particular. It can take time to get used to this. Closing the eyes completely may create a tendency toward sluggishness, sleep, or daydreaming, all of which are obstacles to clear meditations. Zen meditators meditate with the eyes wide open. This is possible, but it only takes a tiny bit of movement to be distracted when you first start.

199

5. Jaw and Mouth
Your jaw and mouth should be relaxed with your teeth slightly apart, not clenched, lips lightly touching. This helps you not tense-up.

6. Tongue
Your tongue should rest lightly on your upper palate, with the tip lightly touching the back of the upper teeth. This reduces the flow of saliva and the need to swallow. These automatic bodily actions can be hindrances to deepening your concentration as they can become distractions.

7. Head <--- Second most important
Your head should be just slightly inclined forward so that your gaze is directed naturally toward the floor in front of you. If your chin is held too high, you may have problems with mental wandering and distraction. If you drop your head too far forward, this can bring mental dullness or sleepiness.

That's it!

***Mahadevananda Breath- Taken from Bo Lozoff's "We're All Doing Time"7* (Must Have. It's FREE for prisoners.):**

OK, here are the details:

Touch your middle finger and index finger of your right hand to your third eye, with your hand in front of your face. Use the thumb to block your right nostril, and the ring finger to block the left. Memorize this pattern before completing this advanced meditation technique, designed to balance your left and right brain. It can be quite energizing.

1. Close right nostril. Breathe out left.
2. Breathe in the left.
3. Hold a few seconds.
4. Close the left nostril. Breathe out right.
5. Breathe in the right.
6. Hold a few seconds.
7. Close right nostril. Breathe out left.

Try ten complete rounds of alternate nostril breathing. (This can be helpful anytime you feel a headache.)

Bhastrika Breath- *Taken from Deepak Chopra:*

A traditional breath exercise in yoga is "bhastrika", which translates in English as "bellows breath." If you feel sluggish, doing a set of bhastrika breaths will clear the clouds from your body and mind. If you are trying to lose weight, doing a few rounds throughout the day will increase your digestive power and help increase your metabolism. However, performing bellows breathing close to bedtime isn't recommended, as it may invigorate your mind and make it difficult to fall asleep.

How to Perform Bellows Breath:

Begin by relaxing your shoulders and take a few deep, full breaths from your abdomen. Now start exhaling forcefully through your nose, followed by forceful, deep inhalations at the rate of one second per cycle. Your breathing is entirely from your diaphragm, keeping your head, neck, shoulders, and chest relatively still while your belly moves in and out. Start by doing a round of 10 bhastrika breaths, then breathe naturally and notice the sensations in your body. After 15 to 30 seconds, begin the next round with 20 breaths. Finally, after pausing for another 30 seconds, complete a third round of 30 breaths. Although bellows breathing is a safe practice, stay tuned in to your body during the process. If you feel light-headed or very uncomfortable, stop for a few moments before resuming in a less intense manner. Practicing bhastrika brings your attention into your body, reminding you how to move energy consciously. The ability to manage your life force or "prana" is essential for all success and fulfillment.

Compassion Meditation- Taken from His Holiness the Dalai Lama:

We have shared with you the easy breathing exercises, beginning meditation techniques and even went a little deeper into practicing pranayama. As your meditation practice develops, you can truly begin to cultivate the inner discipline necessary to train the mind. The Dalai Lama emphasizes inner discipline as the fundamental method of achieving happiness. Inner discipline involves cultivating positive states such as kindness, compassion and tolerance. Here is the Dalai Lama's instructed meditation on compassion:

201

"Begin by visualizing a person who is acutely suffering, someone who is in pain or is in a very unfortunate situation. For the first three minutes of the meditation, reflect on that individual's suffering in a more analytic way – think about their intense suffering and the unfortunate state of that person's existence.

After thinking about that person's suffering for a few minutes, next, try to relate that to yourself, thinking, 'that individual has the same capacity for experiencing pain, joy, happiness and suffering that I do.'

Then try to allow your natural response to arise – a natural feeling of compassion towards that person. Try to arrive at a conclusion: thinking how strongly you wish for that person to be free from that suffering. And resolve that you will help that person to be relieved from their suffering.

Finally, place your mind single-pointedly on that kind of conclusion or resolution, and for the last few minutes of the meditation try to simply generate your mind into a compassionate or loving state."

WITHDRAWING

"You become like those you hang around." This fact is true. No matter who it is, or why we're around them, eventually they will influence us, become part of our nature. The only way to keep yourself from turning into a steaming pile of shit is to constantly DE-PROGRAM and REPROGRAM yourself. Every day, as you improve at mindfulness, every second of every minute of every day. For the man serious about making a way for himself, he needs to regularly ask himself this question:

"What am I listening to?"

The problem with our brains is they are somewhat reactionary. No matter how much we intend to ignore stimuli, once we perceive a sensation, it begins to set off a chemical chain reaction in our brain that leads to certain mental reactions. We can do a lot to lessen this reaction, especially with practice, but still, our brains are PART CHOICE, PART CHEMISTRY.

Meditation and practice will help make them more choice and less chemical reaction, "knee jerk reaction", but never completely. We'll always be some combination of victim and hero, of the influenced and the influencer. Our task is to tip the scales in our favor. In order to effectively de-program, we've got to take a good look at what's coming in. Garbage in, garbage out. We need to look at each portal:

Sight – What are we watching? Jerry Springer? Are we reading an uplifting book or an indulgent car magazine? Are we spending our time watching the lemmings run around their cage, or are we watching our pencil dance around our journal?

Hearing – What are we listening to? This one is the weak point when you're in prison. People are constantly yelling. People are asking you questions, giving their bogus opinions. Guards yelling at you to get back in line. Gates clanging shut, TV blaring. People singing songs, crying, screaming, beating on their door, slamming their tray down. We need some serious work to free ourselves of the parasites that are burrowing into our brain through our ear canals.

203

Four most powerful tools I've found for reducing noise pollution:

1. **Go inside your cell.** Spend less time in common / loud areas.
2. **Ear plugs**- roll up toilet paper to make ear plugs, then tie a shirt over them too to make it even quieter. (Radio, if you got it, but being bombarded by advertisements isn't much better, so look for a public- commercial free station.)
3. **Stay up**- In dorm-style environments, when the sound gets too bad, I just stay up all night writing and sleep during the day while people are loud.
4. **Meditate**- Your meditation practice will reprogram your brain so that sounds do not bother you so much. It can be nice to meditate without distractions, but never let distractions prevent you from meditating. If it's loud, great practice.

REPROGRAMMING

Reprogramming will come in the form of a set of quotes, texts, people, ideas that you constantly come back to. It's time for you to write your own Bible. If something really speaks to you, read and reread it. Come back to it. Copy it down in writing. Write about how it relates to other things, experiences, other parts of your personal "Bible".

Collect quotes

Collect "Greats"- people whom you seek to emulate. (Make a list.) Surround yourself with people you can benefit from. **Not people giving fish, but people teaching fishing, for life.** Shape your relationship with these people in such a way that **maximizes the good** that you create together with them, and at the same time **minimizes the bad.** So that means if you meet an old man who used to be a stock trader and you want to learn about stocks, become his friend. Listen to what he wants to talk about, but try and direct the conversation towards the information you want to learn about. If he wants to be negative and complain about how bad the food is, don't eat lunch with him. Approach him at a different part of the day. Take the good, let the bad go. Don't let people vomit their complaints on you. Find common ground. Humble yourself and be taught.

Read and reread your "sacred texts". Take notes from them. **Make their words, your words**. *Examine your life through the lens of their perspective.* Let them guide your actions and steer you to your personal nirvana, whatever that may be. Be it power, success, self-actualization, enlightenment or just being the best person you can be.

Examples:

Seven Spiritual Laws of Success[2] by Deepak Chopra

The Art of Worldly Wisdom[3] by Jesuit educated Balthazar Gracian

We're All Doing Time[7] by Bo Lozoff, provided free to any inmate by the "Human Kindness Foundation" (Human Kindness Foundation, PO Box 61619, Durham, NC 27715)

A New Earth[6] by Eckhart Tolle (a poetic writing that reminds us how pointless our animalistic, egoic mind is compared to the eternal, principled existence we have in our potential)

Sacred Geometry[9] by Robert Lawlor (a compendium of sacred geometry symbology and understanding from ancient civilizations)

Anything by: His Holiness the Dalai Lama, Einstein, Gandhi, Socrates, Plato, Gracian, Chopra, Tolle, Thich Nhat Hahn, Confucius, Lao Tzu, Jesuits, Pythagoras. More I can't think of.

These are the giants whose shoulders the editor stands on. These are the men who he believes have gone through great lengths to provide me with unbiased truth, powerful wisdom capable of transforming his world. You are free to choose your own- but shoot for the stars. Don't settle for Malcom X or JFK. Scour the history books; look for GREAT men, not just good ones, though they're good too.

LISTING

It's time to look at what got us here. It's time to look at what will get us out. Even when you are set free, you will have problems. They will have multiplied. Going to prison does not take them away, only helps us forget how many they are. "Everywhere you go, there you are." It has been said before by wise men, "You cannot manage what you cannot measure." This is true for our character, standing in relationships, virtuosity in general. There are many different exercises we can use to tease information out of the subconscious stew called human consciousness. Once we've extracted all the concepts, we can do a little alchemy and recreate our humanity. The goal here is to make a list, which gives us elements to give some attention to. We can then also create initiatives/objectives in response to any deficiency or in exploitation of a resource.

"What lists do is give the visual side of your brain a place to store an address to stuff in the subconscious and cerebral parts of the brain. It then becomes much easier to rapidly access this information, store it, process it, communicate it, benefit from it, benefit others with it."

Explanation: There's nothing more clarifying than an exhaustive list. Everyone should have a collection of lists that act as a sort of "operating manual". Not only will you find this activity unexpectedly rewarding, but it will help you to keep mental track of where you see improvement and where you could stand to improve. For me, a direct result of this activity has been greatly improved relations with my "inner circle" of friends and family, since I no longer forget to call them regularly.

Once these lists are created, you are free to take some time elaborating on how to address each, how to invest in improving each in an economy of time, how to set reminders and plan events that will assist.

Here's how I do it:

Listing Responsibilities / Roles / Dreams, etc.

Example:

Roles I play:
-Uncle
-Brother
-Friend
-Entrepreneur
-Salesman
-Steward of a vehicle
-Driver
-Global Citizen
-American

Expanded Example:

Uncle - Facetime Nephew Benny at least once a week.

Brother - Call Bethany after I go swim on Sundays, text Landon to call me when he's free at least once a week.

Friend - Call Corey, Casey, Cole, Bryan, Chris, Scott, Lance, William at least once a month just to talk.

Entrepreneur - Read the latest posts to Ries' blog. Continue to take advantage of all the offerings from local Small Business Association. Attend Bootstrap Entrepreneur meetup.

American - blog about political issues, redirect people's attention to the sentiments of our Founding Fathers. Watch documentaries.

List areas you want to learn more about or continuously grow in:

Entrepreneurship
Symbolic Mysteries
Sacred Geometry
Rising to Political Power
Art of War

Take Inventory:

-Personal Moral Inventory (list strengths and weaknesses)
-Team inventory
-Family inventory
-Friend inventory
-Financial inventory (include possibilities, traction)
-Accident Preparedness
-Jackpot Preparedness

Types of lists:

-Gratitude
-Role
-Life Period
-Most / Least Bothersome
-Accidents
-Malic
-Charity (Cost-Benefit)
-Good (Profit-Profit / Benefit-Benefit)
-Self-serving (Benefit-Cost)
-Resentments
-Debts
-Budget
-To-Do
-Already Done
-Reflections
-List of Lists

LUCID DREAMING, Expanding your day

On average, we spend an average of 6 years of our lives DREAMING. Whether you remember your dreams or not, you have about 6 of them every night. While scientists are unsure of the exact purpose of dreams, many studies suggest dreaming is a necessary part of digesting the memories we have gathered and giving them meaning. It's our brains way of letting the subconscious experiment with different ideas, testing out various interpretations of symbols to result in better understanding. Ever noticed that after you sleep on a decision, it's easier to make? Ever noticed the day after you first attempt a particular skill, you become suddenly much better at it. Ever noticed a skill you had developed, despite a break from it altogether, having gotten better at it? Ever had a dream that came true?

Believe it or not, there are those among us who have trained our brains to allow us to be conscious during a dream. Once we gain consciousness, we have the power to control our dreams, remember them in vivid detail, decide what happens next. We can do anything, to anyone in our dreams, since everyone in our dreams are just products of our imagination. We can also tap directly into our subconscious mind, literally seeing our imagination and interacting with it. We can overcome fears and write music. The possibilities are endless:

What is lucid dreaming?

Lucid Dreaming is the scientifically proven ability to become conscious while dreaming - to "wake up" and take active control of your dreams. In fact, we know much of what we do about dreaming by training people to lucid dream and then use eye movements and breathing to communicate with the outside world during a dream, since both breathing and eye movements in a dream are the same breathing and eye movements we're actually doing in real life. Scientists also know that time passes in a dream much like it does in real life, something they proved by asking subjects to look right to left every second once they started dreaming.

With lucid dreaming you can:

Explore your dream-world with total clarity, where everything you see, hear, touch, taste and smell can be as authentic as reality, and even more so. Colors, sights, smells, sensations can be even more intense than they are in real life.

Fulfill any fantasy like flying, having sex, base jumping, shape-shifting, time traveling, meeting your hero and visiting other worlds.

Overcome personal problems like fears, phobias, anxieties, nightmares, past traumas and recurring dreams.

Tap into your creative genius by playing music, seeking artistic imagery and conversing with your dreaming self.

A word of caution: don't get too attached to just enjoying yourself in dreams. You need dream time to work through things. The most important skills you can learn from lucid dreaming are: remembering your dreams and learning to interpret your dreams, to gain insight on what's really inside your head.

Taken from dreaminglucid.com:
When the first spark of lucid realization illuminates your mind, and you gleefully announce, "Hey, this is a dream!" what happens next? For many beginning lucid dreamers, their success will be determined by how they respond in the first 30 seconds. In those initial crucial moments, taking four important steps can set you on the path to an exciting and lengthy lucid dream. These are the MEME steps:

1) Modulate your emotions.
2) Elevate your awareness.
3) Maintain your focus. And finally,
4) Establish your intent.

The joy or euphoria that often accompanies your realization of being in a dream will lead to its quick demise, unless you rein in the emotional intensity. Lucid dreaming newbies quickly learn to modulate their emotions, since intense emotions lead to the collapse of lucid dreams. Lucid dreamers change their emotions in a number of ways. Some visually focus on something boring, like their hands or the floor; visually neutral stimuli serves to decrease any emotional upsurge. Others mentally tell themselves to "Calm down," before their emotions get too high. While others begin to concentrate their energies on other tasks, which naturally reduces the level of sensed emotion. Once the emotional level has stabilized, you will want to elevate or clarify your awareness. Some do this by performing a 'reality check' (they levitate, put their hand through a wall, etc.) to re-confirm that they exist in the dream state. Some engage in a solidifying ritual, such as rubbing their dream hands together to ground themselves and spark the kinesthetic senses. You can take this further by shouting out a suggestion to the dream, such as "Greater clarity now!" or "More lucid awareness!" These vocalized intents normally show immediate results. An elevated awareness makes the next goal of maintaining your focus much easier. Newbies frequently discover that their focus can wander, and suddenly they will get interested in some aspect of the dream. If not careful, this new aspect can become so interesting (or entrancing) that your lucid awareness vanishes, and you slip back into regular, unaware dreaming. Maintaining your focus requires an 'active' realization of lucid dreaming. Some lucid dreamers perform repetitive actions to remind themselves that they are dreaming. They may repeatedly announce, "This is a lucid dream" or perform reality checks at certain intervals. One caution about focus involves staring at objects in a lucid dream. For some reason, lucid dreamers find that staring fixedly at something for more than a few seconds often causes the dream to feel shaky and then collapse. Some lucid dreamers notice the shaky feeling and immediately look back at their hands or the ground to stabilize the dream state. Others have discovered ways to create a new dream scene (by closing their eyes for a second or spinning around); however, for inexperienced lucid dreamers a new dream environment may feel bewildering. In my book, *Lucid Dreaming: Gateway to the Inner Self*[10], I suggest that the easiest way to maintain your focus involves establishing an intent or goal to accomplish, and then establishing a new intent or goal immediately after the initial accomplishment. You can think of this as the 'focus & re-focus' technique. By re-focusing on a new goal, you maintain an active state of awareness. Without an active focus on a goal, new elements will spontaneously enter the dream and capture your attention. Within seconds, your focus will likely become en-tranced by these new elements and you will lose lucidity, as you slip back into unaware dreaming. By habitually establishing goal after goal, you keep your awareness active. Of course, a lucid dreaming goal may be a very simple thing, such as, "I wonder what is behind this door?" or, "Should I ask that dream figure what it represents?" Each goal focuses your awareness and keeps your conscious activity illuminated. By stringing these simple goals together, a beginner can maintain lucid awareness, and have a surprisingly long lucid dream.

Each of these four MEME steps to successful lucid dreaming -- 1) modulate your emotions, 2) elevate your awareness, 3) maintain your focus and finally 4) establish your intent -- requires you to focus on them for a moment in your lucid dream. Feel free to memorize the MEME – modulate emotions, elevate awareness, maintain focus and establish intent. With practice, these steps become second nature and create a strong foundation for your lucid dreaming. Enjoy your journeys into the larger dimensions of the Self and its incredible creativity.

MORE
Clear your mind. Relax. Repeat to yourself thoughtfully one of the following:

"Tonight in my dreams, I will realize I am dreaming and become consciously aware."

"Tonight in my dreams, when I see _____ (my deceased Aunt Ruth), I will realize I am dreaming and become consciously aware."

Waggoner's Modified Castaneda Technique:
Using the Carlos Castaneda approach consistently each night before sleep is how I had my first lucid dream. I believe it works by establishing a simple stimulus-response associational link. Practicing repeatedly develops the association between the stimulus (the sight of your hands) and the response ("This is a dream!").

1) Sit in your bed, and become mentally settled.
2) Stare softly at the palm of your hands, and tell yourself in a caring manner that, "Tonight while I am dreaming, I will see my hands and realize that I am dreaming."
3) Continue to softly look at your hands and mentally repeat the affirmation, "Tonight while I am dreaming, I will see my hands and realize that I am dreaming."
4) Allow your eyes to cross, and unfocus; remain at peace and continue to repeat slowly.

5) After about five minutes or once you feel too sleepy, quietly end the practice.

6) When you wake up in the middle of the night, gently recall your intention to see your hands and realize that you are dreaming. Try to remember your last dream; did you see your hands?

7) At some point in a dream, suddenly your hands will pop up in front of you and you will instantly make the connection, "This is a dream!" Try to stay calm and explore the dream environment. Later, when you wake from your lucid dream, take a moment and write it down in your dream journal -- write the entire dream; how you realized you were dreaming; what you did while aware that you were dreaming, etc. Congratulations!

Stephen LaBerge's MILD Technique
The following is my interpretation of LaBerge's visualized role-playing technique:

1) Get into the practice of memorizing your last dream in detail, when you spontaneously wake up at night. Simply lie in bed, and recall the last dream in detail.

2) Then LaBerge suggests that you take your recalled dream, and clearly imagine that you have become lucid at an appropriate point. Visualize yourself becoming aware in the remembered dream.

3) Next, intend to become lucid in the next dream by suggesting, "Next time I'm dreaming, I want to recognize I'm dreaming."

4) Do the above until you feel determined. Expect to become lucid and aware in your next dream as you fall back asleep.

LaBerge also recommended that lucid dreamers conduct a "reality check" to verify that they were dreaming. A "reality check" could be something as simple as levitating or flying -- if you can do these actions in the dream state, then obviously it is a dream!

Paul Tholey's – A Critical Question? Or a Lucid Mindset
In 1959, Paul Tholey developed an idea to achieve critical awareness in dreams, writing: "If one develops a critical frame of mind towards the state of consciousness during the waking state, by asking oneself whether one is dreaming or awake, this attitude will be transferred to the dreaming state. It is then possible through the occurrence of unusual experiences to recognize that one is dreaming." Throughout the day when confronted with an odd event, ask yourself, "Am I dreaming or not?" Then consider, "How do I know?" Some have suggested putting a red 'C' on your hand with a

marker, and then each time you see it, ask yourself, "Am I dreaming?" You could then do a reality check, like try and levitate. Eventually, this may transfer over to your dream state, and when you wonder "Am I dreaming?" and do a reality check, you will find yourself levitating, and realize, "This is a dream!"

Nap to Lucidity Technique
Independently noticed by many lucid dreamers (and confirmed by the Lucidity Institute), the Nap to Lucidity Technique significantly increases the probability of a lucid dream.

A) Wake about 90 minutes before your normal waking time.
B) Spend the next 90 minutes reading or thinking about lucid dreaming, then return to sleep with the intent to become lucid.
Using this technique, the number of lucid dreams skyrocketed in the final sleep period, when compared to baseline records. (Lynne Levitan, *Nightlight*, Vol 3, # 1, "Get Up Early, Take a Nap, Be Lucid"[11])

Miscellaneous Thoughts
For some people, lucid dreaming requires some persistence. So try to do one of the above practices consistently. Also, consider what you might like to do in a lucid dream. Get interested, curious and excited about that! This develops emotional energy. If you don't know what you'd like to do, start reading the lucid dreams of others at The Lucid Dream Exchange (www.dreaminglucid.com) and find something that make you wonder, "Could a person really do that in a lucid dream?" If this is your first lucid dream, remember not to get too excited upon becoming lucid, since this normally will wake you up. If getting excited, look at your hands, or the ground or focus on something boring in the lucid dream to stabilize it. Good luck!

FASTING

Taken from allaboutfasting.org:
Can the benefits of fasting really be so broad? Yes, they can, and they are. We are so much more than a physical body, and fasting affects every part of our being. When we cease the over-indulgence that has become so common in our modern world, even for a short while, our lives and our priorities become clearer. Do these "short while"s occasionally, and you have a tool that will greatly add to your life.

Fasting will:
-rest the digestive system
-allow for cleansing and detoxification of the body
-create a break in eating patterns, while shining a spotlight on them
-promote greater mental clarity
-cleanse and heal "stuck" emotional patterns
-lead to a feeling of physical lightness, increasing energy level
-promote an inner stillness, enhancing spiritual connection

These benefits of fasting are not limited to just traditional fasts like water or juice, but can be attained through cleansing diets as well, although the effects will be less pronounced, as they occur over a longer time frame. But they will be there.

"Fasting is the greatest remedy --the physician within." ~Paracelsus

Fasting has been called the "miracle cure" because the list of physical conditions improved by fasting is long and varied. Cited most often are allergies, arthritis, digestive disorders of all kinds, skin conditions, cardiovascular disease, and asthma. Because fasting initiates the body's own healing mechanisms, any ailment may show improvement. Fasting frees up energy so healing can begin. Fasting is a wonderful antidote for our usual over-indulgences. There's nothing wrong with enjoying our food, but excess food on a continuous basis does create a burden for the body. When it must handle more than is comfortable and appropriate for it, it will suffer. Imagine at work how you feel when you're handed a huge work load--more than you can handle in your 8-10 hour day, more than is comfortable and appropriate for your job title (or salary level). You're under duress. But you WILL cope. You MUST cope. You must make decisions. You attend to the most

215

important and urgent of matters and set aside those that can wait for another day. This is what our bodies do when they're overworked; they tuck things away for another day. Whatever tasks can be postponed will be. And more work is dumped on them at every meal- or snack-time, whether they're ready or not. This is why fasting is a beautiful gift you give to yourself. A vacation for your weary, overworked, under-appreciated body. During fasting, we rest our system from the constant onslaught of food stuffs. We usually think of food as giving us energy, so it can be a new way of thinking to understand how the food we eat actually requires energy. Digesting, assimilating and metabolizing--these activities require a great deal of energy. It is estimated that 65% of the body's energy must be directed to the digestive organs after a heavy meal.

Some Benefits of Fasting:
Antiaging effects
Better attitude
Better resistance to disease
Better sleep
Change of habits
Clearer planning
Clearer skin
Creativity
Diet changes
Drug detoxification
Improved senses (vision, hearing, taste)
Inspiration
More clarity (mentally and emotionally)
More energy
More relaxation
New ideas
Purification
Reduction of allergies
Rejuvenation
Rest for digestive organs
Revitalization
Right use of will
Spiritual awareness
Weight loss

Taken from Staying Healthy with Nutrition, by Elson Haas, M.D.:
Free up this energy and it can be diverted to healing and recuperation. It can detox and repair cells, tissues and organs,

eliminating foreign toxins as well as the natural metabolic wastes (which are also toxins) produced even by our healthy cells.

And this is what the body will do during a fast. It will take advantage of that time and energy to do some housecleaning. The overloaded, overworked system, unable to properly handle all the toxins, has been storing any excesses in the tissues where they can be dealt with later. This is one of the great health benefits of fasting in that it offers this opportunity to play "catch up".

Fasting itself isn't necessarily a "cure" for anything. What it does is "set the stage" or create the environment in which healing can occur. Our bodies know how to heal themselves. We just have to "get out of the way", and this means on all levels of our being. Fasting has a way of rebalancing us on all those levels.

Physically, fasting is of high benefit to the chronic degenerative diseases that are plaguing our population and that modern medicine is at loss to cure.

Losing weight

Losing weight is, for many of us, one of the greatest benefits of fasting. Due to differences in metabolism and/or body chemistry (or mental patterns), exact results will vary from person to person. Using fasting to lose weight can create many opportunities to gain insights into your patterns with food and for making changes to your habits and lifestyle much easier to accomplish. Those who have the best luck "going it alone" are usually fasting to "get healthy" rather than to "lose weight". The change in mentality can be the trick.

Sometimes a short 3-day fast is used to "jump start" a new healthy diet plan, because fasting will change your tastes toward more natural and wholesome foods. It will also give you a new perspective on your relationship to food; why and when you eat what you do, what your mental and emotional attachments are, and offer an opportunity for you to heal these issues.

Fasting can give you more energy.

When you've progressed past the stage of dealing with detox symptoms, a fast will have you feeling lighter, more energetic, more enthusiastic, and requiring less sleep.

Mental and emotional benefits of fasting:

Because fasting improves mental clarity and focus, it can become a tool in your life to give you greater freedom, flexibility, and energy to get done the things and projects that are important to you.

Many experienced fasters find it helpful to fast whenever they need an additional boost for a major project or deadline, e.g. writing a paper, preparing for a big presentation, getting ready for a long trip. Artists and writers often talk of foregoing food during great creative inspiration; that it helps to keep the momentum going. (Although, beginners must be warned that this won't be the case at first. Don't fast for a big event until you are more knowledgeable about your fasting reactions, and you're sure you won't get a "detox headache" or such.)

Emotionally, you will feel calmer, clearer and happier. Fasters often report that depression lifts, goals begin to feel more obtainable as obstacles are put into proper focus. Doctors have reported patients experiencing improved concentration, less anxiety, sleeping better and waking more refreshed.

Sometimes it's hard to tell the difference between our emotional and mental aspects, where one begins and the other ends. Am I sad because I had this thought? Or did I have the thought because I've been feeling sad? Fasting has a way of clarifying those issues. Your awareness can focus in more accurately and determine the source of some unpleasantness that then snowballed into a mess. Once the source is identified, it's easy to see how overblown everything else was that came after. In other words, you see things from a clearer, more appropriate perspective.

Spiritual benefits of fasting:

And let's not forget the powerful effects of fasting on our spiritual connection. Another one of the benefits of fasting is that it promotes taking our attention inward and that we listen, become quiet. And that quiet quality time, you with you, will also allow, if you are willing, a greater sense of kinship with your Inner Being.

Without the continual addition of heavy foods into the system (and after any major detox symptoms have passed), the body takes on a lighter, less dense, feeling. This helps to create a subtle separation

218

from ordinary physical reality and all its worldly things, and instead you begin to sense the presence and power of things beyond this world.

Meditation or prayer become clearer, higher states easier to attain, messages or guidance from higher realms clearer. Knowing you are loved and supported every minute of your day and of your life is something you begin to intuitively feel. Recognition that there truly is a higher plan or purpose will become more real as it is intuitively experienced rather than just intellectually understood.

Your experiences will be deeply personal and unique. Sometimes, subtle too. You have to pay attention to the little things, you have to be quiet enough internally to pick up the nuances in a changed attitude or perception.

Begin to experience the benefits of fasting:

You can start with simple, short-term fasting. Even short fasts will help you enjoy the many benefits of fasting, allowing the body, digestive tract and organs a chance to rest and repair and heal, and you to begin the process of rebuilding your inner connection to your physical body, as well as your inner spirit.

The benefits of fasting reach into all areas of our lives. And whether you want to fast for increased health, or increased mental clarity, you will get them both--only maybe not all in the first day. Fasting is an ongoing practice that grows and deepens over time, delivering more and more meaningful benefits.

Taken from http://www.mensjournal.com/magazine/the-benefits-of-occasional-fasting-20121116#ixzz35ExqyYRM:
By now, everyone's heard about the life-extending benefits of caloric restriction. Lab results show that drastically cutting food intake can nearly double longevity in rodents, worms, and flies, and a massive 20-year study on rhesus monkeys, a species closely related to humans, found that the benefits of the diet seem to be universal: a resistance to cancer, heart disease, and age-related cognitive decline.

There's even a Calorie Restriction Society International, with thousands of members who live off roughly 30 percent fewer calories than the number recommended by conventional medicine.

The downside, of course – and it's a big one – is, who wants to live a life of deprivation? But what if there were a shortcut? What if you could get the benefits of calorie restriction without the same degree of sacrifice? Many people now believe you can. The idea is called intermittent fasting (IF), and it's becoming the diet du jour of weightlifters, crossfitters, and the paleo set.

"When people hear the term fasting, they tend to think of a week of not eating," says Brad Pilon, author of the book *Eat Stop Eat*[12]. "Instead, I like to think of it as taking a break from eating."

It is not what most people typically think of as fasting – going without food or sustenance for days. Instead, IFers believe you can reap all the benefits (and more) of chronic calorie restriction after as few as 12 hours without food. Which means that simply skipping breakfast and waiting until lunch to eat any food (most say it's OK to put a splash of cream in your coffee) counts as IF.

It seems counterintuitive, but skipping meals helps you feel more energized, recover better from exercise, blast fat, and retain lean muscle mass, and even protects your body from heart disease, cancer, diabetes, and cognitive decline – which is why NASA is interested in looking at fasting to improve the cognitive functioning of pilots and unmanned-aerial-vehicle operators.

How does skipping meals provide these types of benefits? Because we were once hunters and gatherers who sometimes went days between meals, our bodies were designed to survive in times of feast and famine. Most Americans now live off a constant drip of processed food, which keeps blood sugars elevated and immune systems depressed.

Breaking off this continual drip of refined, high-sugar, high-carbohydrate food isn't as tricky as it might seem, say proponents of IF, who swear the diet's protocol is simple and easy to follow. "Once you get through the first couple of weeks, it's easy," says John Olson, former director of the Strategic Analysis and Integration Division in Human Exploration and Operations at NASA. "If you have a healthy diet going into it, it's not really that big of a deal," he adds. "If you have a junk diet, it's going to be hard. For me, it's been transformational. I would say, anecdotally, the cognitive improvements are noticeable almost immediately."

Weight loss and fitness gains:

We learned in high school biology that the body's fuel source is glucose – blood sugar. We get it in abundance by eating sugar and refined carbohydrates like bread, pasta, and sports drinks. But our body can burn another type of fuel known as ketones. These molecules are created when your body runs out of glucose and starts to burn fat, which happens when you fast. Your system switches fuel sources from sugar to fat without breaking down muscle.

If you exercise during your fasted state, you can supercharge your body's fat-burning potential. Studies show that growth hormone, which has serious muscle-building properties, surges during fasts. The spike of this muscle-molding hormone proves that fasting is not simply about calories in and calories out. The human body appears to have adapted to thrive during short bouts of going without food.

That's not to say, though, that you should attempt a marathon during a fast. Most people do a short stretch – around 45 minutes – of moderate exercise like strength training or bike riding that can run through their blood glucose and turbocharge ketosis. "My clients find fasting not only increases fat burning, but they feel better and feel stronger as they get used to it," says Jon Haas, owner of functional fitness gym Warrior Fitness in Hainesport, New Jersey. Proponents also say the notion of not having to eat three square meals a day is freeing and makes you feel more in control of your body. "It provides another level of mental toughness," says Haas. "This is how your body was designed to function."

The downside of IF is that research shows people who fast are much more likely to reach for high-calorie, carbohydrate-rich foods when they eat again. These foods were never a problem, evolutionarily speaking, until the advent of soda, hoagies, and all-you-can-eat pasta buffets. Still, the research makes sense: If you haven't eaten in 20 hours, why wouldn't your body go for the biggest bang for the caloric buck? But IFers go a step further and claim the science behind bingeing after a fast is faulty. "To my knowledge," says Mark Sisson, author of *The Primal Blueprint*[13] and a proponent of IF, "these studies are not done on people adjusted to burning fat, so it's not surprising that someone on a moderate- to high-carbohydrate diet is going to go for the carbs when they start eating again – the brain of a sugar burner is always expecting sugar." Sisson's

221

comments mirror the reports of the legions of people who claim there's an adaptation period as the body becomes more efficient at converting fat into ketones – or, as Sisson calls it, "becoming a fat-burning beast."

Cancer prevention

An extensive body of research conducted by institutions like the University of California at Berkeley, the University of Southern California, and Chicago's Mount Sinai now shows that IF may help prevent and treat cancer. During a fast, the cells in our bodies go into a protective mode, while cancerous cells continue their metastatic, robotic growth. But the fasted state is hostile to cancer cells in part because their fuel – glucose – disappears from the bloodstream. The same is true of precancerous cells – the type that lead to cancer – says Valter Longo, director of the University of Southern California Longevity Institute. "Imagine someone who has precancerous cells," says Longo. "The process of developing cancer could take years, but if that person fasted, those cells could be killed before they had a chance to spread." Longo, who has shown that the act of fasting itself can kill cancer cells, is now working with the Dr. Otto Buchinger Clinic in Germany, an institute that has promoted therapeutic fasting for almost a century, to develop more human studies to better understand why IF may be beneficial for treating and preventing cancer.

Longevity and neuroprotection

Fasting challenges your brain in a way that's similar to exercising muscle, says Mark Mattson, of the National Institute on Aging. "When the brain goes under energy restriction, we see neural activity that's associated with protection against degeneration from stroke and aging," says Mattson. "Fasting increases BDNF, a protein that's crucial for learning and protection against age-related cognitive decline." There's also evidence that ketone bodies converted from fat and used as fuel during fasting may protect against neurodegenerative diseases like epilepsy, moderate autism, and Alzheimer's.

Master the fast

When Brad Pilon, a major guru of the IF diet, dropped out of his job in the supplement industry to attend graduate school, his goal was to create the ultimate diet. He was astonished to learn the key to longevity was to regularly skip eating. He developed what's since become the main reference title of IF followers: *Eat Stop Eat*[12]. It's updated annually, and it recommends two 24-hour fasts a week. But it's by no means the only protocol in the world of fasting. While most IF adherents have their own method for restricting food, the most popular seems to be skipping breakfast, which allows you to include sleep in your fasting cycle. If you eat dinner by 9 p.m., for example, all you need to do is skip breakfast and then resume eating at 1 pm for a solid 16-hour fast, or push it longer. "Fat loss starts happening at about 12 to 13 hours and plateaus around 18 hours," says Pilon, who also has a master's in human biology and nutritional science from the University of Guelph in Ontario.

Though we've been told for years to fuel up before working out, IF loyalists report that doing strength training mid-fast provides them with more energy than they would have had if they'd eaten breakfast. It does take some getting used to, however. You're essentially switching fuel sources from glucose to ketone molecules, and your body becomes more efficient at doing so over time – something IF advocates call being keto-adapted. It's like tapping into a tank of different fuel, and people report having greater concentration while burning ketones. As with so many things in the health sphere these days, what's old seems to be what's new. Many of the world's great religions call for fasting regimens; Socrates was a fanatical proponent; and Benjamin Franklin may have said it best: "To lengthen thy life, lessen thy meals."

223

Deepak Chopra's Seven Laws of Spiritual Success[2]:

#1 The Law of Pure Potentiality:
Take time each day to be silent. To just be.

Silence and stillness are about "dropping down" into a realm of greater possibility. It's the process of going deeper and deeper to the roots of possibilities. Sometimes when we have a problem, the solution is available, but just not in the set of possibilities we are considering. Stillness is about stopping the mind, letting it stop its momentum, so you can access the deeper controls that solve the problems.

#2 The Law of Giving:
Give gifts. Gratefully receive gifts. Keep the wealth circulating: compliments, knowledge, resources, love, time, listening, tools, etc.

Service to others is a powerful thing. When energy goes from A->B often there is a multiplying effect. This is where the creation of value comes in. When I spend 30 minutes and $30 filling my cooler with waters and ice to wheel down to the Congress Bridge each night, and sell them each for $1, I am turning my $.20 and 1 minute into $1 and great satisfaction from the buyer. Thus I am CREATING value. Even if I were to give them away, I would still be creating value, in multiples of what I put in. Thus GIVING is a way of multiplying the value in the world. If we combine this multiplication of value with an awareness of distribution of limited resources, the result is personal profitability. We need to understand that profit and creation of value are not the same thing. We should strive to FIRST create value. Profit should only serve the purpose of enabling the ongoing production of value. Even if the purpose of the profit is only to help one eat, have shelter, put gas in the tank, still- that's what's needed to continue creating value. The further we remove our profit-making actions from our value-creating actions, the unhappier we will be with our vocation. Think prison guard or someone else who says, "It pays the bills," when asked if they enjoy their job. Refer to the book *Drive*[15] on the three aspects of motivation for more information: autonomy, mastery and interconnectedness.

224

#3 **The Law of Karma**:
Every action generates a force of energy that returns to us in kind.

Choosing actions that bring happiness and success to others ensures the flow of happiness and success to you. Even if you don't believe in some sort of pervasive collection of rights and wrongs that keeps track of everything we do wrong and right and brings it back to us, we certainly can believe in our own mind keeping track. When we do wrong, we set a precedent in our minds that is harmful to us. It is our own nature (as well as other's nature) to reward right-doing and punish wrong-doing. The Law of Karma seeks to reinforce this constructive, righteous part of us, to encourage us to strengthen it above all else.

#4 **The Law of Least Effort**:
Accept people, situations, and events as they occur.

Take responsibility for your situation and for all events seen as problems. Relinquish the need to defend your point of view. Could also be described as "Law of Productive Effort". Refers to releasing any form of thinking without a practical take-away. It's natural to identify problems, things that bother us. We need to release/ accept them when they don't have immediate solutions. Only then can we clear the emotions enough to objectively work towards a solution/ subversion.

#5 **The Law of Intention and Desire**:
Inherent in every intention and desire is the mechanics for its fulfillment.

Make a list of desires. Trust that when things don't seem to go your way, there is a reason. We need to take time to articulate our desires: material desires, career goals, relationship desires, all of it. This articulation will give us a clearer picture of how we should act in order to approach these things. We will often find places desires are currently in contradiction with each other. This will give us the opportunity to recognize those places, then to either release one of them, or invent a novel way that the desires can coexist. Wish-lists are powerful tools. We can use them to create "fishing lists" suitable for Craigslist, eBay. Taking inventory of these things will also bring them to the front of our awareness, so that in our day, as we interact with people, we will remember them, and be far more likely to realize them.

#6 **The Law of Detachment**:
Allow yourself and others the freedom to be who they are. Do not force solutions- allow solutions to spontaneously emerge. Uncertainty is essential, and your path to freedom.

The Law of Detachment (peacefully analyzing situations objectively/ sensibly, not reactively) may seem vague and impractical, since if someone hits us, we naturally think, "they caused me to be angry". What needs to be understood is that our perception of our environment is very multifaceted. There is a "reactionary" component that is a fairly deterministic, chemical reaction style process. If you are insulted, without proper practice, you will automatically feel upset, along with all the physiological feelings associated. Thus this law describes a direction, one we must strive towards proactively with meditation. Before we take time to meditate, increasing the space between stimuli and response, we are likely to see detachment as impossible. We need to understand that simply desiring to be "detached" and objective will start as something theoretical, something we observe only in retrospect. As we continue to practice, it will take less and less time to recognize attachments. With meditation/ mindfulness we can pass the threshold of "first I reacted, then realized my mistake" to stimuli->consideration->mindful response. It's a process; it takes time and constant effort.

#7 **The Law of Dharma:**
Seek your higher Self. Discover your unique talents. Ask yourself how you are best suited to humanity.

Using your unique talents and serving others brings unlimited bliss and abundance. The process of "dharmic alignment" is a process of reviewing your actions, feelings about those actions, consequences, patterns. By spending both daily and periodic time reviewing your roles, experiences, relationships, successes, failures, you will get a clearer picture of who you have been, who you are and who you can be. One must be careful not to confuse what we have done with who we are. The most powerful revelations come from empathizing with the information we compile in this process. What "feels" right? What practices interconnect the best with your life? Which roles have you most enjoyed? Where do you see promise for growth? Focus on these. Your priorities are dynamic, they should constantly change to match your situation. Only through the process of articulating your particular life details (inventory-taking) can we get a clear enough picture to make an educated decision. Thus inventory-taking is a fundamental part of any purpose driven existence. This process requires time, you may find you have to adjust your lifestyle to include more contemplation, writing, review. So be it.

SACRED GEOMETRY

An old Masonic lecture from several centuries ago states:

"If we consider the symmetry and order which govern all the works of creation, we must admit that geometry pervades the universe...By geometry we may curiously trace nature through her various windings to her most concealed recesses; by it we discover how the planets move in their respective orbits and demonstrate their various revolutions; by it we account for the return of the seasons and the variety of the scenes which each season displays to the discerning eye. By it we discover the power, wisdom and goodness of the Grand Artificer of the Universe and view with delight the proportions which connect the vast machine."

"Behind the wall, the gods play, they play with numbers, of which the universe is made up."

As did French architect Paul Jacques Grillo, who wrote:

"The world around us is a world of numbers—numbers that spell life and harmony. They are organized by the geometry of figures, all related to one another according to a sublime order, into dynamic symmetry. Glimpses into this magnificent kingdom form the basis of all our knowledge, and it seems that in this domain the ancient civilizations had gone further than modern science."

"The harmony of the world is made manifest in Form and Number, and the heart and soul and all the poetry of Natural Philosophy are embodied in the concept of mathematical beauty."
— D'Arcy Wentworth Thompson

DESCRIPTION

The term sacred geometry describes the geometrical laws which create everything in existence. It unites the mind and the heart, spirit and matter, science and spirituality. Everything in nature is made up of patterns, structures, and designs from the smallest atom to the infinite universe. Each of nature's creations reveals to us the nature of that object and its own energetic vibration. Thus every creation has a unique vibratory frequency. The interaction of all the vibratory

228

frequencies found in creation show us the intrinsic unity of the part to the whole.

The general belief behind sacred geometry is that geometry and mathematical ratios, harmonics and proportion are also found in music, light, and cosmology. This value system is seen as widespread even in prehistory, a cultural universal knowing of the human condition. It is considered foundational to building sacred structures such as temples, mosques, megaliths, monuments and churches; sacred spaces such as altars, temenoi and tabernacles; meeting places such as sacred groves, village greens and holy wells and the creation of religious art, iconography and using 'divine' proportions. Alternatively, sacred geometry based arts may be ephemeral, such as visualization, sandpainting and medicine wheels.

Kepler's Platonic Solid Model

Sacred geometry may be understood as a worldview of pattern recognition, a complex system of religious symbols and structures involving space, time and form. According to this view the basic patterns of existence are perceived as sacred. By connecting with these, a believer contemplates the Great Mysteries and the Great Design. By studying the nature of these patterns, forms and relationships and their connections, insight may be gained into the mysteries - the laws and lore of the Universe.

Music

The discovery of the relationship of geometry and mathematics to music within the Classical Period is attributed to Pythagoras, who found that a string stopped halfway along its length produced an octave, while a ratio of 3/2 produced a fifth interval and 4/3 produced a fourth. Pythagoreans believed that this gave music powers of healing, as it could "harmonize" the out-of-balance body, and this belief has been revived in modern times.

Hans Jenny, a physician who pioneered the study of geometric figures formed by wave interactions and named that study "cymatics", is often cited in this context.

229

Cosmology

At least as late as Johannes Kepler (1571-1630), a belief in the geometric underpinnings of the cosmos persisted among scientists. Kepler explored the ratios of the planetary orbits, at first in two dimensions (having spotted that the ratio of the orbits of Jupiter and Saturn approximate to the in-circle and out-circle of an equilateral triangle). When this did not give him a neat enough outcome, he tried using the Platonic solids. In fact, planetary orbits can be related using two-dimensional geometric figures, but the figures do not occur in a particularly neat order. Even in his own lifetime (with less accurate data than we now possess) Kepler could see that the fit of the Platonic solids was imperfect. However, other geometric configurations are possible.

Sacred Geometry Natural Forms

Many forms observed in nature can be related to geometry (for sound reasons of resource optimization). For example, the chambered nautilus grows at a constant rate and so its shell forms a logarithmic spiral to accommodate that growth without changing shape. Also, honeybees construct hexagonal cells to hold their honey. These and other correspondences are seen by believers in sacred geometry to be further proof of the cosmic significance of geometric forms. But some scientists see such phenomena as the logical outcome of natural principles.

Art and Architecture

The golden ratio, geometric ratios, and geometric figures were often employed in the design of Egyptian, ancient Indian, Greek and Roman architecture. Medieval European cathedrals also incorporated symbolic geometry. Indian and Himalayan spiritual communities often constructed temples and fortifications on design plans of mandala and yantra. For examples of sacred geometry in art and architecture:

Labyrinth (an Eulerian path, as distinct from a maze)
Mandala
Flower of Life
Parthenon
Taijitu (Yin-Yang)
Tree of Life

Rose Window
Celtic art such as the 'Book of Kells'
Yantra
Swastika
Dharmacakra
Vesica Piscis
Metatron's Cube

Contemporary Usage

Contemporary usage of the term "sacred geometry" describes assertions of a mathematical order to the intrinsic nature of the universe. Scientists see the same geometric and mathematical patterns as arising directly from natural principles.

Some of the most prevalent traditional geometric forms ascribed to sacred geometry include the sine wave, the sphere, the Vesica Piscis, the 5 platonic solids, the torus (donut), the golden spiral, the tesseract (4-dimensional cube), and the merkaba (2 oppositely oriented and interpenetrating tetrahedrons).

Taken from Sacred Geometry International.com:
Most of us tend to think of geometry as a relatively dry, if not altogether boring, subject remembered from our middle school years, consisting of endless axioms, definitions, postulates and proofs, hearkening back, in fact, to the methodology of Euclids Elements, in form and structure a masterly exposition of logical thinking and mental training but not the most thrilling read one might undertake in their leisure time. While the modern, academic approach to the study of geometry sees it as the very embodiment of rationalism and left brain, intellectual processes, which indeed it is, it has neglected the right brain, intuitive, artistic dimension of the subject. Sacred geometry seeks to unite and synthesize these two dynamic and complementary aspects of geometry into an integrated whole. Robert Lawlor addresses this fundamentally dualistic nature of geometry in his essential work: *Sacred Geometry – Philosophy and Practice*[9] (1982), in reference to a medieval representation of geometry as a woman seated at a table, with compasses in hand, surrounded by the implements of the art: The idea, vision rather, of God as a Great Architect and Geometrician has found expression through numerous sources throughout the ages. The great Christian theologian St. Augustine, who held both Pythagoras and Plato in high regard, grasped the significance of geometric form, pattern and

231

proportion, and their representation through numerical symbolism, when he stated:
"Numbers are the thoughts of God."

"The construction of the physical and moral world alike is based on eternal numbers."

Galileo clearly understood this geometrical/numerical dimension of reality when he said:
"Mathematics is the alphabet with which God has written the universe."

And so did Johannes Kepler when he said:

"Geometry existed before the creation. It is co-eternal with the mind of God...Geometry provided God with a model for the Creation..."

Here in the Keplerian view, Geometry is clearly envisioned as existing upon an archetypal level, prior to the manifestation of material creation, and serving as the model utilized by the Great Architect. Through the study and practice of Sacred Geometry, this invisible geometric matrix begins to reveal itself as the template upon which the material universe, expressed through space and time, has been framed by the hand of the Great Architect.

Form Function and Design (1960):
"Geometry as a contemplative practice is personified by an elegant and refined woman, for geometry functions as an intuitive, synthesizing, creative yet exact activity of mind associated with the feminine principle. But when these geometric laws come to be applied in the technology of daily life, they are represented by the rational, masculine principle: contemplative geometry is transformed into practical geometry."

Lawlor here expresses a crucial idea in the definition of Sacred Geometry—it has both a contemplative side and a practical side, and an intuitive and intellectual side, it is an activity both right brained and left brained.

Further differentiating Sacred Geometry from the ordinary geometry of our school days is its relation to number and symbol. This difference, I think, is succinctly expressed by Miranda Lundy in her superb little book entitled simply *Sacred Geometry*[14] (2001):

232

"Sacred Geometry charts the unfolding of number in space. It differs from mundane geometry purely in the sense that the moves and concepts involved are regarded as having symbolic value, and thus, like good music, facilitate the evolution of the soul."

Sacred Geometry, then, charts the unfolding of number in space and has symbolic value and thereby has conferred upon it a qualitative status absent from common geometry. And here I must add that magnifying the inherent power of Sacred Geometry is the fact that it also charts the unfolding of number in time. This is an idea of such compelling ramifications that I must return to it in detail in another article.

At the very earliest appearance of human civilization, we observe the presence and importance of geometry. It is clearly evident that geometry was comprehended and utilized by the ancient Master Builders, who, laboring at the dawn of civilization some four and one half millennia ago, bestowed upon the world such masterworks as the megalithic structures of ancient Europe, the Pyramids and temples of Pharaonic Egypt and the stepped Ziggurats of Sumeria. That geometry continued to be employed throughout the centuries from those earliest times until times historically recent is also clearly evident. That it was made use of by cultures far-flung about the globe is evident as well, finding expression in China, Central and South America, in pre-Columbian North America amongst Native Americans, in Africa, SE Asia and Indonesia, Rome and of course in classical Greece and in Europe, from the Megalithic era some 4000 years ago, as stated, and again some 3000 years later, magnificently expressed during the Gothic era of cathedral building.

Geometry is especially associated with Classical Greece and such illustrious figures as Pythagoras, Plato and Euclid, who wrote the first actual textbook on the subject, the aforementioned Elements. Geometry has also been held in particular reverence and high esteem by the ancient order of Freemasons, which, of course, hearkens back to the great Cathedral Building era of the 12th through the 14th centuries, from whom modern Masons derive their pedigree.

From the foregoing is should be obvious that geometry was, and is, closely associated with architecture, that great manuscript of the human race, which provided the first and primary vehicle for the human employment of geometry. That it is closely associated with art, music and handicraft is obvious as well to the student of the history of these subjects. Ultimately, it must be appreciated that it was apparent to archaic peoples, as it is becoming increasingly apparent to contemporary students of the subject, that geometry is intrinsic to the very order of nature itself, both biological and cosmic, and, now, thanks to scientific inquiry, the realization dawns that geometry lies at the basis of the molecular and atomic levels of creation.

The word Geometry itself means 'Earth measure,' which definition is generally attributed to the fact that the ancient Egyptians regularly utilized geometry to resurvey the fertile farmlands of the Nile river floodplain in late summer, after existing boundaries were buried by the deposition of thick layers of alluvium from the annual flooding of the river. However, I would suggest the possibility that the idea of 'Earth measure' applied not only to the local measure of tracts of agricultural land in Egypt, but also on a much larger scale, literally, to the measure of the Earth itself, in a geodetic sense.

Anecdote has it that over the entrance to Plato's Academy was inscribed the phrase, "Let none enter here who are ignorant of geometry." Whether or not this is a historical fact, the idea should make sense to anyone who has attempted to ascend the heights of metaphysical experience and knowledge, that a form of mental training designed to develop the rational faculties and the reasoning ability to high levels of proficiency, would be a prerequisite for successful completion of the metaphysical journey and avoidance of the many traps, snares and pitfalls that await the inattentive pilgrim who presumes to tread the path of knowledge.

'Demiurge' by William Blake:
We are here introduced to a another fundamental idea lying at the heart of Sacred Geometry— that it provided the means by which God, as the Great Architect of the Universe, was able to frame the template of Creation. Freemasons, Hermeticists and Initiates into the Mysteries have for centuries held the conception of the Universe as the material expression of a hidden reality, an invisible blueprint, set down by the hand of the Grand Geometrician, and to which the study of Geometry provided the key and the means to render visible that which is concealed from the undiscerning and untrained eye, and that these fundamental geometric relations, manifested through form, pattern and number, form the very basis of harmony.

The term 'dynamic symmetry' refers to a concept that we will explore in depth a little further on. For now let it be said that dynamic symmetry describes a way of dividing space such that there is a specific relationship between the parts of a spatial composition and the whole of that composition, a specific relationship that can be expressed by certain constants of proportionality, as for example, the square root of two, or the square root of three, the Phi ratio, and so forth. Stated simply, dynamic symmetry is the idea of dividing space such that the proportions of the whole are found in the parts. Probably the most well-known example of this principle is found in the famous Phi ratio, which, in its simplest representation as a straight line, is divided asymmetrically such that the small segment is to the large segment as the large segment is to the whole line.

The Golden Mean or Phi Ratio

It is extremely interesting that Grillo recognized, back in 1960, when the source of the above quote was published, the significant fact that ancient civilizations were highly knowledgeable of the domain of number and geometry to an extent completely unappreciated by conventional scholarship of his time. Implicit in this idea regarding the degree of advancement of ancient cultures, is the recognition that a study of Sacred Geometry requires an immersion into the history and meaning of the archaic cultures for whom it provided a vehicle to produce some of the most awe-inspiring demonstrations of symbolic and sacred architecture to have been conceived and executed by the mind and hand of mankind, while at the same time providing a path to a deepened spiritual awareness of the fundamental principles of creation.

It could be said of Sacred Geometry that it provides one of the most, if not the most important key to unlocking the great Mysteries of the Ages. According to the famous 17th century Alchemical tract Atalanta Fugiens, the great Hermetic Secret lies concealed behind the 'Wall of Mystery' which can only be penetrated through an astute employment of geometry.

In the lodges of old, as in schools of Plato and Euclid the tools of Geometry were simply an unmarked strait edge and a pair of compasses. That's all. With those two tools it was possible to draw straight lines and circles, or arcs of circles. Out of the combination of straight lines and arcs the entire edifice of Euclidian geometry could be generated. In the archaic conception, God was seen as

235

working only with lines and arcs, or circles, to create the entire manifested universe. In modern language we might think of vector forces and scalar forces. Through a simple act of geometric construction using these two tools, two lines could be drawn that intersect at an angle of 90 degrees. The same act of geometry can yield an intersection forming an angle of 60 degrees. These two angles lie at the base of the two great systems of Masonic geometry, Ad Quadratum and Ad Triangulum, that is 'of the square' and 'of the triangle', respectively, and, through their marriage emerges an infinity of form.

In a small handbook frequently given to newly initiated Freemasons we find a valuable elucidation on the meaning of Geometry:

"Geometry is an 'exact' science. It leaves nothing to chance. Except for its axioms, it can prove everything it teaches. It is precise. It is definite. By it we buy and sell our land, navigate our ships upon the pathless ocean, foretell eclipses, and measure time. All science rests upon mathematics, and mathematics is first and last, geometry, whether we call its extension 'trigonometry' or 'differential calculus' or any other name. Geometry is the ultimate fact we have won out of a puzzling universe....There are no ultimate facts of which the human mind can take cognizance which are more certain, more fundamental, than the facts of geometry."

A study of Sacred Geometry begins with the hands-on experience, the commission of a geometric act of creation, utilizing only the straight-edge for drawing lines and the compasses for the drawing of arcs. Following from engagement of the hand and eye, the most basic of geometric axioms can be easily and intuitively grasped by the mind. Familiarity with the simpler exercises is soon followed by an ever increasing mastery of the more complex principles. A comprehensive program of study would require both deep contemplation of the forms, patterns and proportions of Geometry and their meanings, as well as the ability to apply the knowledge of Geometry in practical applications of problem solving and creative work.

As we trace the manifestations of Sacred Geometry throughout history and around the world, we see that it is infinitely adaptable and constantly evolving. As we continue to recover from the wreckage of ages past and civilizations lost new knowledge and new understanding of our extraordinary cultural heritage, we begin to appreciate that Geometry played a profound role in opening up the mysteries and secrets of Nature to humankind, inspiring our predecessors on this planet to achieve glorious heights of creativity by mimicking the fundamental processes and harmonies of Creation. As modern science becomes ever more proficient at penetrating the finest recesses of Natures' Order, we will have the opportunity to develop new and original applications of this ancient Craft.

It is difficult to convey the power of Sacred Geometry through the written word. It is best experienced first-hand through the process of geometric construction. In my classes and workshops over the years I have endeavored to provide students with the experience of Sacred Geometry by guiding them to a place where they can perceive for themselves the patterns and forms as they emerge beneath straight edge and compasses. And, I have attempted to show them examples of the myriad ways in which Sacred Geometry both conceals and reveals itself throughout the kingdoms of Nature, Art, Architecture and Life, and finally, to suggest the possibility of a revitalization of Sacred Geometry, that it might once again become a force for manifesting greater harmony in the world.

   - Yours Sincerely, Randall Carlson, THE COSMIC BLUEPRINT

Gaia-metry, or geo-metry, is the measure of the Earth. In ancient times, the correct estimation of the physical properties of the host planet was paramount to the success of the temple. As with other planets, the Earth was seen as an expression of super-physical consciousness, the manifestation of spirit and of God: a living organism.

Since the temples were designed as analogs of universal principles, designing them according to the same geometric proportions bound in the planet was to imbue the temple with soul. And so, just like the Earth, the temple was also regarded as a living organism.

The ancients figured out that the apparently physical world was constructed from atoms and molecules, and that each and every one was governed by patterns of order that favored balanced geometric relationships, a view now held by modern physics.

Furthermore, by studying the heavens, and the orbits of planets in particular, the ancients deduced that each mean orbit related one to another in orderly geometric relationships. Since the planets were considered to be living bodies or akousmata ("resonant beings") they were attributed the titles of Gods. And from that point, geometry became sacred.

Therefore, the geometry of life– bio-geometry– was incorporated into the fabric of temples the world over. Much of it is occult ('hidden from the eye'), and yet its presence can be felt by the atoms and molecules of the human body which are built on identical geometric platforms.

To enter an ancient temple is to enter oneself is to know thy Self.

Some of the most celebrated uses of geometry are found in those deceptively simple buildings, the pyramids of Egypt. The Great Pyramid at Giza incorporates a most unusual slope angle of approximately $51.49°$, which neatly references that most unusual of regular geometric figures, the seven-pointed heptagon. Unlike all other regular geometric figures, the heptagon is the only one whose angles cannot bisect a circle to a whole number, and so it has traditionally been associated with sound, the unknowable, and the seeking of wisdom. It has also been described as the geometry of the soul.

The enigmatic Bent Pyramid at Dashur, often portrayed by orthodox archeologists as 'a mistake', is equally encoded with an invisible geometry, and an important one at that. When unfolded like the petal of a flower, the top slope angle reveals a pentagon, the bottom slope a hexagon.

This combination of geometries is inherent in the design of the crystalline structure of human DNA. Since biogeometry is an eddy of energy, or a material expression of consciousness, the energy field of a person walking into the Bent Pyramid is influenced by the actions taking place within that geometric framework.

The same effects are true in Gothic cathedrals and their complex geometry, Chartres being one of the finest examples. Russian scientists monitoring EEG brainwave patterns inside the nave of Chartres discovered that the building's special harmonics have a noticeable effect on peoples' states of awareness. When combined with Gregorian chant—the kind of music these churches were designed to amplify—people's brainwaves went up as much as 4000% above normal waking state.

238

At Stonehenge, the relatively simple series of rings and horseshoe alignments that typify the world's most famous stone circle belie the fact that the positioning of its stones is governed by a complex geometric blueprint. In fact, it may be the only temple in the world that incorporates multiple sacred geometries: triangular, square, pentagonal, hexagonal, and heptagonal.

Stonehenge is the classic example of an organic temple, built and expanded over the course of some 4,000 years, serving to amplify the specific needs and subtle energy requirements of the era. Consequently, only parts of the temple were in use at any given ceremony: adepts would enter the temple with a specific purpose, and consciously 'awaken' only those geometries that served the intent of the moment.

It is also worth noting that, when the temple is not in use or being misused, its subtle energy field shuts down. This is particularly so when thousands of tourists and their clicking cameras and camcorders are present, blissfully unaware of the true purpose of the site. Without the single-minded intent and respect, all that stands in front of them is nothing more than a bunch of upright, inanimate rocks.

But thanks to a common framework in biogeometry, the energy exchange between the stone temple and the human temple only takes place whenever there is sympathetic resonance between the two, and when the intent of the participants matches that of the temple with which they are interacting.

In our era, the new geometric temples are the enigmatic crop circles. Despite the vast amounts of money spent by special interest groups in debunking the subject, crop circles have been scientifically validated as a genuine phenomenon, and that it is intelligently guided.

Like pyramids and Gothic cathedrals, genuine crop circles share the same occult geometric framework, and quite often the shape one sees in the flattened crop conceals a far different geometry. As with the Bent Pyramid, the crop circles favor the use of pentagonal and hexagonal geometry, and so it is not surprising that hundreds of documented cases describe alterations of awareness in people who interact with the designs, as well as healings. Indeed, sacred sites around the world share the same rich tradition.

239

It seems rather timely that, just as the sacred sites are experiencing a sudden resurgence in interest, so the crop circles have sprouted in 29 countries. And wherever they manifest—from the fields of southern Britain to the prairies of Alberta and the rice paddies of Japan—they always do so beside ancient sacred sites.

TO BE A REBEL

A revolutionary is part of the political world; his approach is through politics. His understanding is that changing the social structure is enough to change the human being.

A rebel, is a spiritual phenomenon. His approach is absolutely individual. His vision is that if we want to change the society, we have to change the individual. Society in itself does not exist; it is only a word, like "crowd" – if you go to find it, you will not find it anywhere. Wherever you encounter someone, you will encounter an individual. "Society" is only a collective name – just a name, not a reality – with no substance.

The individual has a soul, has a possibility of evolution, of change, of transformation. Hence, the difference is tremendous.

The rebel is the very essence of spirit. He brings into the world a change of consciousness – and if the consciousness changes, then the structure of the society is bound to follow it. But vice versa is not the case, and it has been proved by all the revolutions because they have failed.

No revolution has yet succeeded in changing human beings; but it seems we are not aware of the fact. We still go on thinking in terms of revolution, of changing society, of changing the government, of changing the bureaucracy, of changing laws, political systems. Feudalism, capitalism, communism, socialism, fascism – they were all in their own way revolutionary. They all have failed, and failed utterly, because man has remained the same.

We have to be rebels, not revolutionaries. The revolutionary belongs to a very mundane sphere; the rebel and his rebelliousness are sacred. The revolutionary cannot stand alone; he needs a crowd, a political party, a government. He needs power – and power corrupts, and absolute power corrupts absolutely.

Human consciousness has not grown for centuries. Only once in a while someone blossoms – but in millions of people, the blossoming of one person is not a rule, it is the exception. And because that person is alone, the crowd cannot tolerate him. His existence becomes a kind of humiliation; his very presence feels insulting because he opens your eyes, makes you aware of your potential and your future. And it hurts your ego that you have done nothing to grow, to be more conscious, to be more loving, more ecstatic, more creative, more silent – to create a beautiful world around you. Hence a Gautam Buddha or a Chuang Tzu hurts you because they have blossomed, and you are just standing there.

The world has known only very few rebels. But now is the time: if humanity proves incapable of producing a large number of rebels, a rebellious spirit, then our days on the earth are numbered. Then the coming decades may become our graveyard. We are coming very close to that point.

We have to change our consciousness, create more meditative energy in the world, create more lovingness. We have to destroy the old – its ugliness, its rotten ideologies, its stupid discriminations, idiotic superstitions – and create a new human being with fresh eyes, with new values. A discontinuity with the past – that's the meaning of rebelliousness.

These three words will help you to understand: reform, revolution, and rebellion.

Reform means a modification. The old remains and you give it a new form, a new shape – it is a kind of renovation to an old building. The original structure remains; you whitewash it, you clean it, you create a few windows, a few new doors.

Revolution goes deeper than reform. The old remains, but more changes are introduced, changes even in its basic structure. You are not only changing its color and opening a few new windows and doors, but perhaps building new stories, taking it higher into the sky. But the old is not destroyed, it remains hidden behind the new; in fact, it remains the very foundation of the new. Revolution is a continuity with the old.

Rebellion is a discontinuity. It is not reform, it is not revolution; it is simply disconnecting yourself from all that is old. The old religions, the old political ideologies, the old human being – all that is old, you disconnect yourself from it. You start life afresh, from scratch.

The revolutionary tries to change the old; the rebel simply comes out of the old, just as a snake slips out of the old skin and never looks back.

The future needs no more revolutions. The future needs a new experiment, which has not been tried yet. Although for thousands of years there have been rebels, they remained alone – individuals. Perhaps the time was not ripe for them. But now the time is not only ripe....if you don't hurry, the time has come to an end. In the coming decades, either mankind will disappear or a new human being with a new vision will appear on the earth. That new human being will be a rebel.

The difference between a revolutionary and a rebel: To be a rebel we need to stand alone – yet together in this aloneness. So easily, with all the expectations raised by so much info coming out – and talk of what is about to happen – we can sit and wait for someone else to do it for us, when this attitude itself is what has got into this mess – giving our power away to governments, conditioning, status quo, the easy option, the safe option, not rocking the boat, etc. Individuals have to take courage and speak up for themselves if we are to see this world change on a sustainable basis. It's just a cautionary point at this time of great expectations.

UPON RELEASE:

It will take time to reconnect your new paradigm with the one around yourself. Your world with have to shrink back to almost nothing. It all will be taken away, and your challenge will be to rebuild it as you remember it in prison. You'll still have the same problems you went in with. You'll have to actually work to fix your life problems so you can implement your dream. Do not post-pone implementing your dream because of these problems, if at all possible. The sooner you start, the sooner you achieve. People won't always understand. Keep your lip tight. Be careful not to raise expectations or proselytize.

Chapter 5: Conclusion

After Cory left prison, he did indeed spend time in a halfway house, but not in his beloved Austin. He was sent instead to San Antonio, Texas. After two months, in March 2013, he made his way back to Austin, but also divided his time between Austin and Houston where his new nephew lived. He was able to take a trip to Spain in May 2013, where he walked an ancient pilgrimage, El Camino de Santiago, with his brother for two weeks. And later that year in September 2013, he traveled to Bulgaria and Greece to celebrate his sister's wedding.

True to his vision, Cory chose not to be attached to a traditional 9 to 5 job. Instead he worked at various jobs for people he knew, initially a lot of construction. He soon began pursuing his entrepreneurial ideas of buying and selling. While he didn't actively get income rolling on some of his ideas by the time of his death, one practice that became his main income during the summer and early fall 2014 was selling water at the Congress Avenue Bridge in Austin, Texas where hundreds of people gather each night to view the bats that live under the bridge which come out at dusk to feed. This endeavor afforded him the ability to make enough money to survive while only working a couple of hours each night. Plus he enjoyed interfacing with the crowds, sharing insights about bat conservation and most of all providing water, essential for life.

The last six months of Cory's life were quite profound as he seemed to have blossomed into an enlightened state. During this time, he chose to live out in nature, intentionally homeless, sleeping in a hammock in the Green Belt of Austin (an extensive natural forest/park that adjoins downtown Austin). He also made significant strides in his growth, healing and overall enjoyment of life. Here are some of his Facebook posts that illustrate this:

I feel really. REALLY. REEEALLLYYY GOOD.

This post is about me, but I am posting because I would like it to be about you...

No I am not on MDMA, madly in some passionate romance (although it's a pretty similar feeling), or manic-depressive.

I just feel, good. So, so, sooo good.

Crisp. Clear. Connected. Fulfilled. Loved. Grateful. Satisfied. At peace yet full of vigor. Vital. Energetic when needed, peaceful when not.

The colors are so bright; the aroma is delight.

I see rainbows more regularly than seems normal, and am actually looking at the rainbow projection of a prism as I type this. Random, I know.

Yes, I'm talking about real rainbows. No I'm not on LSD, though it's quite reminiscent of hallucinogens at times (minus the nausea and weirdness).

I just feel indescribably wonderful, and have for about three weeks now.

The first week or two I was concerned it was just a phase, wasn't sustainable, or eventually I'd "come down".

The thing is I'm not describing over-energetic, or ecstasy, or mania, or euphoria per-se.

I'm talking about feeling "justifiably good". The kind of good feeling that you feel was "meant". The kind that doesn't have to be teased out with drugs or intense exercise, but just exists when you're doing what we're supposed to.

At first I thought it was some magical consciousness shift, and it may be, but the reality is- I'm doing A TON OF STUFF different. Even the most skeptical among us should appreciate this experience, because it's got a major PRACTICAL component as well, regardless of what's really happening on an abstract level.

245

It started with a few things. Small life changes that made a BIG difference for the better. Withdrawing from an occupation I'd grown to dislike - construction. Doing some minor fasting and experiments with dietary changes...

I started to feel pretty good.
Then I had this thought... This kind of crazy, totally unscientific thought. What if I just THREW EVERYTHING I KNEW AT FEELING BETTER?

What if I literally lived like this could be my last day, week, month, year? [He died 7 weeks later.]

What if I started to do not just SOME but ALL those life-changing things I had on my "eventually I should get into" list? (Ok, so as many as possible, still have a long list to be employed.)

Then on my birthday I really started to get in touch with self-service.

And I decided to just do EVERYTHING. Now. Today. $%$* it. YOLO, but in a good way...

Hollllyyyyyyy shit.

It's amazing. I'll never be the same. I will eventually have to "come back down" in a small sense, but I've realized the world I'll come back down to will be vastly improved even. And since they're all healthy, positive changes for the better, there will be no violent impact when I come back to the surface of earth. I will eventually just smoothly drop into normalcy, in my new and improved life. Much of the way I feel is completely sustainable. I liken it to when you're deficient in a particular mineral and you take said mineral. You'll feel like you just took a drug. And eventually the euphoria will wear off, but you'll still land much higher than you were.

So what did I do? Well... Everything I had on my radar just about.

If people express interest I will elaborate.

I want SO badly to be able to convince you, right here, right now, to just drop everything and give yourself completely to these practices. I really believe even the possibility of these things affecting you the way they affect me would be worth trying it all wholeheartedly.

But I know that's not the reality. People are skeptics. They normally have to ease into the waters of the oasis. It takes more willingness than most people have.

So I'll just list a few things, and if people want elaboration, since every one of these I could write a whole page on, they can ask in a comment.

- Alternating Day Fasting Protocol
- Regular Waterfall Massage
- 1hr + Meditation Daily, varied types and durations
- Chewing adaptogenic roots, taking adaptogenic supplements
- Not taking multi-vitamins
- Writing / Journaling
- Elimination of problem foods or even borderline problem foods
- Authenticity (eye contact, physical contact)
- Eliminating mediocre or damaging relationships from my time
- Purposefully targeting, selecting, cultivating fruitful relationships
- Yoga
- Getting in regular contact with loved ones

The list continues, but since people are too fearful/unwilling to employ radical changes, generally speaking, I'll leave it there...

You decide the degree to which your life improves.

My door is open.

———————————

And the following post reveals an entirely new approach to what many may deem an unfortunate circumstance, homelessness:

I'm homeless.

I've spent 3 years of my life or so without technically having a "home".

I haven't kept it a secret per-se, but I certainly haven't made it public until now.

247

Anyways, It's time to "come out of the closet" with my lifestyle. I normally don't even think about it. I just pack my bag and go. It's what's natural to me.

But what does that word even mean? Homeless.

It means you don't have a place to call your own. But that's not exactly true for many "homeless". Personally, I carry my shelter; it's a 2 lb.-rain-proof-double-sized hammock that I sleep better in than I do on a fancy mattress. I like sleeping in the cool breeze and waking up to the sunrise surrounded by majestic pecan groves and walking distance from a spring-fed swimming hole. It matches my idea of living beautifully.

The Greenbelts are my bedroom.

You've got cute furry stuffed animals in your bedroom. I've got actual cute furry animals running around my bedroom.

You've got a light bulb on a lamp for a nightlight. I've got a whole freaking moon and a sea of stars for a nightlight.

You've got air conditioning. I've got a cool evening breeze scented with mountain juniper berries and wildflowers.

You have an alarm. I have a whole Sun to wake me up.

You have a little swimming pool in your back yard. I have a whole spring-fed pool complete with friends hanging out, topless women and waterfall massage. (The actual law here states toplessness is legal unless it incites a riot.)

Homelessness is how I keep life consistently picturesque. Steeped in spontaneous, flowing, endless beauty. There is no room in my life for the disinteresting/boring. It would be a waste for me NOT to live this way.

"But these are public places, you can't just use them as your own, what if everyone did that?"

Exactly, they are public places.

248

By definition, I'm invited. Silly laws about not being in the park after dark would be the equivalent of me roping off a section of the library and telling people they could only enter with my permission. It's silly.

No one owns anything. Period.

No one owns the woods. I own the woods. The sparrows own the woods.

We share. It's the first thing you learned in kindergarten. If it's there and I can take it, it's mine. We CHOOSE to respect ownership in-so-far as it serves us. Now, it serves us well when there's mutual exclusivity, or possibility of damaging the good or space to be "shared". But this is just to make it safer in the park. Safer for who? I assure you, the park is safer with me IN IT. Park curfews and camping laws do not serve me. Veto.

I am welcome.

The Universe has already offered me an open invitation to everything, all the time.

Including the freedom to camp in the Greenbelt, considerately.

When you practice consideration, respect, courtesy, general pleasantness, spontaneity, wit, service, compassion you generate "welcomeness". This "welcomeness" can be for a variety of things: say- attending a police officer bicycle training randomly just because I saw them riding around, or using the super-hip W hotel library room as my own personal meeting room. Having plenty to offer will inspire confidence. Confidence, once practiced will enable you to walk right into any circle, any space, and leave with a handful more friends, a full stomach, and plenty of pleasantries. I am quite confident in my ability to improve the life experience of everyone around me, in every crowd, in every situation, therefore, I feel profoundly welcome. Everywhere. No merit of my own, this is just what developed organically over many years of experience being deeply "in the world". I didn't get almost killed, spend time in prison, suffering just so I could come back and live a life of mediocrity. F@#* that. I went through the fire so I could live GOLDEN. Why would we chose any less?

And of course, I also contribute materially. This isn't just hippy-dippy rainbows and unicorns. I make money, spend money, and do constructive work just like everyone else. Don't get it mixed up.

There's some really neat stuff out there in places the "system" says you don't belong. You can forge your own existence and become comfortable and happy in any lifestyle/environment. It takes practice. For sharing space in general, which homelessness is just an intensified example of: It's quite simple really.

Do no harm.

Hear people out.

Be considerate about how others are experiencing you in the space.

Be pleasant to interact with, or do not interact at all.

Look presentable / sensible / kempt as best as possible.

Contribute as much as possible (time, attention, money, whatever's lacking.)

Serve / make every place a little better than it was when you got there.

Take advantage confidently.

BAM, you're in. Walk right into the nearest fundraiser gala and serve yourself a plate of lamb chops.

Walk right up to that beautiful stranger you see alone at "their" table and have an impromptu date. "Are you attached to the idea of eating alone?" "No" "Great. My name is..."

Go swim in that hotel's awesome rooftop pool even though you haven't stayed there in years.

When you need to use the restroom, don't settle for a public restroom. Walk your ass into the nicest restaurant you can see and go directly to the bathroom. Come on, man, it's there FOR YOU. Take it. You either earned it or are going to earn it.

People love you! You just need to remind them why. They love you because you love them! They just need to be reminded. They'll remember.

Since people love you, they WANT you to enjoy their things. They want you to sit down and eat barbecue with them randomly in the park. They want you to enjoy their beautiful courtyard while you read a book.

They want you to listen to the secrets of how they made their first million.

They want you to walk up to them and just start talking.

They just need to be reminded who you are. You are someone who loves them.

Love = time. Love = consideration. Love = security. Love = beauty. Love = meaningful.
So give time, consideration, security, beauty- meaningfully.

Bam. Easy.

People get it. They really don't care if you're homeless or Donald Trump. They want to feel safe and uplifted when they're around you. If you can do that for them, they really don't care if you're on drugs, poor, rich, even if you've done terrible things.

I know this from prison. I had to live with murderers. Me and them, just the two of us, 23 hours a day, 7 days a week. Watch each other poop. You can't afford to care that they brutally murdered their wife; you want them to be your friend! Your concern is the same as any other two strangers: am I safe around this person? Will this person uplift me? Surprisingly with practice you'll find you can get 99.9% of people to meet these criteria if dealt with correctly. It takes practice. But even the most violent, antisocial people will be your friend if you just listen.

Just listen! It's easy. Nothing special. Just hear their story.

People feel so uncomfortable around the homeless. They have nothing to lose, so they are a threat.

251

This is true. They are a threat. But at least they're a threat you can see. A little security and healthy boundaries can neutralize that handily.

It is possible to make people trust you in a glance if you practice. You can gauge your success according to how much vulnerability people expose to you. Learning to develop trust rapidly is a worthy endeavor, particularly for the transient/many-homed/homeless.

Ramble end.

Since I really don't have the space to elaborate on the impact Cory's life had on many and continues to do so, I encourage you to read the details of his life further in *Beyond This Space: My Son Cory's Story and How He Changed My Life*[1].

Yet, I imagine by now some of you are wondering what happened that caused Cory's death at the age of 27. This is a mystery that may never be solved. (I go into greater detail in my book, *Beyond This Space*[1].) Let's just say it was either an accident or a homicide. Upon hearing of his passing, I was granted the gift of acceptance and perspective, which helped me immensely to avoid additional suffering. I understand that Cory lived a full, rich and complete life in his short life span. And I hope that the same can be said of me when I pass. Here's his obituary:

Cory Gabriel Roussel passed away on Sunday, October 26, 2014, at the age of 27. Born in Wilmington, North Carolina, Cory lived most of his life in Texas, most recently in Austin, Texas. He left behind a powerful legacy of love and compassion that profoundly affected so many lives. Cory's genius and soulfulness made him a rare life-force and an unbelievable socially conscious INDIVIDUAL, more unique, honest and connected than many of us will achieve or experience in a life-time. Cory breathed the air of the Greenbelt in Austin. He loved getting a Barton Springs waterfall massage in the morning, taking in and relishing in the simple beauty and amazing power of nature. His bare feet and toes in soil connected him to a deeper place, a place he was excited to share with others. Sparks of ideas flew from Cory's mind and imagination, out in every direction he took. Nothing was off limits intellectually or philosophically; he compassionately accepted all and took all views into consideration. He was no stranger to strange ideas. He never feared being different, which allowed him to live fully every day and to live in the present, moment to moment. Orthodoxy was thoroughly discarded and the unbridled imagination and passion within him were set free. Whether he was rolling on two wheels of his bike, hair blowing in the wind, or on the ecstatic dance floor, he shared love liberally and artistically. He freed his own mind from the burden of judgement by others and the confines of society, a joy he wanted all to experience. His courage, his gentleness, his humility, positively touched everyone he knew.

He is survived by his parents, Ross and Denise Roussel, his siblings, their spouses and his nephew: Bethany Roussel and Angel Shtarbov; Landon, Amanda Roussel and Benedict Roussel; his paternal grandfather and grandmother: Will and Margaret Roussel; his maternal grandmother: Thia Licona and a very large extended family.

A Celebration of His Life will be held at the East Baton Rouge Main Library Multipurpose Room at 7711 Goodwood Drive, Baton Rouge, on November 1, 2014 at 3:30 pm. For those so inclined, in lieu of flowers, please send donations to the Human Kindness Foundation at *www.humankindness.org* or donate your time to help someone else in his honor.

Today, I along with others, am passing along Cory's legacy of love and compassion by sharing Cory's dream for each of us to BE the Change: to BE love, Be compassion, Be authentic and Be present. This book is an important part of Cory's life purpose, as it is my own. It is my sincere hope that you can know the depth of love and compassion Cory felt towards his fellow man, especially those imprisoned by their own minds and that you can know the freedom that he found and shared with us.

Notes

Chapter 1

1. Denise Roussel with Cory Roussel, *Beyond This Space: My Son Cory's Story and How He Changed My Life,* 2015, Cory's Dream Publishing.
2. Cory Roussel, *The Seed Collection: A Book of Proverbs,* 2014, Cory's Dream Publishing.

Chapter 2

1. Eckhart Tolle, *A New Earth: Awakening to Your Life's Purpose,* 2005, Plume.
2. Francis de Sales, *Introduction to the Devout Life,* 2002, Random House.
3. R.T. Kendall, *Total Forgiveness,* 2007, Charisma House.
4. James Allen, *From Poverty to Power,* 2009, World Classics Books.
5. Timothy Ferris, *The 4-Hour Work Week,* 2009, Crown Publishers.
6. George Jackson, *Soledad Brother,* 1994, Lawrence Hill Books.
7. Michael G. Santos, *Prison! My 8344th Day, A Typical Day in an Ongoing Journey,* 2010, APS Publishing.
8. Wm. Paul Young, *The Shack,* 2007, Windblown Media.
9. Rick Warren, *The Purpose Driven Life,* 2002, Zondervan.
10. John Bradshaw, *Healing the Shame That Binds You,* 1988, Health Communications, Inc.
11. Gerald G. May, *Addiction and Grace: Love and Spirituality in the Healing of Addictions,* 1988, Harper One.
12. Mark Batterson, *Primal: A Quest for the Lost Soul of Christianity,* 2010, Multnomah Books.
13. Elizabeth Gilbert, *Eat, Pray, Love,* 2007, Riverhead Books.

Chapter 3

1. Lee Strobel, *The Case for Christ,* 2013, Thomas Nelson Publishing.

2. Mark Batterson, *In a Pit with a Lion on a Snowy Day*, 2006, Multnomah Books.
3. Philip Baker, *Weird Christians I Have Met*, 2005, Whitaker House.
4. David Platt, *Radical*, 2010, Multnomah.
5. Lynne McTaggert, *The Intention Experiment,* 2007, Atria Books.
6. Michael J. Losier, *The Law of Attraction,* 2010, Grand Central Life & Style.
7. Balthazar Gracian, *The Art of Worldly Wisdom,* 1992, Doubleday.
8. *The Biggest Secrets,* reference not found.
9. Plato, *Republic,* 2000, Dover Publications.
10. Timothy Ferris, *The 4-Hour Work Week,* 2009, Crown Publishers.
11. Eckhart Tolle, *Power of Now*, 2004, Namaste Publishing.
12. Eckhart Tolle, *Practicing Presence*, 2011, Eckhart Teachings.
13. Rhonda Byrne, *The Secret*, 2006, Atria Books/Beyond Words.
14. Eckhart Tolle, *Stillness Speaks,* 2003, New World Library.
15. Robert Lawlor, *Sacred Geometry – Philosophy and Practice*, 1982, Thames and Hudson.
16. Bruce H. Lipton, *The Biology of Belief*, 2008, Hay House.
17. Carl Jung, *The Undiscovered Self,* 2006, Signet.
18. Ilie Cioara, *The Silence of the Mind,* 2011, John Hunt Publishing.
19. Dalai Lama, *How to See Yourself as You Really Are*, 2007, Atria Books.
20. Shakti Gawain, *Creative Visualization*, 2002, New World Library, Nataraj.
21. Bo Lozoff, *We're All Doing Time*, 1985, Human Kindness Foundation.
22. Bo Lozoff, *Lineage and Other Stories*, 1990, Human Kindness Foundation.
23. Ken Follett, *Pillars of the Earth*, 2010, Signet.
24. Deepak Chopra, *The Seven Spiritual Laws of Success: A Practical Guide to the Fulfillment of Your Dreams*, 1994, New World Library.

25. Alexandre Dumas, *The Count of Monte Cristo,* 1985, Bantam Classics.
26. Eknath Easwaran, *Bhagavad Gita,* 2007, Nilgiri Press.
27. Bo Lozoff, *Inside Out,* Human Kindness Foundation.
28. Robert M. Williams, *Psych-K,* 2004, Myrddin Publications.
29. Ram Dass, *Be Here Now,* 1978, Lama Foundation.
30. Albert Einstein, *Ideas and Opinions*, 1995, Broadway Books.
31. Gretchen Rubin, *The Happiness Project,* 2011, Harper Paperbacks.
32. Paul Brunton, *What is Karma?,* 1998, Larson Publications.
33. *Spirituality- Feeble Fiction or Fantastic Fact*, reference not found.
34. Bo Lozoff, *It's a Meaningful Life: It Just Takes Practice,* 2001, Penguin Compass.
35. Elizabeth Gilbert, *Eat, Pray, Love,* 2007, Riverhead Books.
36. Robert Fulghum, *All I Really Need to Know I Learned in Kindergarten*, 2004, Ballentine Books.
37. Cheri Powell, *Seven Tips to Make the Most of the Camino de Santiago*, 2013, R.C. Linnell Publishing.
38. Thich Nhat Hanh, *The Heart of Buddha's Teaching*, 1999, Broadway Books.
39. Francis S. Collins, *The Language of God, 2006, Free Press.*
40. Mitch Albom, *Tuesdays with Morrie*, 2002, Broadway Books.
41. Rick Hanson, *Buddha's Brain*, 2009, New Harbinger Publications.
42. Malcolm Gladwell, *Outliers: The Story of Success,* 2011, Back Bay Books.
43. Hermann Hesse, *Siddhartha*, 1982, Bantam.
44. *Farmers' Almanac 2012*, 2012, Farmers' Almanac.
45. *Mathmatx*, reference not found.
46. James Boswell, *The Life of Samuel Johnson,* 2008, Penguin Classics.
47. Boy Scouts of America, *The Boy Scout Handbook,* 2009, Boy Scouts of America.
48. Gary Taubes, *Why We Get Fat: And What to Do About It,* 2011, Anchor.

49. Brian Browne Walker, *The I-Ching or Book of Changes,* 1992, St. Martin's Griffin.
50. Ellen C. Babbitt, *The Jataka Tales,* 2009, Wilder Publications.
51. William Buck, *Ramayana,* 2000, University of California Press.
52. Laozi, *Tao Te Ching,* 1992, Harper Perennial.
53. Patrick Olivelle, translator, *Upanisads,* 2008, Oxford Paperbacks.
54. Julia Cameron, *The Artist's Way,* 2002, Jeremy Tarcher/Putnam.
55. Luc Ferry, *A Brief History of Thought: A Philosophical Guide to Living,* 2011, Harper Perennial.
56. Twyla Tharp, *Creative Habit: Learn and Use It For Life,* 2006, Simon & Schuster.
57. Daniel Pink, *Drive: The Surprising Truth About What Motivates Us*, 2011, Riverhead Books.

Chapter 4

1. Cory Roussel, *The Seed Collection: A Book of Proverbs*, 2014, Cory's Dream Publishing.
2. Deepak Chopra, *The Seven Spiritual Laws of Success: A Practical Guide to the Fulfillment of Your Dreams*, 1994, New World Library.
3. Viktor Frankl, *Man's Search for Meaning*, 2006, Beacon Press.
4. Rubin Hurricane Carter, *The 16th Round: From Number 1 Contender to Number 45472,* 2011, Chicago Review Press.
5. *The Book of the Phoenix*, citation not found.
6. Eckhart Tolle, *A New Earth: Awakening to Your Life's Purpose,* 2005, Plume.
7. Bo Lozoff, *We're All Doing Time*, 1985, Human Kindness Foundation.
8. Balthazar Gracian, *The Art of Worldly Wisdom,* 1992, Doubleday.
9. Robert Lawlor, *Sacred Geometry – Philosophy and Practice,* 1982, Thames and Hudson.
10. Robert Waggoner, *Lucid Dreaming: Gateway to the Inner Self,* 2008, Moment Point Press.

11. Lynne Levitan, *Nightlight*, Vol 3, # 1, "Get Up Early, Take a Nap, Be Lucid".
12. Brad Pilon, *Eat Stop Eat*, 2014, Helion.
13. Mark Sisson, *The Primal Blueprint*, 2012. Primal Nutrition, Inc.
14. Miranda Lundy, *Sacred Geometry,* 2001, Walker Books.
15. Daniel Pink, *Drive: The Surprising Truth About What Motivates Us*, 2011, Riverhead Books.
16. George Orwell, *Animal Farm,* 2004, Signet.

Chapter 5

1. Denise Roussel with Cory Roussel, *Beyond This Space: My Son Cory's Story and How He Changed My Life,* 2015, Cory's Dream Publishing.

For additional copies of this book
or to purchase

***Beyond This Space: My Son Cory's Story
And How He Changed My Life***
by Denise Roussel
with Cory Roussel

The Seed Collection/ A Book of Proverbs
by Cory Roussel

Do You See What I See?
by Denise Roussel
with Cory Roussel

Please visit: **www.corysdream.org**
or **Amazon.com**

You may also visit and like:
Facebook Page: ***Cory's Dream***
for ongoing inspiration and education.